ON THE PERCEPTION
OF WORSHIP

ON THE PERCEPTION
OF WORSHIP

The ethnography of worship in four Christian
congregations in Manchester

Martin D. Stringer

THE UNIVERSITY
OF BIRMINGHAM

UNIVERSITY PRESS

ISBN 0-902459-04-0

British Library Cataloguing in Publication data
A CIP catalogue record for this book is available from the British Library

Printed in Great Britain by Alden Press Limited

In memoriam
Mark Searle

ABOUT THE AUTHOR

Martin D. Stringer was awarded a PhD from the Department of Theology, University of Manchester in 1987. He then worked for five years as a church-based community worker in east Manchester while also being tutor in Social Anthropology and Honorary Research Fellow in the Department of Social Anthropology at the University of Manchester. In 1993 he was appointed as lecturer in Sociology/Anthropology of Religion in the Department of Theology, University of Birmingham, and in 1997 he became director of the Worship in Birmingham Project. He has published in the areas of liturgy, anthropology and practical theology.

THE WORSHIP IN BIRMINGHAM PROJECT

This book is published in co-operation with the Worship in Birmingham Project, UK

The Worship in Birmingham Project aims to produce a body of data about the nature of worship in different religious traditions within Birmingham. The Project aims to assess this data comparatively in order to add to our knowledge about the way in which worship impacts on the lives of ordinary worshippers and congregations within the city.

CONTENTS

Acknowledgements   *ix*

Introduction   1

PART I

1   On worship   21

2   On ethnography   42

3   On discourse   61

PART II

4   The Baptist chapel   83

5   The Roman Catholic church   109

6   The Independent Christian Fellowship   138

7   The Anglican church   168

PART III

Conclusion   199

Bibliography   221

Index   232

ACKNOWLEDGEMENTS

There are many people who should be thanked for a piece of work such as this. The work reflects fifteen years of study, both in Manchester and in Birmingham, and detailed fieldwork with at least four different congregations. To thank everybody who made a contribution to the work by name would, of course, be impossible.

To start at the beginning, I must thank Kenneth Stevenson without whom the original research would have been impossible, and Mark Searle who offered such stimulation at a very early stage in the process. The original research was made possible through a grant from the British Academy and was undertaken as part of a doctoral thesis in the Faculty of Theology at the University of Manchester. I had essential support from Tony Dyson within the Faculty of Theology and from David Turton, Martin Southwold and Marilyn Strathern in the Department of Anthropology.

My most sincere thanks go, naturally, to the clergy and members of the four congregations in Manchester who allowed me to join them and to study them for so long. I established a number of important friendships within these congregations and gained more from my discussions with individuals and groups within each congregation than they will ever know.

Finally, I must thank David, along with colleagues and students here in Birmingham for their support and for their patience in reading, listening to and commenting on various parts of the texts. I also offer my thanks to Vicki Whittaker at the University of Birmingham Press for her encouragement, effort and professionalism.

INTRODUCTION

The ideas and arguments contained within this book owe their origins to two very different conversations. The first occurred in 1983, towards the end of my undergraduate degree in social anthropology at the University of Manchester. As part of my final year I had taken a course in the history of liturgy taught by Kenneth Stevenson and Richard Buxton. At the end of this course Kenneth asked me what I, as an 'anthropologist', had made of it. I said that I had enjoyed the course and that I had learnt a great deal from it. However, I suggested that if we really wanted to understand worship, then we should not be studying texts from the third, fourth, or any other century. Rather we should be going out into the ordinary churches of Manchester, and elsewhere, and discovering what real people think about their worship and how ordinary churchgoers respond to what happens every Sunday morning in their churches. The ultimate outcome of this particular conversation was that I got the chance to go back to Manchester a year later to undertake just the kind of research into what ordinary Christians understood by their worship which I had been proposing.

The second conversation took place some four years later towards the end of my initial period of research. I was offered the opportunity of spending two months in Chicago as part of my study. While I was there I travelled to the University of Notre Dame and spent a week in discussions with Mark Searle who was, at that time, head of the Liturgy Program. Mark was working on questions relating to the use of semiotics within an understanding of liturgical performance. Most of our conversations, therefore, revolved around the question of 'meaning' in relation to worship. Mark maintained the position that the 'meaning' of any rite rested primarily within the text and the performance of the rite itself. I argued, on the other hand, that the 'meaning' of any act of worship existed primarily within the minds of the worshippers who attended the rite and had very little to do with the specifics of the text or the actions of the liturgy being used. From my current position it is clear that both of us were using a relatively naive understanding of the concept of 'meaning', and that the 'answer', so far as there is an answer, must lie somewhere between the text and the minds of the worshippers who use the text. This question, however, and the discussions which surrounded it, have remained with me beyond the initial writing up of the original fieldwork and will now form the core of the argument within this book (see Stringer 1991 and the critique of this paper in Nichols 1996: 18–21).

It was clear that at the time of my conversation with Kenneth Stevenson there was very little, if any, work that had been done on the nature of liturgy as it actually happened, and nothing which could help me to grasp what it might mean to study how worship was understood by ordinary members of Christian congregations. I had just completed a degree in social anthropology during which I had specialised in the anthropology of religion. We had looked at various forms of ritual from around the world and explored a number of different ways of interpreting these rituals. I hoped, therefore, that there would be something within this material which might be of use to me. I was also aware that ethnography was the primary means of study within anthropology and I was convinced, probably with very little clear theoretical reasoning, that ethnography would be the method that I should use to discover what worship meant to members of different congregations in Manchester. Kenneth acted as my supervisor. His initial training was in classics, and while he always remained somewhat sceptical of what I was trying to do, he was always very supportive of the project itself. I also had support and help from various members of the Department of Anthropology, particularly David Turton and Marilyn Strathern. On the whole, however, like so many postgraduate researchers, I was on my own. I entered the field with a great deal of methodological naivety and I found that I had to establish my own methodology and theoretical frames as I went along if I was ever going to make any sense of, or be able to articulate the kind of information that I was discovering.

It was not surprising, therefore, that by the time of my conversation with Mark Searle, I had developed an understanding of what was going on within worship that was both original and could be seen as controversial. What seemed obvious to me from my fieldwork was completely unthinkable for Mark as a liturgist and a Catholic theologian. Practically every writer on worship or ritual, whether from a liturgical, a theological or a sociological/anthropological[1] point of view, has assumed that the real meaning of any rite exists primarily within the texts and/or the performance of the rite itself. The sole task of the analyst, therefore, as by implication of those who participate in the rite, was either to discover, or to affirm, or to respond to this inner meaning. This is still, I would suggest, the majority position within the literature and, for various reasons which I will discuss below, it is still seen to be the common sense position, especially when it is related to Christian worship. This position did not, however, equate with what I had discovered in the field, and it has taken many years for me to work this through and to construct a range of theoretical approaches and arguments which have subsequently allowed me to express my own position more coherently.

This book, therefore, is the end result of this kind of questioning and exploring. It began in the experience of fieldwork in four different Christian congregations in Manchester between 1985 and 1987 and it has developed through a series of methodological reflections throughout the ten years that have followed. The questions that the book addresses, however, remain fundamentally the same as those that I discussed with Kenneth Stevenson and Mark Searle. That is, how do ordinary members of Christian congregations in Manchester understand their worship, and does the 'meaning' of that worship exist primarily within the performance of the rite, or should we aim to find it within the minds of those who attend that rite? If it is the later, as I am suggesting, then, subsequently, how can this be discovered, articulated or assessed and what can we, as anthropologists, sociologists, theologians, or liturgists, actually say about it?

3

MODELS FOR THE STUDY OF WORSHIP IN PRACTICE

As I have already suggested, when I began my research in the mid-1980s there was very little academic material which was of immediate or obvious use. Nobody had done the kind of study of worship in practice that I was proposing, and nobody had reflected on how such a project might be done. As I looked round for models and methodologies, therefore, it became very clear that the number of alternatives was very limited. Essentially there were just four kinds of study that I could turn to. The first consisted of works by liturgists and theologians that had drawn on anthropological or sociological material to help them in their own analysis of worship. The second included the work of the very few anthropologists or sociologists who had commented, even if only in passing, on Christian worship. The third consisted of the whole area of the anthropological study of ritual, and anything that might be of interest within this. And the fourth consisted of those sociological works that aimed to explore the nature and content of religious perceptions within Britain and other western societies. None of these could provide exactly what I wanted but it was through reviewing all these different kinds of literature that I was able to hone and clarify my own particular questions and establish my own specific approaches to methodology.

Liturgists and theologians using anthropology and sociology

The use of sociological or anthropological ideas by theologians, and even by liturgists, has a long history, almost as old as the disciplines of sociology and anthropology themselves. Much of this borrowing, however, has tended to be implicit and the range of explicit borrowing which has taken place, especially in the study of worship, has always been fairly limited (see Stringer 1989). By the mid-1980s a small number of liturgists had begun to use the work of Victor Turner, Mary Douglas, and to a lesser extent Clifford Geertz, in an explicit fashion. These were largely in the form of papers in journals such as *Worship* (Bell 1989) and *Theology Today* (Randal Nichols 1985). Such borrowing was not particularly surprising as both Douglas and Turner, unlike most other anthropologists, had already made comments on Christian worship in the light of their own studies of ritual in Africa and elsewhere (Douglas 1973, Turner 1974). Many of these papers, however, were of a very tentative nature and they would have needed a great deal more work to be formed into a significant model for the study of Christian worship as a whole. What is more, even in the mid-1980s, both liturgical scholarship and anthropology were already moving beyond the work of Turner and Douglas to ask new, very different and often unrelated questions which once again took the debate away from the study of specifically Christian worship.

Another development of the same kind was found in a more systematic form in the work of theologians such as Harvey Cox and J.G. Davies. Both of these writers were competent sociologists as well as being aware of a range of questions raised by radical theologians within Christianity (see Cox 1969 and Davies 1973). Both writers also assumed a strong form of the secularisation thesis and both worked within a framework based on a combination of Neibuhr's theology of culture and Berger and Luckman's sociology of knowledge (Neibuhr 1952, Berger & Luckman 1966). Within such a framework all knowledge was seen as socially constructed but needing some kind of legitimatisation in order to establish its objectivity. Ritual played an important part in this legitimatisation and in pre-modern societies this ritual was always seen to be religious. Both Cox and Davies, however, understood that while ritual continued to play a significant role within a modern, secularised society, its form was that of the ceremonial, sport, protest rallies, feasting or the carnivalesque rather than the traditional rites of the Christian church. Both writers, therefore, proposed a theology of worship that related liturgy, and particularly the Eucharist, to more contemporary forms of ritual. All this work was essentially theological in nature. It offered a suggestion about where worship should be going, rather than a discussion of how worship was actually being practised. The practice was simply taken for granted and was seen to be out of touch with secular society, theologically moribund and generally in a state of crisis (Davies 1973: 307–18).

One project that did bring together sociologists and theologians to focus on worship was also inspired and led by J.G. Davies. This was the Institute for the Study of Worship and Religious Architecture based at the University of Birmingham between 1973 and 1986. To a certain extent this unit existed to forward

Davies' own approach to worship in a secular society as expressed in the second half of *Everyday God* (1973). The unit also had an emphasis on architecture and supported the building of many of the multi-purpose church plants that were so popular in the 1970s. As part of the project both theologians and sociologists were brought together, along with practising architects, and a series of research bulletins and other publications were produced (Davies 1966–83). However, as with Davies' own work, the primary emphasis of the Institute was the development and improvement of worship within a particular theological frame and very little work was done on what was actually happening in churches Sunday by Sunday (but see Leslie 1983 & Bryant 1983).

In the fourteen years since I began my initial research there has been a growing acceptance of the use of anthropology and sociology in the work of liturgists and liturgical theologians. There has always been a certain sense of scepticism, however, about the value of such insights and a tendency to use the findings of these other disciplines simply to bolster an already existing theological agenda. Aiden Kavanagh (1984), David Power (1984) and Robin Green (1987), along with many others, have all contributed, in their different ways, to this growing tradition. The Liturgical Press even produced a series of books on the sacraments which specifically brought together liturgical and sociological/anthropological scholars (Duffy 1987). Much of this literature has provided some very interesting insights along the way, and I will be drawing on these within the analysis that follows. Such literature cannot, however, provide a starting point for the analysis of worship as it happens within our churches today as it is generally too theological to relate to the views of ordinary worshippers.

Anthropological and sociological comments on Christian liturgy

The work of Cox and Davies shared one thing with the very small number of sociologists and anthropologists who were writing directly about Christian worship in the 1970s and 1980s. This was a general distrust of, and often blatant condemnation of, the extensive liturgical revisions which had been going on in many churches since the mid- to late-1960s. The bulk of the radical liturgical revisions, especially the major revolutions in form and language, followed from the Second Vatican Council and were introduced into the Roman Catholic church from 1967 onwards before they were picked up by the other mainstream churches. These took some time to take root within local churches and in the meantime sociologists and anthropologists were among the most vocal critics of these revisions. Ironically it was the very same anthropologists that the contributors to *Worship* and other journals had been drawing on to inform their understanding of liturgy who were among the most critical voices in the battle against the new rites.

Mary Douglas, for example, wrote a number of very critical papers based on her own understanding of Catholic ritual among those whom she described as the 'bog Irish' (1973: 59–76). Victor Turner also expressed his own distaste for the Catholic revisions and framed his critique in terms of his own work on ritual and symbolism (1974: 231–71). Even Margaret Mead, the famous American anthropologist offered her own critique, as her biographer recalls in a chapter titled 'Bishops Might but Anthropologists Do Not' (Howard 1984).

In Britain, David Martin, a prominent sociologist, made an impassioned plea, on very similar grounds, against the new liturgies within the Church of England, calling for the retention of Prayer Book language and rites which people knew, loved, and used to establish their own sense of identity (1980). Cox and Davies were also vociferous critics of these revised rites but unlike Douglas, Turner and Martin, Cox and Davies did not think that they went far enough (Davies 1973: 243–60). They felt that the new liturgies were merely reworkings of ancient formulas and that in a secular world a completely new form of rite would be needed. Once again, therefore, the debate was expressed in terms of what should or should not happen within liturgy rather than what was actually happening in ordinary churches either in Britain or America (see Davies 1983).

Despite the fact that these critiques were undertaken by a group of well-respected scholars, who were highly skilled in social scientific methodologies, there is no evidence in any of their writing that any of them had ever studied what ordinary people in ordinary churches had to say about their worship. As regular worshippers themselves (Douglas and Turner were both converts to Catholicism, Davies and Martin were committed mem-

bers of the Church of England), all these critics considered themselves to be experts in the field and able to act as their own
informants. This would never have been accepted if they were
talking about ritual activity in Africa or South America (where
Douglas, Turner and Martin have all carried out extensive fieldwork). However this situation reflected a far more general position within anthropology where it was considered perfectly normal to use personal reflections on the home society to explain
or illustrate aspects of the society being studied on the assumption that both the anthropologist and the reader of the analysis
already knew about the home society and did not have to have it
explained. Practically all references to Christian liturgy and
worship within anthropology have been of this kind.

On the whole the sociological literature, which might be expected to focus on this important aspect of our own society, has
had even less to say about worship than the anthropologists.
Sociologists of religion in both Britain and America focused their
attention either on questions of secularisation within society as a
whole, or on the study of semi-Christian and non-Christian cults
on the outer edge of our social world. Neither of these approaches led the sociologists to study worship and none of this material
had any obvious relevance for the kind of question that I wished
to address.

It is interesting to note, therefore, that, as was the case with
the liturgical and theological use of anthropology and sociology, very little has actually changed in the years since I began my
initial fieldwork. There are still very few decent studies of Christian worship in practice. Victor Turner has developed his work
on pilgrimage, some of it within a Christian context (Turner &
Turner 1978) and a small number of other texts have been produced. The only major contribution to this field has been Keir-
en Flanagan's book *Sociology and Liturgy* (1991). This book is
something of a broadside, from a post-modern perspective, on
the liturgical revisions of the1960s and 1970s. Flanagan, however, suffers from all the same problems that we have already seen
in other anthropological and sociological critiques of the revised rites. He draws entirely on his own personal experience in
discussing the liturgy (offering in the process a very plausible
argument for why this can be the only kind of approach (1991:
8–10)) and appears to be almost entirely out of touch with the

situation in most of the churches in Britain today. A small number of theses and other tentative research work have also tried to explore worship in practice in a similar way to my own field-work. Despite this, however, we still remain as ignorant today of how ordinary people actually understand and respond to Christian worship as we were when I held my first conversation with Kenneth Stevenson almost fifteen years ago. It was clear, therefore, right from the start of my own research that I would have to look elsewhere for my methodology.

The anthropological study of ritual

When I began my research I had hoped to turn to the anthropological tradition of the study of ritual for my principal methodology. I knew some of this material from my undergraduate course and I familiarised myself with much more over time. The mid-1980s was, in fact, a good time to become interested in this material as it was at about this time that the study of ritual was beginning to experience something of a renaissance within anthropology. Much of this new work was related to the 'symbolist' analysis used primarily by those who studied ritual in New Guinea (see Lewis 1980), but there was also a great deal of other material from other parts of the world which subsequently proved to be very interesting and relevant.

What has become apparent over the years, however, is that it is not only in the area of Christian worship where there appears to be a lack of information on, or models of how to discover answers to, questions relating to the way ordinary people respond to ritual. I had assumed that while it was clear that anthropologists did not deal with Christian worship in Western cities, they did at least have a methodology for studying, and a procedure for analysing, the way in which ordinary members of a society understood and responded to the rites in which they took part. This methodology was essentially ethnographic. As I began to read this material, however, and came to try and use it for my own purposes, it gradually became more and more apparent that this is not the case. Certainly anthropologists have been among the most prolific writers on ritual; they have probably described and analysed more rituals than any other discipline. It is also true that one of the principal driving forces for ethnography is to try to understand a society from the point of view of the ordinary members of that society. There are, however, with only a very few exceptions (see for example Barth 1975), practically no attempts within the anthropological literature to try to develop a methodology by which the researcher can begin to explore the way in which ordinary people comprehend, perceive or understand the rituals in which they take part.

Practically all the analysis of ritual within anthropology is done from the anthropologist's own, detached and external, point of view (sometimes using 'native exegesis'[2] as part of the data but not asking how this 'native exegesis' is arrived at). More than this, the analysis of ritual is primarily seen as one way in which the researcher can begin to understand the basic values of a society which are thought to be encoded within that ritual, rather than the researcher asking what kind of meaning the ritual has for individual participants and how that meaning is arrived at. If this is not the case then the anthropologists are interested in creating, or improving, a 'theory' of ritual: in other words, exploring the nature of ritual in and of itself, rather than asking how ritual is perceived by those who use it (Humphrey & Laidlaw 1994). There are many reasons for this position which I will be exploring in Chapters One to Three below. What this meant in practice, however, was that I actually had to turn to other methodologies, and even to other disciplines, in order to find a method by which the ordinary perception of worship could be observed, recorded and assessed.

The sociology of religious opinions

What I was looking for was a methodology by which I could explore how questions of religious opinions, perceptions and responses have been approached within the study of our own society, and then to ask how far this can help with the study of perceptions and responses to worship. Many studies of religious opinions within Britain have touched on questions relating to worship but once again, like so many other forms of the literature, they have seldom engaged directly with the problems raised by the understanding of Christian worship from the perspective of the participant.

The most widely used method for gaining religious opinions and responses is the statistical survey. These have been used for many different purposes over the past hundred years or so. At one level the usual batch of church statistics is interesting because they can at least tell us how many people are attending worship at any one time and how that number has changed (Brierely & Hisock 1993). Most versions of membership statistics are related to attendance at worship in some way, and when sociologists discuss declining membership in the mainstream churches then what they are usually discussing is the decline in the number of people attending worship. It is often assumed, therefore, that there is a declining number of people who are getting anything significant out of their worship. There is, however, no direct evidence for this disenchantment within the statistics themselves. The many different theories that have been proposed for the decline in numbers, therefore, generally depend on the personal speculation of the proposers (Davie 1994, Bruce 1995). Such statistics can tell us a great deal about changes in numbers. Other methods are needed, however, to explain how these changes should be interpreted.

Another range of statistics focuses less on attendance at worship, or on membership of particular churches; rather, it aims to discover how widespread beliefs in God, in hell, in the ten commandments or whatever, are within society as a whole (Abrams et al 1985). Once again these numbers are interesting. It is interesting to know, for example, that while 76 per cent of the population claim to believe in God, less than 25 per cent claim to attend public worship in anything like a regular fashion (Thompson 1988: 228–30). This has the potential to reveal a great deal about the way people understand worship, but once again all that it can really say is dependent on the speculative powers of those who wish to interpret it. The numbers alone cannot even tell us a great deal about what they claim to assert: that 76 per cent of people 'believe in God'. Simply asking the question of a random group of people and demanding an instant 'yes/no' answer offers us no understanding as to what the respondents mean by the word 'God' or even by the word 'believe' (Stringer 1997b). We can never be very sure whether such surveys can actually tell us very much about people's real perceptions or opinions at all.

This leads on to a number of approaches which go beyond the widescale asking of simple 'yes/no' questions and focuses, in one way or another, on asking more specific and detailed questions, through interviewing or other similar techniques. One area where the eliciting of opinions from a wide cross section of ordinary churchgoers has been very common in recent years has been in the production of church reports such as *Faith in the City* (ACCUPA 1985), *Faith in the Countryside* (ACRA 1990) and, perhaps most interestingly for our purposes, *Views from the Pews* (BCC 1986). The compilers of *Faith in the City*, and its counter-part for the countryside, placed great stress on the fact that they listened to what ordinary people had to say (ACCUPA 1985: xiv). This 'listening' involved a combined process of open meetings at which individual responses were elicited, direct interviews with significant people and an open invitation for individuals to send their responses direct to the compilers. Many of the direct comments and quotations from 'ordinary' people are contained within the final reports and give them a level of authority and authenticity that they might not otherwise have. In neither report, however, does worship form a major area of interest, although the criticism of the limited space given to worship in *Faith in the City* did lead to some expansion by the time of *Faith in the Countryside* (ACCUPA 1985: 134–6, ACRA 1990: 181–206). What they do say, however, is interesting only because it appears to be the case that what the compilers heard from ordinary people simply reinforced what they already felt to be true from their own observations. Worship was seen to be boring and out of touch. Within such a process it is always possible to ask who was actually being listened to, how that listening was conducted, how it was recorded and what use was being made of the results. It is clear that the respondents themselves were largely self-selected, being primarily those with particular complaints or those who could shout most loudly at public meetings (see Hobson 1993).

Selective listening and open meetings are not only used by the compilers of church reports. They are also used, although in an even less systematic way, by a number of popular liturgists and pastoral theologians to justify their own reflections on worship (see Carr 1985, Cotton & Stevenson 1996, Green 1987 & Ramshaw 1987). A quotation from an 'ordinary member of the congregation', therefore, as with the official reports, gives such reflections a certain relevance and authenticity that might otherwise be lacking. There is, however, nothing objective in such reporting and we hear nothing from those who may be perfectly satisfied with their worship, from those who are unwilling or unable to offer their particular point of view, or from those who see the whole process of consultation as an irrelevant exercise.

On a much larger scale comparative sociology acts as a halfway house between the random interview technique, which underlies the report producing-process, and ethnography in its full form. Researchers who choose the comparative sociological approach tend to be worried about questions of typicality related to the detailed study of particular congregations, and yet want to get beyond the wide-ranging and impersonal questionnaire. Many of the studies in this category are large scale and expensive, involving a large number of researchers and a great deal of organisation and careful analysis of the data. It is not surprising, therefore, that many of the studies of this kind have been carried out in the United States (Leege & Gremillion 1984–87, Livezey 1996).

An interesting example of this kind of study was the Notre Dame Study of Catholic Parish Life based at Notre Dame University with Mark Searle as the liturgical advisor (Searle & Leege 1985a, 1986). This research consisted of a number of identical studies of a carefully selected sample of Catholic parishes across the States. In each case a number of different techniques were used, including mass questionnaires, specific interviewing and participant observation. The participant observation was used primarily for the study of worship. In each of the parishes being studied two researchers, one a practising Catholic with a personal knowledge of the liturgy, the other a trained social science observer, went into the parish to observe one act of worship (Searle & Leege 1985a). This dual observation was then supplemented by questions about worship in the questionnaires and interviews that were carried out alongside the observation.

It may be thought that such a carefully controlled process would have been able to provide a very clear picture of the way in which ordinary members of, in this case Catholic, congregations perceived, understood and responded to their worship. It certainly raised a number of interesting questions. However, the overall shallowness of the data, the superficiality of the techniques, and the need to provide comparative material meant that in the end what was found proved to be little more than could have been predicted by any well-travelled Catholic who attended mass in more than one church and who had a certain interest in what was going on. Questions were asked of those interviewed about the level of congregational participation, about the relationship between formality and levels of congregational singing in the liturgy, and correlations between political views and preferences in liturgical style (Searle & Leege 1985a, 1985b). There is nothing in this material which can begin to ask the deeper, more searching, question about perception or response, and nothing that can distinguish the range of different, and essentially individual, views within any one congregation. One visit and a series of questionnaires and interviews cannot get beneath the surface of a community or explore the particular responses and thought processes of individuals within the congregation. For this something far more long term and in depth is needed.

This brings us back to the process of ethnography, the long term study of a particular community by an individual researcher who aims, so far as it is possible, to be a complete participant observer. We have already noted the process of ethnography as used by anthropologists in their study of ritual, although I have claimed that these anthropologists have generally failed to ask the kind of questions of that ritual, and of those who take part in it, that were of particular interest to me. There have also been a small number of ethnographic studies of congregations in Britain, most of which derive from the series of so-called 'parish studies' which were undertaken in the1950s and 1960s (Crow & Allan 1994: 13–18). These were concerned with the wider questions of the social make-up of congregations and the formation of beliefs and opinions within those congregations so there should have been something within this material that could have been of interest to me.

The earliest of these parish studies, like Conor Ward's study of a Catholic parish in Liverpool (1965), are primarily statistical and suffer from the same kinds of problems that I have already highlighted for other methods. As the method developed, however, so did the sophistication of the analysis and the kind of data that was generated. Robert Moore's study of chapel life and politics in a Durham mining village (1974) and David Clark's study of chapel life and the fishing industry in a North Yorkshire fishing village (1982) are excellent local community studies which raise many interesting questions about the nature of religion and belief in community life. One thing that is very clear about both studies, however, is the complete lack of any data about worship. It is almost as if the authors never actually went into the chapels during worship, or they felt that this was something they could not, or should not, comment on.

It is evident, from all these different kinds of study that the only way in which I could begin to get a clear idea of how ordinary members of local congregations understood their worship was to use an ethnographic type of methodology. In other words I needed to go and worship with a specific congregation for a considerable length of time. It was also important to participate fully in the wider life of the congregation, to get to know individual members of the congregation as people, to observe what was going on in many different kinds of situation, and to listen as clearly and as closely as is possible to everything that was being said. It was only by getting within the congregation, by aiming to understand the members of that congregation from the inside, that any sense of the perception of, or response to worship could have been achieved. This, then, was what I set out to do.

REFLECTING ON AN EXPERIENCE OF FIELDWORK

When I began my initial study I, like many first-time ethnographers, knew very little about the methodology of fieldwork in any technical sense. I had three years full-time research ahead of me and I knew that I wanted to spend as much of that time as possible in the field. I was also persuaded that I should do more than one study during this time so that I could analyse the results in a comparative fashion.[3] I chose, therefore, to undertake four studies, in four very different congregations in the South Manchester area. Each study would last six months, making a total field experience of two years. The four congregations that I chose were Baptist, Roman Catholic, Independent Christian Fellowship and Anglican.[4]

As I began the fieldwork I knew very little of what was expected of me as an 'ethnographer' and to a large extent I had to learn on the job. The fieldwork I undertook was not perfect. It never is. There are always restrictions of time or practical problems relating to the specific context of the fieldwork or to personalities within the community being studied. If I were to have the chance to undertake the study again then I would no doubt do some things differently. The lack of any formal training in fieldwork techniques, however, probably had its advantages as well as its disadvantages. At the most obvious level it did mean that I was free to explore what seemed interesting to me, rather than trying to follow any particular scheme of research, or to answer any specific questions. I am sure that if I had not entered into this initial phase of fieldwork in such a naive fashion I would never have begun to ask the kind of questions which led to my conversation with Mark Searle on the question of meaning.

After completing this initial fieldwork, however, I subsequently worked for five years with thirteen Anglican congregations in East Manchester. In 1993 I took up a post as Lecturer in the Anthropology/Sociology of Religion at the University of Birmingham, where I have subsequently found myself trying to prepare a new generation of first-time fieldworkers for the ethnographic study of worship in different religious communities within Birmingham. My experience of fieldwork and my knowledge of the ethnographic literature has grown enormously since I started out on this project. This has enabled me to be far more critical of my own methods within the different congregations in Manchester. It has also enabled me to draw on that experience, to reflect on it critically, and then to use what I have learnt from that experience to critique the literature on ethnography and fieldwork that I have subsequently read. For this reason, therefore, this book should be seen as both a reflection on the initial period of fieldwork, along with the results and theories that were generated from it, and an engagement with the methodological questions raised by the ethnographic study of worship in general.

In Part II of the book I have outlined what I gained from the fieldwork itself and presented some of the data and analysis that was associated with this. In Part I, however, I have chosen to take up in more detail some of the questions of methodology, ethnography and perception that I have already raised in an initial fashion in this introduction. The aim of Part I is to try to give some indication of what it is possible to discover during fieldwork about the perception of worship within a congregation and the implications that this might have for the way in which the whole topic of worship is approached in the future. In Chapter One, I ask what it is that is being studied: what is worship? In Chapter Two, I explore the concept of ethnography and ask what this can offer a study of worship. In Chapter Three, I explore the nature of the data that I had to work with and the different discourses that surrounded worship in the different congregations that I studied. In each of these chapters the conversation with Mark Searle concerning the question of 'meaning' in worship hovers in the background, never fully coming to rest at any point, but never being far away from any of the discussions.

Part II consists of an outline of the kinds of data that I discovered from the research and some of my own reflections on this data at that time. It is here that the question of meaning finally comes to the fore. As it became more and more impossible to talk in terms of specific meanings for worship in the four congregations that I was dealing with, I became more and more interested in the process by which particular meanings could be generated by individual members of the different congregations. In Part III, therefore, I try to draw together some of the theoretical questions raised within Part I and the data explored in Part II and aim to create an understanding of worship, not in terms of its nature or form, but rather in terms of how worship is perceived by those who take part in it every week or every day of their lives.

NOTES

1   Throughout this book I have made very little distinction between specifically sociological or specifically anthropological contributions to the discussion of worship or ritual. In recent years these two traditions have been coming together, especially in areas such as the study of ritual, and it is not always possible to distinguish one from the other. I have therefore used the two terms almost interchangeably unless it is clear from the text that a particular approach is being used, or if a specific author is clearly identified with a particular discipline.

2   'Native exegesis' is the term that Victor Turner coined to de-

scribe the way in which the people who perform a rite talk about, and explain that rite to each other (see Turner 1967a).

3   This still remains one of the major distinctions between sociology and anthropology so far as fieldwork is concerned. An anthropologist will generally aim to undertake a study of one specific community and to spend as long as possible within that community. The sociologist, on the other hand, usually feels the need for some kind of comparative data and will tend towards a number of shorter, more small-scale studies. When I began this research I was working within a Faculty of Theology which felt that it was important that I should work within a sociological rather than an anthropological frame as this was the approach with which the Faculty was most familiar. If I were to do the study again I would probably move more towards the anthropological and aim to undertake one long study within one specific congregation.

4   Throughout this book I have retained the anonymity of the specific churches that I studied through the use of generic titles. All four churches were in the South Manchester area within a four-mile radius of the University.

PART I

CHAPTER ONE
ON WORSHIP

The first question that must be asked in any book that claims to be about the way members of a congregation understand worship is what is meant by 'worship'. Or, to phrase the same question in a different way, why have I chosen to use the popularist word 'worship' as opposed to the academically more acceptable terms of 'ritual', 'liturgy' or 'rite'? In many of the works of anthropologists, sociologists, theologians and liturgists, the term 'worship' is shunned. There are probably many reasons for this but the two which are most common, and most pertinent, are that the word 'worship' is seen to be too specific, or that the word 'worship' is seen to be too general. 'Worship', it is sometimes assumed, is what is done through liturgy, what happens within the rite. It is one aspect of ritual which may or may not be present in any specific context. 'Worship' in this view could be considered to be too 'Christian' to explain what non-Christians do when they perform rituals: it is too specific. A variation on this argument suggests that 'worship' is a mode of behaviour, a stance towards some external object which, like religious experience in general, cannot easily be studied by social scientists (Turner & Bruner 1986). The alternative view, that which sees worship as too general, sees worship as something that can be done anywhere and at any time and is not restricted to the context of liturgy, rite or ritual at all. All Christians, according to this view, as well as those of other faiths, are called on to worship God at all times and in all places. The communal 'act of worship', therefore, is only a more specific example of the general practice.

Given these objections, I need to restate my initial question: why have I chosen to use the word 'worship' over and against those other words which are more commonly used, those which appear to be more precise, and those which are more generally accepted within the different academic discourses? My answer lies precisely in the use to which the other words have been put, and the semantic baggage that each of the other terms has inherited. It might be instructive, therefore, to look at the roots of some of the various terms that I could have chosen – 'ritual', 'liturgy' or 'rite' – and to see what implications and assumptions they carry. This should then help to explain why these terms have been rejected. Finally, I will come back to 'worship' itself and explain, in a more positive sense, why I find this particular word to be more helpful for my own purposes.

THE SOCIOLOGICAL ROOTS OF 'RITUAL'

In trying to investigate the distinctions between the use of the word 'ritual' and the use of the word 'worship' we need to go back to the middle of the nineteenth century. It is not that either word was coined at this time, nor that either was clearly redefined, but that the two words began at this time to be used more specifically within a more technical kind of discourse. It was within the discussion of 'religion' as applied to other, i.e. non-Christian, religions, that the two words began to drift apart and to develop subtle differences of meaning. In response to the growing awareness of, and need to react to, the presence of 'other' religions in the world a number of different approaches were developed which were originally very closely related (Jordon 1905: 15–22). All these different approaches focused primarily on what people 'did' within the other religions and only incidentally on what they believed.[1] What travellers and missionaries first discovered when they travelled to India, or the South Seas, or Africa were 'rituals', that is acts of worship which could be observed and described in journals, but which, to the outsider, appeared totally meaningless and bizarre, if not cruel and depraved. There were essentially two responses to these activities that went on to provide the origins of the distinction between 'ritual' and 'worship'. Either the acts were considered as something different from, and entirely other than, Christian worship (especially as understood by the Protestant missions) and were therefore defined as 'ritual', or they were of the same kind as Christian worship but were wrongly focused, and were therefore defined as 'worship', but as 'wrong' worship, the giving of worth to the wrong object, seen either as demonic or as a false and lifeless 'idol'.

Underlying this distinction were, of course, many other assumptions, not least the kinds of discourses that different Christian bodies in Britain already used to define the worship/ritual practised by the others.[2] For the British Protestant the use of the word 'ritual' to define the meaninglessness and bizarre acts of the other had a certain attraction. The same word was often applied to Roman Catholic liturgy, even by the Catholics themselves, and this was also dismissed by the Protestants as equally meaningless, corrupt and bizarre. It was, however, only when those who stood outside the religious debate altogether, the growing band of anti-religious social scientists, came to utilise these terms that the underlying distinctions of the Catholic/Protestant divide became fixed as part of a supposedly 'scientific' discourse.

For the sociological writers on religion in the middle of the nineteenth century all activity that was focused on that which was not rational or empirical could be dismissed as meaningless, bizarre and illusory. In this context, therefore, the use of the word 'ritual' for such activity appeared to be the most obvious choice.[3] The fact that this was a disputed term within Christian discourse made very little impact on these early writers, and they soon colonised the term as their own, such that the churches eventually had to carry the baggage of the social scientists when they began to use the term as an insult, or clarion call, within the 'ritualist' debates of the second half of the nineteenth century. This clearly played into Protestant hands as far as the popular conception of worship was concerned. Roman Catholics, on the other hand, or those with Catholic leanings, had to find alternative language. Fortunately there were a number of alternatives available. Walter Frere, Aiden Fortescue, and other more moderate writers, followed one longstanding tradition and used the word 'ceremonial' (Frere 1906, Fortescue 1919). J.M. Neale (1863) F.E. Brightman (1896) and Edmund Bishop (1918), all writing for a more academic audience, used the term 'liturgy'. The more conservative element, however, stuck doggedly to the word 'ritual' and arguably suffered as a consequence (see Cairncross et al 1935).

Within the sociological tradition, however, things were not quite as clear cut as they might have appeared. Edward Tylor, for example, was always very ambiguous in his use of terminology and tended to use whichever term best suited his own particular needs at any particular time, either for academic or literary purposes. This is especially true of words that related to religion. 'Ritual' and 'worship' are no exception. Tylor very rarely uses the word 'ritual' and gives the title 'Rites and Ceremonies' to the chapter of his book *Primitive Culture* (1871: 328), which deals with acts of worship. However, there is also a discussion of 'worship' within the book, especially as this relates to apparently inanimate objects (1871: 194–223). Here again, therefore, we see the distinction between meaningless 'ritual' (or rite) and wrong 'worship' which was inherited from the early missionaries. Tylor, however, would probably be far more ambiguous about the notion of rites being 'meaningless' or the worship of idols being 'wrong' than his choice of language might suggest. It is only in the hands of other, less subtle or ambiguous, writers that these terms came to develop their distinctly negative feel in relation to the religious practices of non-Christian others.

Three works in particular emphasised the apparent meaninglessness of ritual, although all three gave the term a distinctly different feel. James Frazer, in *The Golden Bough* (1911), associates ritual most clearly with magic. Ritual, therefore, like magic, is essentially functional, although, again like magic, it is wrongly directed. It does not achieve those functions that its protractors claim that it achieves. The 'ritual' of magic is clearly seen in Frazer's work to be meaningless, or perhaps 'pointless'. The process that leads to ritual, however, through the understanding of sympathetic or contagious magic, may be understandable and even be seen as 'rational' or comprehensible in itself. In Frazer's view, therefore, ritual is seen as being mistaken. For other writers this is not the case.

R.R. Marett, for example, places a great emphasis on ritual in his book *The Threshold of Religion* (1914). For Marett ritual is not seen as a misguided attempt to do something, rather it is understood as a practical response to the overwhelming emotions that are seen to be at the root of religion. 'Religion', in Marett's words, 'is something not so much thought out as danced out' (1914: xxxi). For Marett raw emotions are such that they cannot be handled in a rational, thinking kind of way. They demand a response that is instinctive and physical. A good example of this came in the aftermath of the death of Diana, Princess of Wales. The emotional response that many individuals felt could not be put adequately into words, rather there was the demand to 'do something', to sign a book, or to lay flowers, or simply to be at the roadside or watch the funeral on television. It is this incoherent need to 'do something', no matter what, that Marett saw to be at the root of ritual, and subsequently of religion. Ritual for Marett, therefore, is entirely meaningless, not in the sense that it is wrong as Frazer suggested, but rather in that it expresses something that is beyond words.

Building on Marett's understanding of religion, and therefore of ritual, are the writings of other contemporary theorists such as Robert Lowie (1936) who saw the roots of religion in the specific emotion of 'awe' (what Rudolf Otto was to define as the 'numinous' (1928)). Lowie's theory of religion as 'awe' is based on a study of religion among the Crow, a Native American people. The 'spirit quest', for example, or the process of individual asceticism leading to a self-induced trance state, led Lowie to place the concept of 'awe' at the heart of religion. Consequently the central image of Indian braves, all dressed up in feathered headdresses and dancing round the totem pole emphasised the nature of ritual as, in Marett's terms, the 'dancing out' of emotional turmoil. This image of the dancing brave is still one of the primary images associated with the word 'ritual' even in our contemporary society. Alongside this we also have the 'African' image of the 'witchdoctor', complete with a bone through his nose, dancing round the oversized cooking pot in which the missionary boils for the cannibal feast. These colonialised images continue to hover around the use of the word 'ritual' even in modern academic discourse. However hard anthropologists and others have tried to stress the word as a technical term, the underlying image of Marett's dancing savages will never quite go away.

It was another author, however, who finally fixed the word 'ritual' firmly within the anthropological literature. This was W. Robertson Smith in his influential *Lectures on the Religion of the*

Semites (1907). The central theme of these lectures was 'sacri-fice' and Robertson Smith came to the conclusion that, as he looked over the whole of what he assumed to be the history of the Semite peoples, the action and process of sacrifice remained practically unchanged while the meaning that was given to the act, and the stories which were told around it, changed dramat-ically over time and space. This led Robertson Smith to stress that the act, the 'ritual' in his terms, remained static and prima-ry, while the meaning, the 'post hoc justification' changed dra-matically depending on context (1907: 439). Once again, there-fore, ritual is seen to be inherently meaningless, although in Robertson Smith's case it is seen to be an action that demands the creation of meaning, or at the very least acts as a magnet to attract meaning. Robertson Smith's emphasis on the primacy of action, that is of 'ritual', over meaning has remained fundamen-tal to the development of the anthropology of religion. A direct line can be traced from Robertson Smith, through Emile Dur-kheim (1915), who saw the given meaning of the rite as second-ary to the collective nature of that rite, to E.E. Evans Pritchard (1956) and beyond. Underlying this tradition is the idea of the essential meaninglessness of ritual in and of itself.

In the1950s and 1960s, however, this situation was to change, primarily through the work of Victor Turner. Turner, like a number of other anthropological writers of the time, drew on the philosophical work of Susanne Langer (1942) who had de-veloped an understanding of symbolism based on the similari-ties between 'symbolic language' and music or art. It was through an initial emphasis on the 'symbol', therefore, which Turner saw as the smallest element of any ritual action, and which Lang-er emphasised as that which carries meaning, that the concept of meaning was once again introduced into the study of ritual (1942). For Turner ritual was still essentially functional, but not in the sense used by Frazer. The function of ritual, for Turner, was primarily to resolve social conflict. It did this through the manipulation of symbols that carried meanings related to the emotive and the ideological elements of society such that the positive elements of the emotional became attached to the diffi-cult elements of the ideological (1967a). Turner went to some lengths to identify and to catalogue the specific meanings of in-dividual symbols within the rituals of the Ndembu people from

Zambia (1968). These meanings, however, particularly in Turner's early work, still existed at one remove from the ritual itself. The meanings were associated with 'symbols' (which in Turner's case were almost entirely of a material nature, things in the world rather than actions or words). Each 'symbol' was associated with a range of meanings, even an ambiguity of meanings. It was these symbols, however, with their associated meanings, which were manipulated in ritual to achieve the functional end that the ritual was supposed to achieve. The ritual, as such, was still seen to be meaningless, or at best merely the framework into which symbolic meanings could be introduced.

It was only when later writers, influenced by the linguistics of Ferdinand de Saussure (1959), began to look at ritual from the perspective of structuralism or semiotics that a more direct link between ritual, symbol and meaning was established (see, for example, Gell 1975, Hugh-Jones 1979). For these writers symbols did not exist in isolation, each with its own range of meanings. Rather symbols formed distinct systems of meaning, after the Saussurian model for language. The manipulation or juxtaposition of these symbols within ritual did not 'do' anything in the functionalist sense, rather they 'said' something. Ritual began to be understood as something that communicated messages through symbolic languages (Leach 1976). Meaning, therefore, far from being something that was absent from ritual, began to be seen as the very heart of ritual, as that which ritual was about. Edmund Leach took this approach to its extreme by suggesting that ritual was the communicative, or aesthetic, element of any action (1968). This extreme position, however, has very rarely been held and developed by anthropologists studying 'rituals' in the field. The logic of this position on the other hand has been widely accepted. The task of the anthropologist who studied ritual, therefore, was seen as a process of decoding the 'meaning' of the act, uncovering its essential message, and making it apparent for all to see. What was less clear, however, was that if ritual was essentially about meaning, was a form of communication, then who was communicating to whom, and why was there such a need to wrap this communication up in such a complex and incomprehensible form?

What becomes very clear in the light of this question is that the meaning of ritual within this tradition was thought to be accessible only to the anthropologist, that is to the one who had the tools to decode the message (see Lewis 1980). This, however, only had the effect of making the rite itself essentially meaningless for the participants, or rather of making any meaning which those participants might have gained from the rite theoretically irrelevant. This position therefore reverted to a Robertson Smith kind of approach such that the meaning of the rite is always established post hoc, by the academic outsider. At another level the 'symbolic' was associated with the 'emotional' (following Marett?) and it was the emotive element of the symbolic that was seen to give significance to the message even when the message itself was not always understood by the participants themselves (Richards 1956). In both cases there was still the suggestion that the rite itself, or by implication ritual in general, was felt to be meaningless, at least for those who participated in it. Any meaning that was derived from the rite existed either in the analysis of the anthropologist or in the purely emotive response of the participants.

One final point which may be worth noting before I leave this particular discussion is that it was clearly the possibility of ritual being meaningful, as containing a message, that eventually enabled the discussion of ritual to be taken up by liturgists and others working from a Christian perspective. It is interesting, however, to recall that it was the work of Victor Turner that was most widely used. Turner, as we have seen, placed the meaning of the ritual within the symbols that went to form that ritual and this sat very easily with a particularly Catholic understanding of the symbolic. The work of structuralists, and symbolists, however, who placed the meaning of the rite within the analysis of the one who is able to decode the symbolic language, was very rarely taken up.[4] This is probably because these writers appeared to deny, or at least to downplay the meanings which participants gave to their own rites and substituted other, from their view more fundamental, meanings in their place. This is not a position which those committed to Christian worship would ever be very happy with. What this shows, however, is that for these writers, like many within the anthropological tradition before them, the meaninglessness of ritual for the participant was a stumbling block for the liturgists and theologians.

This is not the end of the development of ideas about ritual within anthropology. However, as the next stage in the story begins to interact more closely with the work which was being undertaken by liturgists and others, the roots of some of the other terms in the debate need to be explored before we can take this discussion forward

THE LITURGISTS' REJECTION OF 'RITUAL'

To explore the other primarily academic term that I could have chosen we need once again to go back into the nineteenth century. 'Liturgy' has come to be the principal term used by academics within the Christian tradition to talk about their own rites and about worship more generally. 'Liturgy' as a technical term finds its roots in the nineteenth century at about the same time as those in the social sciences were fixing on the term 'ritual'. 'The Liturgy' was the title that has always been used by the Greek-speaking part of the church to refer to the Eucharistic rite. At the beginning of the nineteenth century the word was used by William Palmer and others to refer to the rites of the ancient church (Palmer 1832, Hammond 1878). All that remained of these rites, however, were the texts of the prayers that were used, and in a small number of cases the rubrics and other related texts. The study of the ancient liturgies, therefore, was essentially the study of texts. Palmer, however, was not particularly interested in the content of the texts but more in their similarity to contemporary liturgical texts and the order of these texts within the rite (Stringer 1994). Liturgists since Palmer, on the other hand, have always engaged in a theological debate about the meaning of the rites they studied. This always appears to have taken second place, however, to the study of the rites as texts, almost irrespective of the meaning of those texts in and of themselves.

John Mason Neale, a mid nineteenth-century linguist, hymn writer and Anglican clergyman, claims to have been the first to use the term 'Comparative Liturgy' to describe what he and other liturgists did (Neale 1863: 123–4). It is clear, however, that it is the 'comparative' element of this term that was original to Neale, not the use of the word 'liturgy' (Stringer 1997a). What Neale did by coining this particular term was to link the study of liturgy to the growing number of other aspects of social life which were being studied using the 'comparative method'. These included language, social institutions and religion Tylor (1871) provides an excellent example of this kind of method in anthropology). Using this method Neale catalogued the rites contained within the textual record and set them into families based primarily on questions of style and content (Neale 1869). This method was later developed by Anton Baumstark at the turn of the century (Baumstark 1958). Baumstark went further than Neale in that he not only aimed to classify rites into specific families but he also devised 'laws' which governed the way in which rites changed over time. This link with social science methodologies has always remained somewhere in the background of the study of liturgy throughout the twentieth century. It was not until comparatively recently, however, that liturgists have drawn specifically on sociological and anthropological models for the analysis of Christian rites, and then, as I have already suggested, they have tended to be very selective.

The academic analysis of liturgical texts, however, is only one of two traditions that have colonised the word 'liturgy' and made it the principle academic term for Christian worship. The second tradition had a far more practical origin and developed at the turn of the century into what became known as the 'Liturgical Movement' (Fenwick & Spinks 1995). This movement had its origins in the re-establishment of the Benedictine monasteries in France following their closure during the French Revolution. Within these monasteries there was a growing interest in the kind of worship that was being performing and in questions of community and contemporary relevance. Abbé Prosper Gueranger from the Abbey at Solesmes was the founding influence of this movement, although the organised form of the Liturgical Movement only emerged in Belgium at the turn of the current century (Botte 1988). Gueranger was a Benedictine and was interested in the role of the Office, and in questions of community within a Benedictine monastic tradition (Flanagan 1991: 325–6). He wanted to explore ways of bringing the rite back into what he saw as its original communal form and away from the individualistic act of piety that it had become following the Council of Trent. One of Gueranger's main interests was in music, and he encouraged the re-emergence of plainchant as the principle means for developing communal, participative Christian worship within the monastery.

The primary concern of the founders of the Liturgical Movement was for the rediscovery of the communal in worship (Fenwick & Spinks 1995: 5–7). In part this had to do with the presentation of the rite, and hence the continued interest in musical forms and questions of space and movement. However, it also had to do with the understanding of the rite by those who participated in it and it is here that many of the more recent trends in liturgical revision find their roots. At the end of the nineteenth century all Catholic liturgy was still performed in Latin, and while the founders of the Liturgical Movement were not originally concerned with the translation of the rite, they were concerned that it should be made meaningful for those who took part. Participation was the key to this process and some way of understanding the text, and the actions which surrounded that text, was felt to be necessary for full participation. Various methods were developed to enable this process, including the provision of written translations which could be followed during the rite, commentaries on the rite in the vernacular, and the simplification of the actions by the clergy and others during the rites themselves. Alongside this there developed a programme of education and formation which was aimed at instructing more people in the nature of the rite, to help them to understand what was going on and hence to enable them to participate more fully (Botte 1988).

Within the Roman Catholic Church the work of the Liturgical Movement carried on with more or less official support as a minority interest on the margins of the continental church until the Second Vatican Council. Throughout the twentieth century various minor changes were made to the liturgy itself by various popes, and some of the principles of the movement filtered through into these changes (Bugnini 1990). It was Vatican II, however, which saw the major breakthrough and a change to a situation where the principles of the Liturgical Movement began to dictate the direction of change within the worship of the church. Underlying this change were, once again, the principles of participation and understandability that had been at the heart of the Liturgical Movement from its inception. This led on to more specific questions of translation and simplification. The rite had to be made communal, it had to be approachable by ordinary worshippers, and it had to involve the whole worshipping community. This was a radical, and in many cases total, reworking of the principles on which Christian worship had been based and the effects of this change are still being worked out within the Roman Catholic Church today (Caldecott 1998).

It was not just within the Catholic Church, however, that the Liturgical Movement had its impact. It also affected the Church of England through the Parish Communion Movement and the writings of Gabriel Hebert (Irvine 1993). It affected the Continental and American Lutheran churches and even affected the churches of India and southern Africa, both of whom were among the first to integrate some of its principles into their own liturgical revisions (Jasper 1989: 132–42). In each case worship was understood first and foremost as a communal activity, even as a community-making activity. A premium was placed on the question of understandability (although it was only after the rejection of Latin in the Catholic Church, in favour of contemporary English, that the other churches began to move away from the archaic English in which much of non-Catholic English liturgy had been phrased) and on the question of simplicity and structure (Jasper 1989).

In all these changes, and in the principles that underlie them, we can see the changes and developments in the sociological and anthropological study of ritual coming through. This is seen most clearly in the question of understandability, although the connections are still somewhat complex. I have already shown that the nineteenth century understanding of ritual within sociological writings was that of a meaningless activity. This clearly had its impact on writers such as Gueranger and others who were concerned about the potential meaninglessness of Catholic ritual, much of which had developed in an entirely arbitrary fashion and had become fossilised by the revisions which followed the Council of Trent in the sixteenth century (Flanagan 1991: 48–9). Some kind of 'symbolic' or allegorical meaning had long been associated with this ritual and this medieval approach to symbolic interpretation was resurrected and emphasised by Neale and others involved in the Gothic revival in England in the later nineteenth century (Neale 1843, White 1962). This kind of approach was probably too esoteric, and too close to that which the sociologists were trying to reject, for it to catch on in any major way in Britain. The principles which lay behind it, however, the idea that each symbol had its meaning and that there was a direct and tangible link between the visible symbol and invisible truth which it revealed, continued to remain strong within the popular Catholic imagination. This has also remained the primary way in which ordinary Catholics continued to understand the 'meaning' of their rite even when I was interviewing them as part of my fieldwork in the 1980s.

This kind of symbolic treatment of ritual, however, failed to appeal to the more intellectual and rational traditions of the late nineteenth century and was largely rejected even by those who wished to maintain the ceremonial which it claimed to interpret (see Frere 1906). The explicit rejection of 'meaningless' ritual, therefore, led to an emphasis on the need for liturgy to be 'understood' by those who used it. This could not, however, refer to the explanation of esoteric symbolic meanings but rather to a demand for a more direct form of understandability rooted in the following of the texts themselves. The emphasis on the texts came from the more academic study of liturgy in an historical perspective, and the two traditions, the need for understandability, and an emphasis on the text at the expense of the performance, eventually led to the particular nature of the revisions which took place in all the mainstream churches in the 1960s and 1970s. What were produced were supposedly understandable rites, written in modern English and assuming a fully participating community of worshippers.

It was at exactly this time, however, just as the liturgists were finally rejecting the process of symbolic interpretation and meaning, that anthropologists and sociologists were rediscovering it through the work of Turner and others (Turner 1974).[5] However, as I have already suggested, it may actually have been the liturgists' continued emphasis on the fact that liturgical texts must have meaning, albeit theological rather than symbolic, that made the social scientists begin to explore the possibility that the rituals of other communities may contain messages and have a communicative meaning (even a 'theology') of their own. The traditions of liturgy and sociology/anthropology can never be fully disentangled, but neither can they really be seen as part of a single discourse. The two sides seldom talked directly to each other and the primary drive for development on both sides was arguably a process of mutual misunderstanding.

FOCUSING ON 'RITE'

It is only in recent years that this process of mutual misunderstanding has begun to relax, although there is still a considerable level of suspicion on both sides of the debate. Anthropologists and sociologists rejected the revisions of the liturgists in the 1960s by reverting to a nineteenth-century symbolist approach to ritual (Turner 1974, Martin 1980). Meanwhile liturgists have always felt that any tradition which tries to study Christian worship on the same basis as that used for other religions (especially 'primitive religions', those who have real 'rituals' and dance around totem poles or cannibal pots, unlike Jews who also have 'liturgy' and Muslims and the religions of India who at least have 'worship') should be rejected. Despite this, however, there have been some situations and contexts where the social scientists and the liturgists or theologians have been able to come together on some kind of common ground. What is interesting is that in almost all these cases the terminology that has been used has not been that of either 'ritual' or 'liturgy', but rather the more neutral term 'rite'.

'Rite' has its origins, as a technical term in English, in the writings of French sociologists and liturgists at the turn of the century. The word in French has many similarities to the English word 'ritual', although it does not share all the negative elements of that term as France, with its Catholic tradition, never had the problem of a strong anti-ritualist faction. It was possible within a French context, therefore, for liturgists such as Gueranger and sociologists such as Durkheim to use the same word for the same kind of activity, with only very subtle differences in meaning (Franklin 1976, Durkheim 1915). It is clearly only within the English-speaking traditions that the words have caused so many problems. 'Rite', as a word, also has a history within the English-speaking traditions, but more as a neutral term to avoid the use of 'ritual' or 'liturgy' in the writings of some nineteenth-century English liturgists (Brightman 1915). The word became more popular in the English-speaking traditions, however, through the work of Arnold Van Gennep (1960). Van Gennep's title 'Les Rites de Passage' came to be used in its French form almost as often as it was given an English translation. When his book came to be translated into English, therefore, it retained the word 'rite' in the title and so gave the concept a broader and less prejudiced meaning than it would have done had the translator chosen to use the social scientists' 'ritual'.

Van Gennep's book actually shared a number of similarities with some of the work undertaken by liturgists of about the same time. *Rites of Passage* uses the same kind of comparative methodology as Baumstark (Van Gennep 1960, Baumstark 1958). In both cases the methodology led to the statement of one or more very simple rules which have stood the test of time. In Baumstark's case these were the rules of liturgical development. For Van Gennep the rule consisted in the outlining of a structure for all rites of passage, which had a threefold shape comprising 'rites of segregation', 'rites of transition' and 'rites of integration', along with certain principles based on the nature of transitions and the use of the imagery of death and rebirth in all rites of passage. This same emphasis on shape or structure, although building on the work of Baumstark rather than Van Gennep, can also be seen in Gregory Dix's classic work, *The Shape of the Liturgy* (1945). In this work the concept of 'shape' is used to express the basic structure of all Eucharistic rites. The fundamental emphasis on structures has been maintained in both the anthropological and the liturgical traditions, although the comparative method that led to its early development has since been rejected by both (Bradshaw 1992: 57–63). The use of the word 'rite' as a neutral term within the debate also continued, however, to the point where the revisers of the various liturgies within the different churches in the 1960s and 1970s were able to use the word 'rite' as a technical term for their different texts: for example, the use of 'Rite A' and 'Rite B' as titles for different versions of the Anglican Eucharist (*ASB* 1980), and the use of the term 'rite' in the 'Rite of Christian Initiation of Adults' within the Catholic Church (*RCIA* 1985).

Another area which probably owes its roots to the use of the word 'rite' but which has been growing as a common form of analysis within both liturgy and the anthropological/sociological study of ritual, is the analysis of rite as 'performance' (Bradshaw 1993, Tambiah 1981, Flanagan 1991). This has been an

interesting development that has opened up many different possibilities in all areas of the discussion. The emphasis on performance, with its overtones of 'theatre' and the arts, clearly
overcomes at least one area of dispute between the liturgist and
the anthropologist in the way that it brings together both text
and action without giving priority to either. At its heart, however, the emphasis on 'performance' suggests that all rites must
have some kind of meaning or message and that they use some
kind of symbolic code, as well as a written text, to communicate
that message to the audience. Much of the analysis that derives
from this tradition originated in the study of ritual in India or
Indonesia, where the use of large-scale performance, as understood in a Western sense, is widely used within a ritual context
(Tambiah 1981, Schechner 1993). This has clearly developed
out of a particular strand within anthropology, but has become
increasingly widely developed within both liturgy and anthropology. In anthropology this approach was taken up by Victor
Turner as he moved away from a strictly symbolic approach to
meaning to develop his own concepts of social drama and liminality within rites such as pilgrimage that have always contained
a high level of 'performance' (Turner & Turner 1978). In liturgy it has led to a richer, thicker text that was felt to be necessary
to replace the rather shallow theological treatises that formed
the texts of the 1960s and 1970s (Perham 1993).

This emphasis on performance also draws on another tradition that in very recent years has allowed the study of ritual/
liturgy to develop considerably. This final tradition has many
different roots and can probably look to different origins in different disciplines, but once again it emphasises the importance
of meaning within the rite, although 'meaning' within this tradition is understood neither symbolically nor strictly theologically. This is the hermeneutical tradition. This is related in some
ways to Clifford Geertz's interpretavist approach to anthropology with its roots in Wilhelm Dewey and the American pragma-
tists (Geertz 1973). It is also linked to the work of Hans-Georg
Gadamar, Paul Ricoeur and the development of hermeneutical
interpretation within theology and literary criticism (Gadamar
1979, Ricoeur 1976). From within this tradition all rites are seen
as texts, both in a literal sense and in terms of text as performance. It is at this point therefore that the two traditions, socio-

logical and liturgical finally combine, and merge with the theological in the work of Hans Urs von Balthasar (1988) and others, to form a common contemporary approach (Nichols 1996). This convergence, however, has occurred only at the level of meaning and interpretation and has developed a strongly theological bent (see Flanagan 1991) which actually takes it some way away from the ordinary perspective of the average member of an ordinary congregation. Hermeneutics, as even its name implies, is a highly obscure theoretical approach to rites which dialogues easily with other elements of 'theory' in literary criticism, cultural studies and differing forms of post-modern social thinking, all of which is out of reach, and I might suggest out of touch, for ordinary people getting on with their ordinary lives.

What this means in practice, therefore, is that the kind of 'meaning' which is associated with ritual or liturgy in the performance/hermeneutic tradition is almost identical in type to that which was explained for the structuralist/symbolist tradition. This is not surprising because the use of some form of semiotics underlies both traditions, although with far more sophistication in the former. What is interesting, however, is that while the structuralist/symbolist tradition claimed that only the analyst could decode the meaning of the rite, and that the meaning which was decoded related to some fundamental aspect of society, culture or the subconscious, the performance/hermeneutic tradition, whilst still relying on the power of the analyst to discover the meaning of the text, frames this meaning in far more theological terms. This means that liturgists rejected the former while the latter has been embraced. In principle, however, the two are identical – both place the meaning of the rite, in theory, at the heart of the rite itself – but in practice the meaning of the rite is constructed within the mind, and according to the prejudices of whoever happens to be carrying out the analysis (see Nichols 1996).

WHY 'WORSHIP'?

Within this book I am primarily interested in the way in which ordinary members of Christian congregations in England today understand and respond to the worship they experience every Sunday, and often more frequently. What they experience could be described as 'ritual', although this term would seem very odd to them, and would be a word which all those, from all the churches I studied (including the Roman Catholics), would think of as being dismissive and derogatory. 'Ritual' still has too many overtones of the dancing savages to be a term which ordinary Christians would be happy to use of their everyday worship. 'Ritual' is also treated with suspicion by liturgists and theologians because of the assumptions of meaninglessness and illusion that it still continues to carry. While I do go on to use, and develop, the tradition of 'meaningless ritual' quite extensively in the text that follows, 'ritual' is not a term that I would choose to use as a primary descriptive term for what it is that I am discussing.

'Liturgy' has even less to say for itself. It is a technical term that is largely unknown to ordinary worshippers. It refers primarily to a textual tradition with an inbuilt suspicion of performance and the problems raised by the actual practice of the rite on the ground. It is also a term which is largely meaningless outside a Christian tradition and for these reasons I have tended to avoid it except when I am using it for technical purposes.

So, what about the term 'rite'? This could be a possibility. The term is both neutral and used by ordinary worshippers to describe specific acts of worship. The recent association of the term with the performative and hermeneutical tradition, however, continues to makes me wary. Both the performative and the hermeneutical place far too much stress on 'meaning' for my purposes, especially as this is a 'meaning' which is read into (or out of) the rite by the analyst, rather than claiming to be a reflection of the kinds of meaning which ordinary worshippers may or may not be gaining from their experience of worship. As with 'liturgy' I will be using the term in its technical sense within this book, but as with 'ritual' the word 'rite' does not really capture the essence of what it is that I am primarily interested in.

This leaves me with the word 'worship'. Having largely rejected the other possible terms in the light of the history of their use and the baggage that they carry with them, I do have to acknowledge that the word 'worship' also has a history and therefore carries its own share of semantic baggage. 'Worship' has largely been rejected by the more academic liturgists because it is felt to be too popular. Although it is still used in popular titles, therefore, it is gradually disappearing at all levels of the discussion as 'liturgy' begins to have a wider audience, along with 'formation', 'catechises' and other technical terms related to Christian education (Bishop's Conference 1991). Anthropologists have largely rejected the term because it is too 'Christian'. This is understandable and is a position that I would also be drawn to if I were not studying specifically Christian congregations.[6]

If we look back at those writers who use 'worship' as a technical term then we will find that they come either from a particular strand of liturgical writing, best represented by Evelyn Underhill's book *Worship* (1937), or from the religious studies tradition with its emphasis on phenomenology and the comparative study of religion (Davies 1994). Within both these contexts the choice of the word 'worship' as opposed to 'rite', 'ritual' or 'liturgy', is significant. 'Worship' implies something other than, or perhaps something more than, the rite, the ritual or the liturgy. The use of the word 'worship' places the emphasis not on the text or the performance as a thing in itself, as something in the world that can be recorded and analysed in an abstract form, but implies some level of engagement or experience of that thing, an approach to the ritual, rite or liturgy which can, going back to my original discussion of the early nineteenth-century missionaries, be either 'right' or 'wrong'. Underhill always placed an emphasis on the experience of worship and developed her analysis along lines that were very similar to her study of mysticism (which once again she understood primarily as an experience rather than a theological position (1911)). This same stress on experience (in both mysticism and worship) can also be found within the religious studies tradition, but rooted in the work of William James (1912). Within this tradition, however, the focus is far more on that which is being worshipped, and worship as a specific kind of attitude towards some other object, rather than on the analysis of the experience in and of itself (Davies 1994).

To some extent I would want to draw on the associations of both these traditions by using the word 'worship' in preference to the words 'ritual', 'rite' or 'liturgy'. I would certainly want to endorse the distinction between an attitude towards that which is done or observed, and the event as an objective thing in itself. I would also want to stress the importance of experience. Where I might want to part company with these traditions, however, is in the attempt to be precise about what kind of experience or attitude it is that we might be talking about. It is clear from my research that people have many different experiences within worship, and of worship. People also take many different stances towards worship, not all of which would be recognised by Underhill, or the religious studies tradition, as 'worship'. This is part of what it is that I want to explore. However as it is questions of experience, or attitude, which will form the heart of my analysis, rather than questions of meaning, then I have chosen the term 'worship' to provide the primary referent for what it is that I am aiming to study.

Ultimately, however, it is not the word that matters. It is what is actually going on in churches Sunday by Sunday. Words are simply handles that allow us to discuss this activity in more detail. Much of the discussion of religion generally gets very bogged down by the way in which particular words have come to be given certain technical meanings which have then been opened up for dispute and definitional confusion. This can be seen most clearly in the case of the word 'ritual'. A number of books have been written attempting to define what 'ritual' is, or claiming that this is impossible (see, for example, Lewis 1980). Caroline Humphrey & James Laidlaw, in what is probably the most recent book of this kind, come to the conclusion that there is no such thing as 'ritual' that can be defined in relation to everything that we might want to call 'ritual'. Rather they suggest that we have to talk about the 'ritualisation' of many different activities (1994). This appears to make a great deal of sense, and I will be discussing these ideas again in Chapter Three and in the conclusion. However, even to call what is happening in many different contexts, in many different societies, by the same term, 'ritualisation', probably assumes a continuity which may or may not exist and which can only be established by the careful study of what is actually happening in each and every context. Humphrey and Laidlaw are clearly aware of this and claim that their own work is only specifically relevant for the Jain situation that they set out to study (1994: 1). The same arguments may not make sense of other contexts in other parts of the world. What they do begin with, however, is a detailed study of their own particular situation, without being weighed down by the methodological baggage which goes with assuming that we know what 'ritual' is and that what we are observing and analysing is in fact 'ritual' (1994: 64–87). Within this book I am attempting to undertake exactly the same kind of close observation and analysis of a specific context, in this case in relation to Christian worship in England. Only when that analysis has been completed can we then come back to ask whether this is best described as 'ritual' or 'liturgy' or 'rite' or 'worship'.

NOTES

1   The emphasis on 'belief' within comparative religion only really came about through the work of Max Müller and his publication of the sacred texts of the East in the mid-nineteenth century. The earlier missionaries clearly focused on what they could actually observe, the rituals, and came to their own conclusions concerning the supposedly 'demonic' nature of that which was being worshipped.

2   This distinction is primarily a function of the English language as it developed within a nineteenth century British ecclesial context. As I explain below the French context produced a slightly different range of terms and a different set of understandings.

3   Practically all the early sociologists of religion in Britain – Max Müller, Herbert Spencer, Edward Tylor, James Frazer etc. – while not being practising Christians themselves, came from strongly Protestant backgrounds (Evans-Pritchard 1965: 14).

4   The work of certain theologians, such as Rahner and Schillebeeckx, has taken up this symbolic tradition and clearly did have some influence on the way in which symbols were understood within liturgy and theology more generally (Worgul 1983).

5   It is interesting to speculate about Turner's own conversion to Catholicism at this point, alongside the way in which he appears to pick up a method of symbolic analysis which had been rejected by liturgists but which remained as a common way of thinking about the liturgy among ordinary mass-going Catholics.

6   I would, however, be inclined to use the term more widely because of the other factors which distinguish worship from ritual, liturgy and rite within the different academic traditions.

CHAPTER TWO
ON ETHNOGRAPHY

At the end of the introduction, I suggested that the most suitable method for the analysis of worship was probably ethnography. In this chapter, I wish to justify that claim in a rather unusual way. I need to begin, however, by defining more specifically what I mean by ethnography. This is not as straightforward as it may sound. Martyn Hammersley, in a book called *What's Wrong With Ethnography* (Hammersley 1992), deliberately refuses to address the question of what ethnography is, and chooses to use the term to cover all kinds of qualitative, as opposed to quantitative, research.[1] This use of the term, however, is far too wide for my purposes. Ethnography clearly has its roots within anthropology where it has been the principal method of research since the foundation of the discipline at the turn of the century. There is, therefore, a considerable literature within anthropology on the nature and practice of ethnography. This tradition, however, is driven by the need to do ethnography and has many sub-traditions each relating to distinct practical difficulties in differing kinds of society. There is little within the anthropological literature, therefore, which provides a unified theoretical framework. Anthropologists have, on the whole, simply got on with the doing of ethnography, only making comments on method when they need to justify or explain other aspects of their work.[2]

In recent years something called ethnography has also been taken up by other disciplines: sociology, social psychology, media and cultural studies and so on (Hammersley & Atkinson 1983). In each of these other disciplines the discussion of meth-

od is far more advanced than is traditional within anthropology.
The use of the word 'ethnography', however, has been far less
precise, as with Hammersley's definition referred to earlier. It is
also arguable that what is generally referred to as 'ethnography'
among these other disciplines is not the same as that which is
generally meant within anthropology. For the anthropologist
there are three assumptions which are considered essential for
'ideal' ethnographic study. All of these find their roots in the
work of Bronislaw Malinowski (Malinowski 1922, Kaberry 1957).
The first assumption relates to time. Ethnography demands an
extended period in the field, ideally years rather than months.
The second concerns breadth. Ethnography, unlike surveys,
questionnaires or other methodologies, tries to take account of
everything that is happening within a specific social context and
aims, ultimately, to provide an account which offers a holistic
understanding of that context. The third assumption focuses on
the attempt, at least in theory, to understand the situation being
researched from what Malinowski calls 'the native's point of view'
(Malinowski 1922: 25). In a world of funding councils, and the
subsequent limitations on time, such ideal ethnographic study is
only very rarely achieved. However, because of the assumptions
behind this ideal, and the consequent fact that the majority of
anthropological research has consisted of attempts to provide
holistic accounts of small-scale societies, almost all discussion of
ethnography within anthropology offers very little scope for the
understanding of ethnography within a more limited context,
such as that presumed in the study of worship. It is in this somewhat more limited focus that the sociological, psychological and
cultural studies application of ethnography has come to be far
more significant.

For this reason, therefore, I am going to leave the anthropological roots of ethnography for the present and come at the
question of ethnography and its definition from the direction of
media studies, in particular through the study of soap operas.[3]
This may seem an odd place to begin a discussion of ethnography within the study of worship but I hope that the reasons for
my choice will become clear as the argument develops. I am
not, however, going to offer a theoretical definition of ethnography within the context of media studies. Rather I am going to
present, very briefly, a history of the study of soap operas high-

lighting the different methodologies which have been used within this study over the years. This will conclude with the use of ethnography and should, therefore, illustrate what ethnography can offer to the study of soap operas that the other methods can not. The assumption I am making is that different methodologies offer different ways of asking distinct kinds of questions. No one method should be seen as 'better' in any distinctive sense. Rather it will depend on the kind of question that is being asked as to the kind of method that will be chosen. Within this context, ethnography will be seen to focus on specific kinds of question that cannot be answered by any other kind of methodology.

THE STUDY OF SOAP OPERAS

The study of soap operas is almost as old as the soap opera itself.[4] The earliest soaps were, of course, designed for radio and *The Archers* is the longest running series on any media in Britain. My interest, however, will focus primarily on the television soaps. The first phase of study that interests me is what I would want to call a 'textual analysis' of the soap. The earliest debates over *EastEnders*, for example, revolved around internal textual matters (Buckingham 1987). These were not related specifically to a written text, the script as such. Soap operas, as with all television, and most performance, is a visual medium and so the text is as much a visual text as a written one. The concerns, however, were internal to the text and did not relate to any other external factor. The biggest issue concerned the representation of ethnic minorities and the role that members of the ethnic minorities were allowed to play within the plots of the soap itself. The 'reality' for textual analysis exists only in the constructed object of the text. The text, however, is purporting to be a representation of another reality, but this other reality is of an entirely fictional nature. All texts are representations and it is at the level of the representation, therefore, that textual analysis has to function. Questions can be asked of the author of the text, about the intentions of the author and how far the finished text actually represents those intentions.[5] Questions can also be asked about the message or meaning that is being given within the text, especially in the case of the representation of ethnic minorities for example. All these questions, however, treat the soap opera like any other text, literary, biblical or liturgical, and cannot really take us beyond the text, or ask how the text performs when it is read or viewed by the audience.

When the audience of a soap opera is taken into account, as a distinct voice within the study of the soap, then other interesting questions begin to emerge. The first problem, however, concerns the question of how to identify the audience and how to discover what the audience actually thinks about the soap. This has traditionally been done through questionnaires and surveys. Audience analysis, therefore, provides an example of a second type of study. At a very simplistic level, it is always interesting to note what the audience of a particular programme may be. It might not always be that which is expected, for example, or that at which the programme was originally aimed. One case in point comes from a study of the *Cosby Show* in the United States (Jhally & Lewis 1992). This show, which has many similarities to soaps, represents a middle-class Afro-American family and the programme's creators consciously constructed the show to appeal to 'poor blacks' in an attempt to give them a role model which represented the kind of 'progress' they could make. Audience analysis, however, showed that the primary audience for the *Cosby Show* is not Afro-Americans from poorer neighbourhoods but rather middle-class white families. It appears that common class values mattered far more than colour in the appeal of the programme to its audience. What the actual audience made of the questions of colour and class raised by the programme is another question. In this kind of research, what needs to be studied are answers to questionnaires. The analyst has to ask how far the answers given to the questionnaire match onto any kind of 'reality', either in terms of the people viewing, or more complexly in terms of viewers' opinions. The raw data provided by the questionnaire, however, can never get the analyst very far in itself. All data of this kind needs to be interpreted in relation to some kind of theoretical model and the validity of that interpretation then needs to be tested by further work of the same kind. The outcome is theories, or explanations of the data, that may or may not be plausible and may or may not be interesting or relevant.

Another way in which a particular soap, or any television show, can be viewed in a wider context is to combine textual

45

analysis with audience analysis and so to place the programme within a wider televisual or cultural context. One thing about any television show is that it does not simply exist in isolation. Each show forms part of a schedule with other programmes and trailers being shown before and after it, and, at least on commercial television, with adverts framing and interrupting the action. It is clear from audience surveys that the placing of a programme, its timing in the schedule, the way it interacts with other programmes and with adverts, is essential to the way in which a programme is understood and viewed by the audience. Another factor in this kind of analysis comes from the fact that elements of any show, and particularly of soaps, spill over, out of the television, and into other media. The audience is just as likely to read about the private lives of the stars in women's magazines as they are to watch the show, and very often, at the level of textual analysis, the two texts provide interesting and subversive commentaries on each other. To be a *Coronation Street* fan is not just to watch the show four or five times a week, to know the characters and their intimate lives (and histories). It is also to be aware of off-screen rivalries, of similarities or dissimilarities between the cast and the characters that they play, and the way in which the 'brand image' of the programme and its stars is used to draw attention to other products. The lives of the actors become almost as significant as the lives of the characters. It is in this context that the Royal Family can be understood as a soap. This is not simply in terms of a show which is watched three or four times a week from the safe distance of the sofa, but as a spectacle which is open to constant comment and speculation, dissection and behind-the-scenes revelation in many different media at the same time. To understand the show, and the appeal of the show to the audience, therefore, demands more than a simple analysis of the text of the show itself or a series of naive questions asked about the opinions of the audience.

In all these various forms of audience analysis, the 'reality' that is being studied is no longer confined to the limited situation of the text. It has moved beyond the text to the reception of the text by the audience. The medium, however, is still principally one of representation. The difference is that the representation is no longer the primary object of study. What is of interest is the reception of that representation by an audience and the dialogue that is set up between the representation within the text (and we must assume the author of that representation) and the representation as perceived by those who are receiving the text and remoulding it for their own purposes. It is in this kind of context that we can perhaps talk about the death (or at least the irrelevancy) of the author and draw on the tools of literary theory. One reason for this is that the 'reality' that we are trying to grasp in this kind of audience analysis does not in fact exist in any empirical sense. It is no longer rooted in the text. Nor does it exist primarily within the minds of the audience. The 'audience' in this kind of analysis is never given enough individuality or identity for it to posess a 'mind', let alone for the object of study to be that which exists within that mind. What exists, the 'reality' which is being studied, are answers to surveys, written or spoken opinions, statistics, theoretical constructs and assumptions on the part of the investigator in relation to these surveys, opinions, statistics etc. Audience analysis, I would suggest, is most clearly open to theoretical development and can often leave any kind of empirical reality far behind.

One of the questions which audience analysis can never answer is what a specific audience does with that which it takes away from the watching of a particular soap. The data are not concrete enough to answer these kinds of specific questions. What is more, it is arguably impossible for audience analysis to make any kind of theoretical pronouncements on the reception of a soap unless certain assumptions about the specific situations in which the programme is produced, broadcast and received are made, and generalised. It is at this level, therefore, that media studies has turned to ethnography.

One of the most interesting and informative studies in the ethnographic analysis of soaps consists of a project undertaken by a student in the Department of Theology here in Birmingham (D'Aeth 1999). In this study, the researcher began to investigate the role of *Brookside* in the lives of a group of lesbian viewers in the Greater London area. *Brookside* had at the time of the study a very highly publicised and controversial lesbian storyline. Audience and textual analysis had already been done to show (a) that lesbians were watching these episodes and (b) that the representation of lesbians within the programme was controversial. The ethnographic study, however, went further than this

47

in that the researcher spent a considerable amount of time with a specific group of lesbians. She observed the way in which the group watched the programmes along with their comments and interactions at the time of viewing. She observed the way in which the programmes, and the storyline, were deliberately discussed by the group, and how the issues were woven into conversations that were ostensibly about other things. More importantly the researcher observed the way in which the individuals within the group each used the programme, the viewing, and the discussions surrounding the storyline to question and to negotiate their own identity as lesbians and as individuals. There was no clear condemnation of the images within the soap and yet not all those who formed the group identified with the lesbians on screen. The conversations, analysis and negotiations went far beyond the relatively simplistic writings (condemnations or justifications) of those who used other methodologies and who were coming from a clear theoretical position. When the programme hit the streets, when the story line interacted with real life, then things were never quite so simple and so straightforward. It was only ethnography, I would suggest, which could uncover these other discourses, interactions and negotiations between individuals watching the soap and particular programmes.

This discussion also allows us to make at least a stab at what ethnographic study is, even if only in contradistinction to what it is not. Ethnographic study is time bound but, as we saw with the anthropological tradition, aims at the longest possible span of time while acknowledging the falsity of the boundaries in time which are imposed upon it. Ethnographic study is also bound in social space. Anthropologists have traditionally studied small-scale communities that generate and maintain their own boundaries. In the case just cited the boundaries are defined by the group of lesbians themselves and can be somewhat porous. In all cases, however, a specific social group provides the focus for the study. Thirdly, ethnographic study tends, at least in recent years, to have a specific focus, although the study itself can never be limited to that focus and must spread as far as the group under investigation will allow the researcher to go. It is a very common experience for ethnographers to enter 'the field', the social group in question, with one particular question, only to find that within the group there are other more fundamental, or often far more interesting questions which need to be pursued. The particular focus with which the ethnographer begins the study, therefore, may not be a defining feature of ethnography. However, given that the study must be written up and presented to a wider academic community before it can be 'ethnography' in the strict sense of the term, then some focus, at some point within the process, is essential.

With textual analysis, and even with audience analysis, that which is being studied, the text or the data collected, is fairly clear cut. In both of these cases, the kind of analysis, the form of explanation or interpretation that is expected, is also relatively straightforward. With ethnography, neither of these elements is as obvious or as clear cut. What it is that is being studied cannot be reduced simply to a representation within a clear frame of space or time. The kind of explanation that might be offered is very rarely a testable theory that can be explored further through subsequent study. What is more, ethnographic study as a process raises questions of an ethical nature that are not raised to such a great extent when the subject of the study is a text or a series of numbers or anonymous opinions. Likewise, the relevance of the research is not immediately obvious. Who actually wants to know how a group of lesbians watch *Brookside* and how they integrate their responses to that watching into their wider lives? What kind of knowledge does this contribute? It cannot offer obvious critiques of the programmes themselves, primarily because the programme becomes little more than a secondary text into which meaning is read. It cannot say all that much about lesbians, lesbianism or still less the 'lesbian community' in any generalised sense because what ethnography does, beyond any other kind of study, is to highlight the diversity and complexity of real life where simplistic theories no long apply. What, then, is the relevance of such study to 'real' life? What is it that ethnography sets out to study? These are the questions that I wish to tackle in the rest of this chapter, while turning my attention away from soaps and back to my primary interest in worship.

THE 'REALITY' BEING STUDIED

The first question we must ask of ethnography is what is it that is actually being studied? It is not, as I have already said, a bounded text, but is it a text in any shape of form? More philosophical-ly, is that which is being studied more 'real' than the text *per se* (which is acknowledged to be a fabrication)? Are we studying real people doing real things? Or are we studying what people say about what they are doing and what it means to them? Or are we studying the person undertaking the study and their understanding of the reality before them? The answer must be all these things and far more besides.

A distinction can be made, when discussing what the ethnographer is studying, between 'what a person says they should be doing', 'what they say they are doing' and 'what they are actually doing'.[6] The ethnographer must be interested in all three of these things and must attempt to provide some kind of analysis that links them. At first sight, this seems very clear and obvious. In relation to what I have been saying about soap operas, then what 'should' be is related to textual analysis. What people 'say' they are doing is best discovered through surveys, and when it comes to what people actually do, which is not always what they say they are doing, then only ethnography, full participant observation, can provide an answer. Within the study of worship, this may begin to look even more obvious. We know what 'should' happen in worship, it is written down for all to read. What people 'say' they are doing can be discovered through surveys and questionnaires, and what is 'actually' happening can be observed in any church on any Sunday morning. The only real difficulty appears to be to decide how these three things should be related. However, even at this level things are not as clear as they might appear.

The text itself, what people 'should' be doing, ought to be fairly easy to ascertain. In a literate culture, the text exists and can be discussed or debated as a thing in itself. When we are talking about performance, however, as in the case of both worship and soap operas, then the performance is clearly open to negotiation and discussion. What ought to happen is never entirely clear. What is more, some perception of what ought to happen is always maintained by individuals involved in the participation or reception of the performance and this can be used to judge, or to interpret that performance. Where a clear sense of what 'should' happen exists then the performance takes on a whole new character and the edges between the performance and its ideal form become blurred. In the case of soap opera, this is not so much of a problem as the majority of the audience do not see the original script and that script becomes irrelevant once the performance has been produced. In the case of worship, however, even in churches which do not have a full liturgical tradition, what 'ought' to happen is often known and debated by the congregation, and needs to be taken fully into account within any analysis of the worship as event.

Discussion of what people 'say' they are doing, or more normally, what people say they have been doing, leads us in a very different direction. This is into the realm of perception, of memory and of the memory of the perception, which inevitably produces many layers of complication and distortion between the original performance and any individual's description of that performance, and their role within that performance, at some later date. All this happens before we ask people to describe the 'meaning' that a particular performance has for them (as opposed to the official meanings that would be contained within what 'should' happen). At this stage, all kinds of complications begin to cut in. Are we, for example, asking people to describe what the performance meant at the moment of perception? Could they ever do this? Is this ever recoverable? Is it a meaningful concept? Are we asking them to say what the performance means to them at this precise moment, as we talk to them? Does that meaning change as we ask the question and force the person being questioned to consider an answer? Meaning, I would suggest, is highly situational, at least in part, and cannot be grasped and defined in a once-and-for-all manner (see Nichols 1996).

This leads me on to consider what people 'actually' do. What do they do? They watch. They perform. They react to the performance. They describe the performance. They argue about the performance. They retell and constantly renegotiate the performance. They live out the performance in their lives. These are all complex processes and cannot be classified easily, if at all. In reacting to all of these, however, the ethnographer has a similar problem to the people being studied. How should the ethnographer interpret the action being performed and should that ethnographer take account of what should happen and what the performer says is happening (including the meanings they place on what is happening) in interpreting what is actually happening? This is an impossible question, principally because the ethnographer cannot help offering an interpretation, and, invariably, that interpretation will depend on the ethnographer's own perception of the events as they happen, including the discussion and textual framework within which those events take place. This, however, takes us on to the kind of analysis offered by ethnographers and before doing that I wish to raise one further question which relates specifically to the context of worship.

In the case of a soap opera, the text in question is very specific and its status as fiction is undisputed by all, or practically all, of those involved. In the case of worship, however, there is another layer of reality that is postulated as being behind that which can be observed or perceived. What form this reality is understood to take will clearly have an important bearing upon the way in which the action itself is perceived, either by the participant or by the ethnographer. This other reality, however, is, almost by definition, not observable by the ethnographer in Malonowskian terms. We cannot 'observe' that which is postulated as 'really' happening at a theological or spiritual level. We can only listen to what people say about this other reality, or, depending on the standpoint of the ethnographer, by observing the impact of this other reality on the participants during the course of the action. In either case the ethnographer, *qua* ethnographer, has very little to offer. This other reality cannot, however, be ignored, especially in so far as it forms part of the other three discourses which we have already been looking at (what should happen, what people say is happening and what is happening). Focusing on the potential impact of this other reality, however, does, I think, help us to focus on what the ethnographer can, and should, be studying; the 'reality' which potentially forms the data for ethnography.

Clearly the observation of action is important to the ethnographer, and this must always be present in the background, as must the ethnographer's self-conscious awareness of their own perception of what is happening and their own responses (emotional and intellectual) to what is going on. These, however, are background, and, except in exceptional circumstances, do not form the heart of what the ethnographer is studying. The ethnographer is interested primarily in the details of the discourses that are going on in and around a specific focus. They are interested in what people are saying, how they are saying it, in what context they are saying it and the responses and reactions that such saying has on those around them. The contexts for the saying can change, and can be more or less contrived at different moments within the research (so long as the context is taken into account in the final analysis). What is important, however, is that over time the same issues are explored with the same people in many different contexts and with differing levels of self-consciousness on the part of the people under scrutiny. In this way, the ethnographer can develop a clear view of the range of discourses involved within the discussion of the topic being studied. Everything must be noted and forms part of the data. All aspects of the context and all levels of discourse, including the jokes and the throwaway remarks, must be included within the study. It is only if a complete framework of discourses is available, along with the contexts in which those discourses are delivered, that any kind of analysis can hope to take place.

In placing this emphasis on discourse, however, I am not intending to imply that the discourse is all that there is, or that the discourse does not relate to some other reality. In my view the discourse both frames and is framed by the reality of the world in which people act. It is an important element within that reality but does not encompass that reality entirely. What is more, there is not one single unified or unifying discourse. The world which human beings inhabit is saturated by discourses of many different kinds, not all of which are public. These discourses, however, are part of a more complex whole which, as I have already indicated, the ethnographer must always bear in mind. Another element relates to yet another kind of reality which lies behind the discourses and which, like that 'other reality' which is assumed within worship, is not directly accessible to the ethnographer, or for that matter to any other kind of researcher. This is the reality of what exists in the minds of individual human beings. If I was to say what it was, fundamentally, that ethnography takes as its object then it is this interior world, or the interaction between these interior realities and the outer realities of the world.[7] It is only through discourse, I would argue, and an exploration of the functioning of discourse (including those points where discourse breaks down as so often happens in relation to worship), that we can begin to uncover the inner reality of the mind. This, in part, is what I would see the ethno-graphic study of worship as aiming to do. This leads me on to the kind of analysis that such ethnography makes possible.

THREE KINDS OF ANALYSIS

In reviewing the literature on ethnography, including the many ethnographies that have been written by anthropologists and others, it is clear that there are three kinds of analysis which have traditionally been undertaken in relation to ethnography. These can loosely be labelled as 'translation/description', 'interpretation/explanation' and 'theory/generalisation'. I would not want to see these as distinct types of analysis. Rather I would want to understand them as forming something of a continuum along which any one ethnography might be placed.

The first and easiest form of analysis to deal with is that of 'translation/description' as this is what many ethnographies actually end up being, unless they specifically set out to be something else. I use the word 'translation' in this context in the loosest possible sense to try and capture Malinowski's third aim for ethnography, that is to try and present the material from the 'native's point of view'. This means that we are trying to understand what it is like to be the individual, or part of the social group, that is under investigation. As it is assumed that the 'end user' of the ethnography is not going to be a part of the same social group then some kind of translation is required, such that the life of a Trobraind Islander, or a lesbian watching *Brookside*, or a Catholic attending Mass or whatever, can be conveyed to those who are interested. This is, in principle, a process of translation similar to that between languages, but it relies far more heavily on contextualised description. What the reader needs is both facts about the people under scrutiny, and guideposts that help to make the world, as they understand it, intelligible. There is an art to this kind of ethnography and, when done well, the result can be both enjoyable and illuminating. In terms of deeper knowledge, however, this kind of analysis does not actually take us very far, although it must always be present to underpin the other kinds of analysis.

Interpretation and explanation, my second form of analysis, are often treated as distinct forms of analysis in the methodological literature (see Hammersley 1992). Interpretation is seen as more suited to social sciences, where the emphasis is placed primarily on meaning, and explanation is associated with the natural sciences with the emphasis on laws and predictability.[8] This, I think, is misplaced. Certainly, what we normally think of as 'interpretation' is probably closer to what I have called 'translation' (translation is a weak form of interpretation) and what we normally think of as 'explanation' always tends towards theorising and generalisation. I find it unhelpful, however, to separate the two too distinctly as this tends to hide their common features which are, in my view, far more interesting. In both cases, the data under review is no longer accepted on its own terms. Some other element is assumed to be needed to help the reader to understand what is 'really' going on. Both interpretation and explanation move beyond mere description and aim to get behind the surface reality of the situation being described.[9] The distinction, if we were to look for one, is that 'interpretation' tends to go further by providing a context of 'meaning' for the events, while 'explanation' tends to explore the situation through questions of 'causes' and underlying patterns. In both cases, however, a wider theoretical frame is necessary before the analysis can begin. We need to have some idea of what kind of meanings or causes we would expect to be at work within the situation, and we need to bring this theoretical frame to bear on the subject under scrutiny.

The problem with both interpretation and explanation, therefore, is that they both assume that there is 'something else', something beyond the observable situation through which the observable situation can be made to make sense. Either the situation is 'explained' in terms of some thing else, a cause, whether social, economic or psychological, or it is assumed to 'mean' something else, something beyond the observable. In both cases, that 'something else' cannot be discovered within the situation under investigation. It must be assumed and imported by the researcher. Once assumed, however, this 'something else' can then be used to 'explain everything' or 'interpret everything' as if the 'something else' were the most important thing about the whole situation.[10] Why, we might ask, do we need this 'something else' at all? Can we not accept things simply as they are, without demanding explanations? Does everything have to have a meaning? Ironically, I would argue that it is perhaps the attempt to analyse worship which can do most to challenge this kind of approach. We all assume that worship must 'mean' something to the worshippers, as I have already suggested, and we can all make our own assumptions about what it is that it must mean (Nichols 1996). If we assume that this meaning is wrong in some way (i.e. if we do not accept the 'other reality' which is assumed to be present within the context of worship and which is often assumed to provide the basis for the meaning of worship) then we have to assume that worship must 'do' something, that it must perform some function, either social or psychological. If it neither means anything nor does something by way of a function then we would assume that it would have died out long ago. We actually find it very difficult to accept worship simply as it is, without cause or effect, open to the meanings that people wish to impose upon it. Increasingly, however, analysts are beginning to talk about worship in this way and there is the possibility that worship, or ritual in general, is the one action which defies 'interpretation' or 'explanation' of any kind (Humphrey & Laidlaw 1994).

This leads me on to my final kind of analysis, that of theory or generalisation. If we have already challenged interpretation or explanation, then what hope is there for theory building, abstraction, or any other kind of generalisation? Surely these must build on either the interpretation or the explanation offered in the previous kind of analysis. Theory is the bedrock that makes the explanation work. Interpretation is significant only in so far as it can be generalised. This is the way in which ethnographic analysis is usually presented, but the truth of the matter, as I have already suggested, is that things are often approached the opposite way around. We need a theory to make an explanation plausible. We have to make assumptions about the general to make the specifics of interpretation attractive. Explanation and interpretation assume the presence of a theory. They may test it or challenge it but they cannot come before it. What is more the theories that are chosen are often constructed at some distance from the ethnographic context. Is there, therefore, any kind of analysis, within the realm of ethnography itself, which can lead from the situation as observed to theories and generalisations without going through the stage of explanation or interpretation. I would suggest that there might be, but that we probably need to go back to what I was saying about the kind of 'reality' which ethnography aims to study, and what I have already said about translation and description, in order to find it.

We have to assume that there is some kind of external 'reality' out there. We have to assume that this 'reality' is accessible through observation and through careful listening to those discourses that interact with that reality. We may also assume that there is some other reality. Not, in this case, the other reality of worship, but rather that reality which lies behind the discourse, the internal reality of the mind that produces that discourse. If this is the case then an understanding of the situation being studied, a description if you like, coupled with a close reading of the many different discourses functioning within that situation can, if approached in an appropriate way, tell us a great deal about the kind of mind that might produce any particular discourse within that context. This cannot be done simply through a textual analysis of the discourse. If all that exists is text then there is no way of understanding the mind that produced that text. Without a reality external to the text there is no author, there is no mind. To understand the mind, therefore, we need to explore both the texts and the situations within which those texts become discourse (see Ricoeur 1981). This involves description/translation but it also demands more. It demands the development of a theory of the mind.

If I were to say, therefore, what ethnography can teach us, it has to be that ethnography has the potential, probably unlike any other methodology (including I would suggest philosophy, psychology and computer simulation) to lead us to a theory of the mind. The theory of the mind that is ultimately produced, however, will always be a theory of the mind in action, a theory about the way in which human beings function as whole persons in real situations and in social interaction, and not simply a theory of the mind in isolation. What is more that theory will be filtered through a particular mind, that of the ethnographer, and will inevitably say as much about that mind as about 'mind' in general. This cannot be avoided. That is why we need many ethnographers, many different minds at work, slowly moving towards an increasingly complex theory. Within this construction of a theory of the mind, I would argue, the study of worship should take a central place. Worship is an action that is set apart from the ordinary run of things.[11] It is, I would argue, an action without cause and without inherent meaning. It is an action that cannot be interpreted or explained (explained away?) in any easy fashion and cannot therefore be reduced to the functions or meanings of explanation or interpretation. In worship, therefore, and in discourse about worship, we can see more clearly how individual minds are working and interacting with different kinds of reality. Above all we can see the kind of realities which the human mind needs to construct, beyond that which is given, and can ask what impact these other realities have on the workings of the mind, and on the workings of the human person as a whole.

This, clearly, is an ultimate goal, and in the analysis that I am providing within this book I will be moving some way towards this kind of theory in relation to the specific contexts of worship which I have studied. Along the way to this 'ultimate goal', however, there are still many practical and ethical questions involved in ethnography, and many other things which can be discovered which may be significant in themselves. These are the focus of the next chapter where I shall be looking at the 'doing' of ethnography rather than the theorising about it.

NOTES

1   Towards the end of his book Hammersley even rejects this broad definition by collapsing the distinction between qualitative and quantitative research and seeing no particular role for a specifically 'ethnographic' form of research (Hammersley 1992: 202).
2   Anthropologists have traditionally offered some account of their fieldwork at some point within their ethnographic writing. This has generally served the purpose of adding authority to the text, and has seldom consisted of a detailed analysis or critique of the process of ethnography in itself (see Clifford & Marcus 1986). It is only recently that the process of ethnography has come in for comment and criticism within anthropology (Clifford & Marcus 1986, Okely & Callaway 1992).
3   In taking this view I wish to acknowledge the suggestions offered in a doctoral thesis by Lucy D'Aeth on soap operas and

pastoral theology which I was asked to examine (D'Aeth 1999). The thesis takes these ideas in a very different direction from that which I am pursuing but reading it got me interested in the questions raised by the study of soap operas which form the basis for my discussion.

4   The development of media studies and the subsequent study of television as a medium, or soap opera as a genre, is highly complex. The account that I am offering, therefore, is only a summary to highlight particular questions of methodology. For more detailed accounts see Allen 1987, Morley 1992 and Nightingale 1996.

5   Questions of the 'author' in relation to soaps or any television programme or film are never easy. The original author of the script or screenplay is not the only figure making decisions that relate to the finished product. We must also question the role of the director, the casting director, the producer and many other figures within the process. The same questions of intention and message can, however, still be asked even in this more complex situation.

6   I think that this distinction was originally made by Malinowski in his work on the Trobriand Islanders but I have failed to track down a specific reference.

7   It is no coincidence that many anthropologists, as they near or enter retirement, move away from the details of ethnographic study into what can only be called the philosophy of humanity, asking what it is to be truly human in the world. In many cases this relates directly to a philosophy of mind, in others the understanding of the mind is merely implied.

8   This distinction goes back to Dilthey who distinguished between natural and cultural sciences to make a similar point (Morris 1987: 57).

9   This is seen most clearly in Geertz's interpretavist stand in which he talks in terms of 'thick description' and in the explicit distinction between 'surface structure' and 'deep structure', with the latter forming an explanation or interpretation of the former (Geertz 1971).

10 It is also clear that much of the ethnographic analysis that takes this kind of approach tends to be circular in appearance. 'Something else' is postulated as being needed to 'explain' or 'interpret' the situation, only to find that what we discover at the end of the work is that it is this 'something else' which is presented as the significant discovery.

11 For my use of the word 'action' see the discussion in Humphrey & Laidlaw (1994: 2–5)

CHAPTER THREE
ON DISCOURSE

At the end of the previous chapter I suggested that the process of ethnography consisted in listening to, recording, and interpreting layers of discourse as they related to certain aspects of social behaviour, in my case, worship. The question remains, however, as to which kinds of discourse might be of interest and what process may be used to study these discourses.

Before doing this, however, I need to state briefly what it is that I mean by the word 'discourse'. 'Discourse' is one of those words that has been widely used within the academic literature in recent years. The more we look at the different authors who use the word, however, the clearer it becomes that each writer appears to use the word to mean something entirely different. Michel Foucault, for example, uses discourse to refer to domains of language that exist almost independently of those who use them (Foucault 1972). Gerd Baumann uses the word to discuss the way in which different words, used in different contexts (within different discourses) can take on different meanings (Baumann 1996). Paul Ricoeur on the other hand distinguishes between discourse and text such that discourse is the spoken utterance that is subsequently textualised (Ricoeur 1981). In this chapter I am not intending to follow any of these specific uses of the term 'discourse'. Rather I want to use the word much more loosely and more in line with the way in which 'discourse analysis' uses the term (Coulthard 1985), that it is to refer to elements of spoken, and occasionally written language, as they appear in the world. Discourse in my terms consists of actual statements, or a series of statements, which exist in the world, can be recorded and can be analysed by the scholar. It is these discourses which, I wish to argue, form the basis of ethnography.

QUESTIONS OF STANCE

When reading any book on worship, particularly those which claim to offer an interpretation of worship from the perspective of those who participate in it, then it soon becomes clear that each individual author only ever offers an interpretation which reflects their own particular point of view. This is not surprising. Any kind of study is always going to be undertaken from the particular point of view of the researcher in question, with all the prejudices and assumptions that go with this. What becomes clear in the context of worship, however, is that this is not simply a question of prejudices and assumptions, rather it is a question of stance: from whose perspective within the rite is the study being assessed? If we take a work like Aiden Kavanagh's *On Liturgical Theology* (1984), for example, this work is clearly a study of liturgy from the perspective of the celebrant. It is a theologically informed study that dismisses the supposed 'suburbanisation' of contemporary American liturgy in a very perfunctory manner. Kavanagh is a Benedictine monk and the constant, repetitive, even meditative, approach to worship that is central to the Benedictine life, is clearly present throughout the text.

It is not, however, just those who come from a deeply engrained theological position who take a particular stance within their work. Keiren Flanagan, for example, in *Sociology and Liturgy* (1991), claims to be approaching the rite from the perspective of a sociologist. This, however, is impossible, as his own understanding and approach to the liturgy is coloured by the fact that he is, himself, a practitioner. He tells us quite explicitly that he acts as a trainer of altar servers at the Catholic Cathedral in Clifton, Bristol. The book clearly reflects this and becomes little more, at times, than a discourse of worship from the perspective of the traditional MC at a Tridentine Mass. Flanagan is constantly worrying over details, questioning the validity of what is going on (has he got it right?) and obsessed with questions of piety and deception. Flanagan can never simply relax into the rite, or let it pass over him. He has to constantly question what is going on and is always concerned as to whether the liturgy is a 'success' (whatever that might mean).

Even a book which is supposedly written with the ordinary member of the congregation in mind, can be influenced by the particular stance of the authors. In Robert Cotton and Kenneth Stevenson's book *On the Receiving End* (1996), the subtitle of which is 'A View of Liturgy from the Pews', the argument clearly reflects the position of the authors, both of whom are clergy who, at the time of writing, were in charge of a busy Anglican parish in Guildford and Bishop of Portsmouth respectively. They do quote parishioners directly and reproduce stories of what particular individuals have said to them about the worship they have experienced. However, like a number of other books of this kind, written by clergy but claiming to reflect the views of ordinary churchgoers, the stance that they present is that of those few members of the congregation who will actually take the time to talk to the clergy and raise questions or problems in relation to the worship. There is no sense in this, or in similar texts, of what the ordinary member of the congregation ('the silent majority') is thinking, feeling, or saying about the worship in question.

To some extent each of the books that I have just mentioned does offer a valid perspective in its own right, and all three must be taken into account. What is also clear, however, is that none of the authors ever went out and systematically asked, or listened to, what ordinary people had to say about the worship. This was not relevant to Kavanagh as he was clearly writing a work of theology, albeit one that aimed to reflect an experiential approach to liturgy. The possibility of listening to ordinary people was considered by Flanagan and then dismissed as unworkable because of the lack of typicality of any one liturgy and the impracticality of a wider comparative study (1991: 64). In the case of Cotton and Stevenson, and those of a similar mould, it was assumed that because people were talking to them, then what they were hearing reflected the congregational view. No attempt was made, however, to test this more widely (which would have been irrelevant anyway as what these authors were writing was as much a work of theology as that of Kavanagh). Each of these texts, and many others I could mention, offer a partial view of what is happening within worship, a view from the per-

spective of the informed celebrant, the paranoid altar server, or
the concerned lay person. None of them, and no other text that
I have yet read, actually aims to understand, or even to listen to,
the perspective of the ordinary member of the congregation.

On closer reflection this might not be all that surprising. It is
not only in the case of studies of Christian worship where the
perspective of the ordinary worshipper is ignored. This has been
a constant problem in the study of ritual within anthropology.
Victor Turner has become notorious for relying heavily on a
particular ritual specialist, Muchona the Hornet, for his own
interpretation of the rites of the Ndembu. In a paper on method (1967b) he tells of how he and Muchona would sit up for
hours on end in his tent discussing the meanings of symbols and
the finer points of Ndembu 'theology'. It also becomes clear
that a large amount of what is being said by Muchona is being
made up on the spot, simply because the questions, and the
ideas that they generated, had never occurred to him before.
Barbara Myerhoff's book on the Peyote Hunt among the Huichol Indians of Central Mexico (1974) is also, very explicitly,
presented and interpreted through Myerhoff's own conversations with Ramon, the shaman and leader of the pilgrimage being
studied. Myerhoff even says that she had very little chance to talk
to any other member of the group and therefore had to rely
almost entirely on Ramon for the wider context for her analysis
(1974: 29–51).

At a broader level, therefore, a very different kind of question begins to arise. To whom exactly should the ethnographer
be listening? It is very easy to focus on ritual specialists such as
Muchona or Ramon, the Kavanaghs or Flanagans of their own
society; they are easily accessible and they often have a great
deal to say. Another look at Flanagan's book, however, raises
another possibility which is commonly taken up by anthropologists, especially where there is no obvious ritual specialist available to offer the kind of explanations that Turner and Myerhoff
were looking for. Flanagan compensates for the lack of any real
evidence about how the liturgy is understood by ordinary members of the congregation, by immersing himself in flights of theoretical fancy. At one level this appears to give the book a surprisingly theological air. There is very little difference between
Flanagan's and Kavanagh's work in this sense. At another level

it begins to make much of what is being said appear to be ludicrously irrelevant. Flanagan talks at length about choirboys, angels and 'innocence' (1991: 84–114), or about altar servers, waiters and 'deception' (1991: 207–33), elements of the rite which actually have very little relevance for most of those attending, and which do not even occur outside of the Cathedral/Benedictine tradition which he claims to represent. This would not be so bad if the theoretical analysis itself did not depend so much on these minor irrelevancies of the rite, rather than the serious question of how the congregation actually perceived what was going on.

The same process often occurs within anthropological studies of ritual, particularly those of ritual in New Guinea, where the level of local interpretation and exegesis is clearly very low. Frederick Barth, for example, makes this very explicit in his work on the Baktaman (1975), where local discussion of the rites simply does not take place. The same is also true of the work of Gilbert Lewis, Alfred Gell and others (Lewis 1980, Gell 1975). This leaves the way open for these authors to present their own interpretations of the rites, or alternatively to engage in theoretical discussions on the nature of ritual, rather than in specific analysis of what the people concerned actually do say about the rites they are engaged in.

Something similar might also be said of Caroline Humphrey's and James Laidlaw's study of Jain ritual in southern India (1994). This is also a highly theoretical study of the nature of ritual, or rather of ritualisation. What distinguishes this work, however, from the point of view of method, is that the theoretical questions are raised, not because of a lack of discussion about the rite by ordinary members of the community, but because of an excess of discussion and debate, much of which was contradictory and disconnected. Those Jains who took part in the Puja clearly felt that it was necessary for them to offer a meaning for what they were doing. That meaning, however, was clearly acknowledged to be personal and ascribed, rather than inherent in the action itself (Humphrey & Laidlaw 1994: 34–6). It was through the very careful listening, therefore, to many different people talking about the rites in many different contexts that the authors of this particular study began to see the complexity and uncertainty of what was actually going on. And it was through reflection on these multiple discourses that the final theory of ritual action was developed.

The ethnographic study of ritual, or worship, therefore, must always involve the careful listening to all those discourses that occur in and around the worship itself. It cannot begin with an assumption about the meanings of these discourses, or of the rite itself. It must move from the listening to the discourses, to their interpretation, and then on to an understanding of worship. This still leaves the problem, however, of exactly which discourses should be listened to, or even more fundamentally, of what forms the different discourses that surround worship in contemporary Christian traditions take.

In the rest of this chapter I wish to outline a number of the different, and often contradictory, kinds of discourses, which can be found in and around worship. I will also offer an initial assessment of these discourses, before going on to outline my own research and the background to the worked example that appears in Part II of this book.

THE INDIVIDUAL AND THE COMMUNAL

The first distinction in any understanding of discourses is that between the individual and the communal. This is a difficult field and an area that has generated a great deal of discussion within the sociological and anthropological literature (Cohen 1994). There are, however, a few things which can be said and which need to be born in mind in terms of discourses and worship. At one level it is clear that every member of a congregation is a unique individual and has a unique view of what is happening within worship. If this position is taken to its extreme, however, then it would be impossible to say anything in general about worship at all. On the other hand, many of the works on ritual and worship tend to work from the assumption that there is a common, congregational, view of worship that is shared by every member of the congregation, irrespective of personal views and approaches. Clearly these cannot both be correct. In most cases it is the second statement that is misleading. The view that is often presented as the communal or 'congregational' view is better described as an 'official' or 'formal' understanding of worship, that which is held authoritatively by those who have the right to make this kind of statement, and therefore may not be held by any single individual within the congregation at all. I will come back to the question of official and unofficial discourses in the following section; for now I wish to stick more strictly to the question of individual and communal discourses.

Clearly it is not the case that any one congregation is simply a collection of individuals with disparate and unrelated views on worship, or any other matter. There must be some kind of communal discourse, or at least some kind of limit which is set within the collective. The problem, however, comes when we try to define what this collective discourse might actually consist of. Hopewell in a book on the study of congregations (1987), suggests that the identity of a congregation can be summed up collectively, and symbolically, in relation to a particular story which expresses that which is shared within the congregation (1987: 40–54). Behind this view are two assumptions, both of which are valid and need to be accepted. The first is that a congregation, as a social unit, has a common history and a shared discourse on that history, its own identity, and that which distinguishes it from other similar social units. How well defined this particular story or identity might be will depend on the number of members, the amount of social contact between members, and wider factors such as the integration of members into a broader set of social norms, or a clear identity derived from ethnic, religious or other factors within society as a whole. The second assumption is that any one congregation will tend, over time, to attract to itself people of like mind and temperament and therefore develop a collective identity based on the principle of self-selection. Even given these two factors, however, it is clear that within any congregation there will be a range of opinions and views. There will be differences between those at the core of the congregation and those at the edge, for example, and differences related to many other factors such as education, age, gender, ethnic origin and so on.

What is important is to understand the different contexts within which different kinds of discourse are operating and how far these discourses reflect a collective or an individual view. Within a discussion group, for example, especially one which contains influential members of the congregation, then the discourse which will be heard may be described as the dominant discourse of the congregation (Baumann 1996). It may still be voiced in different ways by different members of the group, but a collective perspective is more likely to be expressed, one which leads towards consensus rather than dispute.[1] In another context, such as in an individual's home or during an informal discussion over coffee, then dissent from this collective view might also be expressed, or some form of qualification of the collective discourse could be made to accommodate an individual's own opinions. These are tricky areas as it is clear that, even in a fully informal individual context, the views of particular members of the congregation will be affected, either positively or negatively, either consciously or unconsciously, by the perceived views of the collective. The two can never be fully separated. This, however, is unnecessary and would provide a false reading of the situation.

Interestingly enough, it is actually the collective view that is more difficult to distil and to articulate. Conversations with individuals, if those individuals are relaxed and unthreatened, can easily produce a series of individual discourses. The collective view, however, can never be simply a combination of these individual perspectives. The collective exists at a different kind of level that is not always easy to observe. It is far easier at times to assume that there is no collective discourse at all, simply a range of individual perspectives, but this is also a misreading of the situation. Each individual constructs their own understanding in relation to what they think others are saying or thinking, in relation to what they have heard influential members of the congregation saying, and in relation to common discourses within the congregation as a whole. These collective discourses may not be easily identifiable but we must always assume that they are present and aim to account for them within our analysis.

This is an area I explore more fully in Chapter Four when I come to discuss my time with the Baptist congregation. It was here, more than in any of the other churches, where I was able to talk individually and privately to the majority of the congregation, and it was here that the members of the congregation felt least constrained by any kind of official discourse about their worship. While I obviously had to acknowledge the individuality of each of the discourses that I was listening to, it was also clear that this congregation, more than perhaps any of the others, had a clear sense of common identity and common story. This was the congregation that had the strongest sense of history. This was the congregation which placed most emphasis on the individual's own decision to join on the basis of compatibility with other congregational members. And this was the congregation that spent most of its time discussing questions of belief and identity in an open and honest way. The same questions, however, also emerged in the other three churches, although in very different ways.

OFFICIAL AND UNOFFICIAL DISCOURSES

I have already suggested that what is often taken to be the 'collective' discourse about worship within a congregation is often better understood to be the 'official' discourse – that is the kind of language and understanding of the rite that is given status and authority within the congregation, which makes it distinct from the discourses of ordinary individuals. It is not always obvious, however, exactly what form the official discourse, or discourses, actually takes and we must not be led to assume that this is any easier to find than the collective discourses mentioned in the previous section.

At one level the official discourse on worship within any congregation will consist of those discourses which actually form part of the worship itself, the text of the liturgy, the prayers, the sermon and so on, as well as the performative and visual texts involved within the worship. This is an official discourse and one to which the congregation is exposed every time they come to worship. Whether this is 'the' official discourse on worship is, however, much more difficult to determine. Within most Christian contexts there has always existed a level of 'official' discourse which acts as a commentary upon the texts used in worship, as well as on the texts of the Bible and other kinds of texts which form the whole range of Christian theology. All these 'theological' discourses assume that what is said and done within worship cannot be taken at face value and needs to be interpreted in some other way. Christianity is a literate religion and the level of secondary literature is so high that the need for interpretation, and the assumption that there is an official interpretation for all the texts and actions which make up worship, is accepted almost universally. What is not so well known is what this 'official' version consists of, and what impact this might have on individuals' own discourses in relation to worship.

If we stick at this stage simply to those discourses which happen within and around worship at the local level, those discourses which the ordinary members of the congregation are actually going to hear and be able to respond to, then I think that it is possible to simplify the situation quite considerably. It is more than clear that the majority of ordinary members of most congregations, even those which are more theologically literate, are not going to be aware of all the 'official' discourses on worship produced by international theologians, or even by church documents or reports. This material simply is not available in a direct form to most ordinary members of most congregations and therefore cannot form part of the discourse that they can take as being 'official'. What can be the case, however, is that an awareness that such discourses are produced, and that ordinary members of the congregation should not comment for themselves because others have already done it for them, does exist; as does the perception that those who have provided the 'official' discourse, even where this is unknown to the individuals concerned, are bound to be right while the individual's own musings are more than likely to be wrong. This is possible, but the evidence that I have found suggests that this strict division of 'right' and 'wrong' is not widely held even in a church such as the Roman Catholic Church, which has a strong sense of ecclesial authority. I will be exploring this issue in more detail in Chapter Five.

If we come back to those official discourses which can be heard by the ordinary members of the congregation, therefore, then we come back to the text of the rites themselves and the various commentaries on them made by clergy or other church leaders in sermons, confirmation classes or other instruction, and discussion groups where these exist. The text of the rite clearly forms the basis of much of the discourse on worship at this level, but only as that which needs to be interpreted, or that through which other events and experiences can be interpreted. The way in which the text itself is appropriated and utilised is a complex issue and I will come back to this in the conclusion when I have discussed the specific examples in Part II. This leaves us with the commentary on the text, or on worship as such, which is provided by clergy in the context of sermons, classes or discussion groups.

When I began my study of worship, and the discourses that surrounded it, I had expected to find references to the official discourse, as mediated by the clergy, to be the most dominant element of all these discourses. There was, I assumed, no other means by which individuals could come to any understanding of their own except through that which they had been taught by clergy and others in positions of authority. What surprised me, in all four of the congregations that I studied, was just how little impact such discourses had on the conversations and language of ordinary worshippers. One reason for this is that worship was not a subject that was often talked about in sermons. This may seem odd as the sermon is itself a part of worship. However this is clearly the case, and was true for all four churches. I never heard any sermon that touched specifically on worship and the response to worship that was expected by the congregation. There were a number of allusions, or references to specific elements within the worship (such as the introduction of the cup during communion in the Catholic church) but even in these cases there was no framework offered for the understanding of worship itself.

This leaves classes and discussion groups. Again I found very little direct reference to such groups in ordinary conversation and, while I have no direct evidence from any of the churches for the way in which worship was discussed in these contexts, it was clear that this made very little impact on the congregations. Where comments were made which did reflect what might be assumed to be an official discourse on worship, then these could probably be best expressed as 'folk' views, common statements which were known by all members of the congregation and were accepted by them as the position of the 'church' (whether they were in fact the 'official' view or not). The Baptists, for example, stressed that all worship was 'free', the Catholics had some understanding of 'transubstantiation' (usually of a realist nature) and members of the Independent Christian Fellowship maintained that all worship was 'Spirit led'. What these folk views actually meant for people, or how they used them within their own individual discourses on worship, is a much more complex topic.

Having said all this, there clearly was some form of 'official' discourse within all four congregations which, while it did not touch directly on worship, was present and maintained the possibility of an official discourse on worship itself. While the sermons were only very rarely about worship they did offer interpretations of biblical texts and an 'official' account of doctrine and the Christian life. This wider official discourse was clearly available for all members of the congregation and obviously presented a context within which any unofficial, or individual, discourse on worship had to be framed. It was not always easy to identify the full form of this official theological discourse. Just like the collective discourse of the previous section, it was never presented in full and was only ever seen in fragments and through allusions. It was always present, however, and always influenced the language, and in many cases the structure, of individual discourses on other topics. This was most clear with the Independent Christian Fellowship and it is in Chapter Six that I pick up this kind of discussion again.

INSIDE AND OUTSIDE OF WORSHIP

Practically all discussions of worship, liturgy or ritual attempt to provide a discussion of the rite from within the context of the rite itself. It is assumed that what is meaningful is meaningful within the context of the event, or the individual or collective experience of that event. This raises a problem for the kind of ethnographic approach that I have outlined because it is impossible to question or interview people while they are actually involved in the process of worship. Turner suggests that it is necessary to at least try to do this when he says that we should ask people what symbols mean as they are used (1967a: 20–2). His paper on Muchona, on the other hand, makes it clear that in his own fieldwork the questioning did not take place within the rite but at some time after the rite, after a glass of warm honey beer in the anthropologist's grass hut (1967b). Flanagan emphasises the same point as part of his own argument that an ethnography of worship cannot be undertaken (1991: 64). We cannot get a first-hand expression of the experience of worship as it is happening and therefore we must look at the event from a theoretical point of view to say what 'should' be experienced or understood. This, I feel, misunderstands what can and cannot be gained through ethnography.

It is clear that any one act of worship is a distinct experience, or series of experiences, which involves those individuals who are taking part in it to a greater or lesser extent as it is actually happening. By being present, by observing and by participating in the event the ethnographer can gain some insights into what appears to be happening, and how the different individuals appear to be responding, at least with regard to what they are doing and how they are looking (bored, interested, excited, pious or whatever). Within the context of the worship itself, however, very little else can be said from the ethnographic point of view, all the rest is speculation and theology. This, however, does not matter as much as we might imagine because it is not only to the ethnographer that what happens within any one act of worship might seem marginal and uneventful. The same is often the case for the participants as well. We cannot assume that any one individual involved in worship is indulging in great feats of theological speculation, or sociological interpretation of what is going on, while it is actually happening. Most people appear to be unaware of the subtleties of the event as it is happening and the theologian or sociologists must themselves stand outside of the experience of the event if they are to interpret that experience for others. What happens within the rite is only a part, and arguably only a small part, of what is happening within or around worship.

One of the major contributions that Humphrey and Laidlaw make to the study of ritual in their book on Jain worship (1994), is that for the Jains the actual act of doing Puja is the least important element of the whole process. What is of equal, if not more, importance is that the Jains themselves are expected to offer an interpretation or meaning for that act (1994: 191). This process of providing meaning, however, cannot be done at the time of doing Puja itself, it has to be a separate, and even a detached, process which is undertaken either in meditation at the temple or in discussion, or private reflection, at some other time. I would want to suggest that much the same has to be true of Christian worship, with the probable exception that many Christians assume that this process of meaning-making is being done for them by professional theologians (also outside the context of worship) and therefore does not necessarily concern them directly. If individuals are going to provide a meaning or interpretation of worship for themselves then this will, inevitably, take place outside the context of worship. It is therefore of little concern to the ethnographer that the actual event of worship can only be observed. All the relevant discourses on worship occur elsewhere and these, it is assumed, can be made available through careful listening and discussion.

If this line of argument is accepted then this only really raises a further question. In what form, and at what point, are individual discourses on worship stated and how do we recognise them when we see them? This is not easy. One of the problems is that there is very unlikely to be a coherent individual discourse on worship any more than there is a coherent collective discourse, or even a coherent 'official' discourse. The discourses on worship that can be offered by individuals may be many, diverse and even contradictory depending on the context in which they are delivered. Of course it is easy for the ethnographer to disguise this by providing a context for the production of a coherent discourse, by setting up an interview with leading questions and subsequent discussion for qualification. This is a false situation and will provide a false understanding of the way in which discourses about worship are actually being constructed and used within everyday life. If people are listened to in different contexts, formal and informal, in contexts where worship or faith is the main topic of conversation and those where it is not, in discussions with different people who have different assumptions about worship, and so on, then many different elements of discourse can be generated, and a series of different kinds of discourse become apparent. In practical terms this means that the ethnographer has to be prepared to eavesdrop on a wide range of different discussions and conversations, or to set up situations in which differing kinds of discourse become apparent. This suggests long-term work, as I have already proposed.

What the ethnographer is left with, however, may well be a very disparate set of data consisting of many different and disconnected elements of discourse that have no apparent logic or internal coherency. This will cause a problem in terms of the writing up of the research and in terms of any theoretical discussion which can be derived from the material that has been collected. These are the questions that are raised by the final two sections of this chapter.

QUESTIONS OF THE DIALOGIC IN DISCOURSES ON WORSHIP

What we appear to be left with at the end of this analysis is a series of fragments of discourse, none of which can be easily constructed, or even re-constructed, to form a continuous narrative. These fragments consist of elements of collective discourse, stories, histories, turns of phrase etc., which are common to the whole congregation. They could be elements of official discourses, folk theologies, statements of faith, the use of particular words or phrases that become associated with a particular tradition of the church, or elements of individual discourses which are dependent on who is talking to whom and in what context. Each of these fragments exists in the light of each of the others. This is particularly true of the relationship between the individual and the collective or the official. In each case the collective or official may become part of the individual within a particular context, such that the two become indistinguishable. More probably the individual is determined by, or expressed in reaction to, either the collective or the official or both. Added to all these we also have the texts, or discourses, of the worship itself. In the light of what I have just expressed, these worship-based discourses, however apparently disconnected in themselves, will probably be the most coherent of any of the discourses that the ethnographer has to work with. It is not surprising therefore to find that most analysts simply resort to an analysis of the discourses inherent in the rite, be they verbal, performative, or in the form of images. However even these worship based discourses only take on significance in relation to the individual, collective, and official discourses that surround them and are themselves in a constant dialogic relationship to these other forms of discourse.

What this means in practice is that it is practically impossible to say what any one liturgical performance means for any one individual at any one time, even if we can say that it means anything at all. Even less can we talk about what worship means to a particular congregation or what worship means in and of itself. 'Meaning' begins to get dissipated amongst the many different discourses that are taking place in and around worship and the attempt to pin it down in any one place simply opens up another series of relationships which make it totally uncertain once again. The attempt to search after meaning in relation to ritual, therefore, as suggested by Humphrey and Laidlaw, is something of a pointless endeavour (1994: 68). If meaning does exist, then it is constructed momentarily for a particular individual, at a particular time, within a particular conversation or personal reflection.

Having said this, however, it is clear, as Humphrey and Laidlaw also point out, that any meanings which may emerge at particular times and places are never entirely arbitrary (1994: 193). The various discourses that do exist in and around worship do begin to set limits on the form and nature of the kinds of meanings that can be generated. Official discourses are particularly important in this regard, especially if they appear to be backed up by some kind of external authority (be that the Church, the Bible or the clergy). Communal discourses and the discourses of worship can also have the same limiting effect when they are allowed to enter into dialogue with individual and official meanings within a particular context. What we can begin to explore, therefore, I would suggest, is not so much the content of specific meanings in specific contexts – these are transitory and unreachable – but rather the different ways in which meanings can be generated within the worshipping context. We can investigate the way in which the discourses surrounding worship can limit the range and form of meanings that are possible, and the impact of these meanings on wider forms of discourse within the lives of individuals and congregations.

It is this process of dialogue and meaning formation which I attempt to explore within the case studies which follow in the next four chapters. As a conclusion to this chapter, therefore, I wish to outline the nature of the fieldwork that was undertaken and some of the questions which were raised for me about the way in which this fieldwork was to be recorded. In doing this I hope to provide a brief introduction to the five chapters which form Parts II and III of this book.

RESEARCH INTO THE PERCEPTION OF WORSHIP

I undertook the research that makes up Part II over two years from January 1985 to March 1987. During this time I spent six months with each of the four churches which made up the study. I choose to do the studies back-to-back with little or no break between them which, in retrospect, was probably not a good idea. I took considerable notes within each study and played with various ideas as I was going along, but I did not really get the chance to stand back from the whole process until I reached the end. It was very fortunate, therefore, that as I got towards the end of my fieldwork I had the opportunity to spend two months in Chicago, during which time I spent a week with Mark Searle in the University of Notre Dame. It was only in this context, many miles away from Manchester and the fieldwork itself, that the ideas that came to make up the following chapters began to come together. Most importantly, it was only during this time that I began to see a way forward to the actual process of writing about that which I was sure, by this stage, went beyond words.

While I was in Chicago I had two seminal experiences. The first was my conversations with Mark Searle which clarified what it was that I actually wanted to argue and which I have already mentioned. The second was the opportunity to read through a transcript of the text of Michael Taussig's *Shamanism, Colonialism and the Wild Man* (1987). Taussig had visited the Department of Anthropology in Manchester earlier in the year and talked about some of his ideas on montage with members of the department. I had already begun to use some of these issues to try to make sense of my experience of the Independent Christian Fellowship. Reading his finished text, however, was something of a revelation, partly because of the sheer power of his writing and the subject matter that he was dealing with, but more significantly because it opened my eyes to the possibility of a very different way of writing ethnography. This was not in terms of 'objective' academic discourse, but more in terms of magic realism and other genres more normally associated with the novel.

On returning to Manchester I attended a seminar in the Department of Anthropology run by Marilyn Strathern in which we looked at reflexive anthropology and the increasingly wide range of ways in which fieldwork could be written up. This literature challenged the traditional ways of writing ethnography and provided a critique of the source of authority within the text

(Clifford & Marcus 1986), the gendered nature of the text (Visweswaran 1994), and the lack of the anthropologist's own self as a significant character within the text (Okely & Calloway 1992). Since that time I have continued to develop my own interest in this literature, particularly as it has tried to explore ways of writing about religion and experience (Young & Goulet 1994), and I have drawn on this widely in the way in which the following chapters are constructed.

My first thoughts were to try to write each chapter in a way that might reflect or capture the very distinct way in which worship was structured and experienced in each particular church. This, however, proved too complex and too contrived for what I was trying to achieve. When I came to reflect on what I was doing more carefully I chose to draw together and combine three separate strands in my writing which could have been separated but which would have made little sense if they had been. These strands reflect (a) the narrative of my own study, the problems that it raised and the attempts that I made to overcome these problems at a practical and theoretical level, (b) the data that I was gathering from those whom I talked to and listened to and the kind of analysis that I was attempting to bring to that data in each distinct context, and (c) my own self-reflection on the actual experience of worshipping in the different churches and the correlations between my own experiences and those of the individuals that I was listening to within each congregation. It is clear that as the ideas which underlie these chapters developed, almost organically, as I was actually engaged within the process of fieldwork, then that process should be expressed, alongside my own reflections upon it, just as much as the experience of worship and the ideas themselves.

The result is that the style and emphasis of each of the four chapters that make up Part II is very different and distinct. This reflects my own response to the congregation in question and the different atmosphere and feelings within the different congregations. It will also be clear that I never stick strictly to either a sociological/anthropological discourse or to a specifically theological one and my language slips between the two with greater or lesser ease depending on the context. I came to this study as a practising Christian, having been brought up within the Church of England and having played a very active role within that church for many years. I was a fully participating observer in each of the four churches and that, clearly, had an impact on what I was thinking and on how I am now expressing those thoughts. I make no apologies for this very personal approach and will come back to a number of the issues that this might raise when I come to draw all these ideas together again in Part III, my conclusion.

NOTES

1   It is also possible that those who express the dominant discourse will suppress other more individual discourses so that certain voices within the group, such as those of women or ethnic minorities or children, are never heard. In this case the definition of this discourse as 'dominant' becomes even more apparent.

PART II

CHAPTER FOUR
THE BAPTIST CHAPEL

The Baptist chapel that I chose to study has a membership of just over seventy, almost all of whom attend worship at the chapel on a regular basis. The chapel is situated two miles south of the city centre close to the university and in an area that is populated largely by students and university staff. The site consists of the chapel with a meeting room, a couple of offices and a kitchen. A hostel for overseas students had recently been built in the grounds.

There are two services on a Sunday. Most people attend the morning service and about half the congregation also comes in the evening. There are a handful of people who attend only the evening service. There is also an Early Session Discussion Group which meets before the morning service and which is attended by about twenty members of the congregation. During the week there is a Wednesday afternoon Bible study (with about six regular, elderly members) and the young people's group, 'Mustard Seed', which meets on Friday evenings. After the morning service on a Sunday the majority of the congregation go to lunch with one of three families (changing each week so no one family has the same group of people every week).

The congregation is dominated by four families. Two of these consist of a husband, wife and teenage children, one of which also has extended family members at the church. A third has a number of adopted children between seven and fifteen and the fourth is a young couple without children of their own. All the church officers and group leaders come from one or other of these families. All the working adults from these families work either at the university as lecturers or researchers, or are involved in the health service in a professional capacity. The rest of the congregation are either elderly, mostly women who have been at the church a long time, or overseas students who live at the hostel on church property. The congregation is entirely white apart from two of the adopted children of the third family and several of the overseas students. The gender ratio, apart from the preponderance of elderly women, is about equal.

The worship is generally planned, organised and presented by the minister. The minister told me that he prepares for each service by reading the lessons from the Joint Liturgical Group lectionary on the Sunday before, reflecting on them throughout the week, discussing them with the Bible study group on the Wednesday and then sitting down and writing the sermon, prayers etc. on the Saturday evening before the services. The congregation would consider themselves to be liberal theologically and this is reflected by the minister who comes from an intellectual, liberal tradition.

I attended the Baptist chapel from January to June 1985. I attended all services during this time, as well as Bible study and Early Session Discussion Group and the Mustard Seed group. I also went away with the congregation for a weekend retreat in the Lake District in April 1985. I continued to keep contact with the congregation during the rest of my research in the other churches and have been back occasionally since completing the project.

INTRODUCTION

When I began my research, I looked around for a church in which to start my fieldwork. I chose to begin at the Baptist chapel for three reasons:

- Because I knew next to nothing about the Baptists and that, I felt, would be an advantage
- Because they had a form of worship that did not utilise formal texts and this, I thought, would get me away from the liturgical establishment

- Because the congregation there was friendly, helpful, academic, and already had an interest in worship

All these answers, taken from notes written before I began to attend the Baptist chapel, prejudge in some way what it was that I was looking for. They also highlight several of my own hidden presuppositions. I was interested in discovering how the congregation understood its worship. The most obvious assumption behind this was that the congregation did have an understanding of worship and that this understanding could be discovered. It also presupposed that such an understanding was in some way different from, and potentially more 'real' than, that of the minister, the theologian, or the anthropologist. There is probably some truth in both these assumptions, but neither of them was clear to me when I first approached the Baptist chapel. I wanted to study the congregational understanding of worship, not because it was different, or any more real, than any other understanding, but simply because such an understanding had not been studied before.

Having accepted this, I still had to ask whether it was possible to talk about a 'congregational understanding of worship' at all? Did individual members of the congregation have their own individual 'understandings' of worship? Could these diverse individual understandings ever be brought together to form a single 'congregational' understanding? When I looked back on my own involvement in worship since childhood, I was aware that I had my own thoughts about what was happening long before I developed any academic interests in the subject. If I had had my own understandings, therefore, derived from my own participation in worship then, I assumed, the members of the Baptist congregation should also have their own understandings drawn from their own particular experiences. Even if I was correct, however, and each member of the congregation did have their own individual understandings of worship, I was still faced with the problem of how I was going to collect the particular understandings of seventy or more members of one congregation and bring them together to create one specific 'congregational' understanding. When I look back to the notes that I made before I began my study, my position on this issue appeared to be fairly clear. I was aware of my own understandings of worship and I was reasonably certain that these understandings could be written down. I had assumed, therefore, that I could also write down, or record on tape, what other people told me about their own understandings of worship. If these individual, subjective, understandings could then be edited and turned from vague ideas, loosely held, into concrete 'texts', then, I assumed, these 'texts' could form a body of data that I would then be able to analyse as the 'congregational understanding of worship'.

As far as I understood it, this was the way in which all anthropologists worked. The anthropologist would go into the field and collect 'data': comments, observations, answers to questionnaires, interviews, tapes of rituals or whatever. This data was then brought home to the university and analysed as 'facts'. Behind such a process, there were numerous questions that could be asked about the authenticity and the reliability of the data. These, however, as far as I was aware at the time, were generally a function of their collection and did not arise out of their inherent nature as 'facts', and it was facts of this kind that I set out to collect.

SEARCHING FOR CONCRETE DATA

In my search for facts I took notes at all the services I attended, I recorded and transcribed several of the sermons, I listened carefully and took notes during discussion groups, I even recorded and videotaped four or five complete acts of worship. All this note-taking, recording and transcribing provided me with very concrete data, but it was not the kind of data that I was looking for. I wanted to know what the congregation thought, not what actually happened. It was concrete data on this point that I was looking for, and it was this data that I was not finding.

I could have sat down at the start of my fieldwork and drawn up a questionnaire to give to members of the congregation. This would have provided concrete, quantifiable, data. But this, I felt, would only have resulted in superficial answers that would have been little more than a reflection of the kinds of questions that I had set. What would have been the value, for example, of asking what a person thought about worship if that person did not generally think about it at all? Obviously, such a person would have given some answer to the question. The question itself would have demanded that such a person thought about worship. Also, I took it for granted, although with very little evidence in retrospect, that the congregation would have had access to what I might call 'pat answers', those snappy summaries that had been taught in Sunday School or were heard in sermons. I was not particularly interested in these pat answers at this stage of my work. I was more interested in the personal, idiosyncratic understandings of individual people, and questionnaires I felt could not provide these.

My problem was one which, in one form or another, appears to have confronted most anthropologists who were interested in religion. There were, therefore, a number of precedents that I felt I could follow. The one which looked most promising for me was that of Frederick Barth in his study of the Baktaman of New Guinea (Barth 1975). Having become dissatisfied with the kind of response that Victor Turner had received from the direct questioning of ritual specialists among the Ndembu (Turner 1967b), Barth decided that he needed to discover what the Baktaman themselves really thought about their rituals. He chose, therefore, not to discuss matters of ritual and religion with the Baktaman, but simply to listen to what they had to say about it in the course of their everyday conversations. In doing this, Barth found that ritual was not a topic of everyday conversation. This left Barth with a problem. He either had to offer his own interpretation of Baktaman ritual without any reference to the Baktaman themselves, or he had to try to overcome the problem of silence in some other way. Barth's own solution was to take a full and active part in all the rituals himself and then to analyse his own experience alongside the few hints that he had got from those involved in the rituals alongside him. From my own perspective, this radical solution did not seem to be entirely satisfactory. As I have already suggested, I was not convinced that even if a group of people do not talk openly about a subject such as religion (especially in front of a foreign anthropologist) this does not necessarily mean that they do not have any views. What is more, those views are very unlikely to be identical to those of the anthropologist. How, then, was I going to discover these views unless I asked?

My own solution was to go half way with Barth. I decided to spend the first half of my time with the Baptists (and subsequently with each of the other churches) simply being around; attending everything that went on, making notes, listening to conversations and so on. During this time I would discover which issues were being discussed and try to ascertain how worship was understood in terms of everyday conversation. Only then, during the second three months of each study, would I begin to ask questions and conduct more formal interviews. The questions I would ask could then be based upon the conversational evidence of the first three months. By this stage, I assumed, I would know enough about the general understanding of worship within the congregation not to prejudge any answers.

That was the theory. However, with the Baptists, and to an even greater extent with the other three churches, things never worked out quite so simply. Ironically a number of people actually broached the subject of worship with me during my first three months at the Baptist chapel simply because they knew that the subject interested me. During the second three months, however, whilst I was actually asking questions, worship was hardly ever mentioned in everyday conversation. Worship was not, I had to conclude, a major topic of normal conversation within the church.

After three months, therefore, I was back to square one and had to try toconstruct some questions in order to discover the 'congregational understanding of worship' which I was desperately seeking. The interviews were, in many ways, my last chance. I was still concerned about the kind of answers that I would be given. I decided, therefore, that the best solution was simply to ask one or two vague questions. This, I thought, would give the members of the congregation the chance to interpret the questions as they saw fit, and so provide me with slightly more impartial answers.

The first question was obvious. From my own experience I knew that what I had understood of the content of a particular act of worship was largely determined by the role that I had performed within that worship. It was not until I began to study liturgy academically that I became aware of the full content of any one service. My first question, therefore, was to ask each person what they remembered from the act of worship on the previous Sunday. This could have provided very concrete, almost quantifiable, data of the kind such that '75 per cent of the congregation did not remember the words of the second verse of the third hymn'. Such statistics could still be provided if I chose to work them out. However, as my example shows, I doubt very much if this would produce anything very useful.

The second question was more of a problem. This would be the important one, the question that would produce the texts that said what people actually thought about worship. I wanted one question that was ambiguous enough to allow the interviewee to move off in any direction that they might choose and yet would focus their attention on worship. Eventually I narrowed the question down to 'What does worship mean to you?'. This was certainly ambiguous enough – the range of answers that I received proved that – and the word 'mean' in this question did not seem to concern people. For a social scientist, this would have caused a great deal of difficulty. What, they would ask, do we understand by the word 'mean'? Some of the more academic members of the Baptist congregation did ask such questions, but in general I found it to be a usefully ambiguous term that generated a wide variety of responses. This, then, was the question that I hoped would provide me with texts about the congregational understanding of worship, with concrete data which I could then go away and analyse.

Towards the end of my time at the Baptist chapel, after having conducted interviews with almost two thirds of the congregation, I was given the opportunity to lead a couple of the Early Session Discussion Groups. I agreed to lead two sessions. In the first I recounted my own experiences within the Baptist chapel and told them what I, personally, had learnt over the previous five months. In the second I presented some of my data, suitably refined by anthropological theory, and opened it up for discussion. I threw back at the congregation what they had told me during the interviews. 'This,' I told them, 'is what worship means to you'. The only problem was that it wasn't! In the discussion that followed individual members of the congregation rejected most of what I had just been saying. It seemed that what I had been told, previously, in the interviews was now, in the context of the discussion group, all wrong. That is to say, not wrong as such ... it was right ... but not right, if you understood what they meant. It all seemed to depend on how I looked at it.

The question I had to ask myself therefore was 'how exactly should I be looking at it?'. What was the real significance of the texts that I had been gathering during the interviews? Did they really contain the 'congregational understanding of worship' that I had been looking for? At one level, that of the interview itself, they obviously did. At another level, however, as seen in the discussion group, they appeared to bear little or no resemblance to what was really being thought, if we could say that anything was 'really' being thought.[1]

REVIEWING THE INTERVIEWS

On reflection, after the experience of the discussion group, there was one point that struck me concerning all the interviews that I had held. I was conscious that, having arranged to see a particular person or family, I would go through in my own mind exactly how I expected those people to respond to my questions. What had intrigued me, and perhaps should also have disturbed me, was that in almost every case I was correct, give or take a few minor details. One member of the congregation asked me whether I had discovered anything interesting or surprising during the interviews. I had certainly found plenty that was interesting, but I had to say that I had discovered nothing that I could honestly say was surprising. It was almost as if I did not need to ask the questions or conduct the interviews at all. It could, of course, be argued that, by going in with this kind of attitude, I was predetermining the answers that I received, or, perhaps more to the point, only hearing those answers that I wanted to hear and overlooking those which I did not. There must certainly be some truth in this. However, I think that the solution is actually much simpler, and certainly much less devious. Quite simply I knew the people to whom I was talking and I did know, at least in principle, how each one of them would respond.[2]

I had been with these people for three months, we had worshipped together, we had shared meals together, we had discussed important political and ethical issues together. I knew these people. I knew how they were going to answer my questions. I knew because I knew in each case what issues interested them. I knew the kind of language that they would use. I knew the ways in which they would interpret the question. Much of the ground had already been covered in other, more informal, conversations over the previous few months. They knew that I was interested in worship and so that was what they had talked to me about. It was obvious, even as I was doing it, that the only purpose for conducting the interviews was to confirm my own suspicions. I wanted to collect useable quotes, words from the horses' mouths, phrases that would look good in a book and which I could place in quotation marks: that is, 'concrete', 'objective' facts.

This, I think, is the heart of the issue. I thought that I was asking them 'What does worship mean to you?', and in one sense, I was: these were the words that I was using. However, when looked at more closely, what I was in fact asking, using exactly the same words, was more akin to 'What quotes, what "formulations", do you use when talking about worship?'. I was not asking about 'meanings'. I was not even asking about 'understandings'. I was asking about 'formulations'. It was not surprising therefore that it was 'formulations', neat pre-packaged ideas, that I received. This is not to say that a 'formulation' about worship is not interesting. It is. It is a 'text' and it does have a certain value. Nothing that I was told was a lie as such. It was a 'fabrication', given to serve a certain purpose, but it was not a lie. And yet, when I came to present these 'formulations' back to the congregation, suitably distilled and purified through the filter of academic theory, they were largely rejected, and rightly so. This was not how the congregation 'understood' worship, it was how they 'expressed that understanding' when asked to do so in an interview.

Some hint of this was given within the interviews themselves. There was always a sense during any conversation that there was something beyond what was actually being said, something that could not be said, something that was implied, shared as common knowledge between interviewer and interviewee. What was unsaid, however, could never become part of the formulation, it could never be trapped within my quotation marks. There was a 'gap' between what was said and what was communicated through other means, a gap that was only hinted at in the vagaries of conversation within the interview, but a gap that became a gaping chasm when the interview was distilled into academic formulations. Such a gap, however, as I came to see, was essential to the way in which the Baptists understood their worship. The formulations were not wrong, but they were not right either, and between 'not wrong' and 'not right' there lies a gaping chasm.

Up to this point, I have concentrated on what the transcripts that I collected during the interviews were not. They were not accounts of how people really 'understood' worship. I have said that they were 'formulations' about that understanding, but the transcripts themselves, if we go back to the raw material, were not even formulations. The formulations were those quotations that I distilled from the transcripts by isolating those issues that I felt to be important in the light of academic theory. The transcripts in their raw state were more than simply formulations. The interviews were wide-ranging conversations containing much more than the quotable formulations, and, within each interview, there was clearly as much left unsaid as was said. If I were to reproduce a complete transcript of any one interview, most readers would be confused and puzzled by the results. The reader would not know what it was that was not being said. The reader would only be confused by the transcripts, however, if they were accepted at face value. From within the environment that produced them, where it was possible to reconstruct what was 'not said', I should have been able to find some way of knowing, or at least thinking that I might know, what the interviewee meant and did not mean by what was being said.

I have already claimed that as I came to each interview I knew, at least in vague terms, what each person was going to say. I also claimed that I had this 'knowledge' because by the time I came to the interview I 'knew' these people as individuals; I knew the issues that were important to them, I knew the language that they were going to use and so on. I would call this kind of knowledge 'intuitive' or 'implicit'. It is knowledge that I picked up over time, not through the direct observation of recordable facts, but through the gradual assimilation of the whole environment within the church, an assimilation that went by almost unrecognised. There are, I would suggest, various levels, or elements, to this 'intuitive' knowledge.

The first element is an understanding of language. I claimed that I knew the language that the various people were going to use during the interviews. At one level, this was the same as that which they had used during meals or over coffee when I had been invited to their houses on other occasions. It was relaxed and informal. Often we would become side-tracked, we talked about personalities, we joked and we laughed. In a very real sense, therefore, these were 'informal' interviews. It was, therefore, an 'informal' view of the worship that I was getting, an understanding that was phrased in the language of the everyday. Everyday language, however, did not seem to have the terms available to talk about the special, the religious, or the unusual. Some terms were borrowed from other forms of discourse; from the discussion groups for example, or from academic theology, or even from the worship itself. Such borrowing was, in fact, rarely used but when it was it was always treated with a certain amount of caution and respect.

This use of a special language, or at least of words from within the discourse of worship, indicates that there may have been some kind of 'religious language' at work within the interviews that behaved in peculiar ways, or that covered up those areas where ordinary, everyday, language could not cope. What I found to be particularly interesting, when I came to review these interviews in the light of the rejection of my formulations, was the fact that it was often these 'worship' words that were the trigger for me in constructing my formulations. Those parts of the interviews that contained these words were obviously those parts of the conversations that dealt with worship. This, in hindsight, appears to be very naive.

There is much more to any interview, however, than the formality or informality of the language that is used. There are also many different kinds of assumptions that lie behind the language, and behind the discourse of the interview itself. These assumptions must also be known if we are to understand what is being said and what is not being said. One set of assumptions is that made about the congregation, most specifically the assumptions that lie behind my statement that I 'knew' the members of this congregation as people. I assumed knowledge of the various tensions that existed within the congregation, the internal 'dynamics' of the group. These only needed to be hinted at during the interviews, and when they were considered to be 'delicate' they would only ever be hinted at. It was still assumed, however, that I, as a regular member of the congregation, would know all about them. It is hints and assumptions of this kind that make entering any unknown group or congregation disconcerting for the first few weeks. After three months, however, I was fairly clear about what was being hinted at and I could share many of these common assumptions in my own conversation.

Unfortunately, however, there is no way in which I could reproduce the full network of seventy specific individuals and their interrelations here. Not only would it take far too long, but it would also be unfair to the congregation in question. What I could do is to outline some of the factors which underlie this network and which determine at least some of its dynamics. I could mention, for example, the basic 'social' make up of the group, its socio-economic background. I could mention the openness and friendliness of the congregation, especially to foreign students. I could talk about the four families that dominated the life of the chapel. I could discuss the diverse religious roots of its members; the sense, often expressed, that any one of them would feel out of place in any other church; the intellectual and academic nature of most of the members; their reluctance to discuss issues of belief; the emphasis that was placed on social values, political and ethical issues and so on. These could all be developed at length and they would all be part of any underlying intuitive knowledge that could go to create an understanding of the internal dynamics of the congregation.

I could also look at the assumptions that underlie, and come together to define, the 'self-identity' of the congregation as a whole. The congregation sees itself, for example, as a voluntary association. Even those who have joined the church from outside the Baptist tradition would support this view, probably because they have chosen to come to this church in preference to some other. The voluntary nature of the group also leads on to the second element of the congregation's self-identity: the stress on the individuality of each person and the upholding of that individuality by the group as a whole. The group would never impose its own ideas, even in a democratic form, upon specific individuals. Each person was 'accepted' as they were, irrespective of their background or present views. What we have in this Baptist congregation, therefore, from its own point of view, is a group of individuals, each having a unique character, background, gifts and roles within the church, all of whom have consciously chosen to be members of, and hence to offer their support to, this particular congregation.

All these assumptions about the social aspects of the congregation are very important and should never be overlooked. I was always fully aware of these assumptions and did, to some extent at least, take them into consideration in distilling the transcripts of the interviews into formulations. They formed the basis for the 'academic framework', through which the formulations were distilled. These are, after all, just the kind of underlying assumptions that anthropologists are trained to look out for and take into account. There is, however, yet another set of assumptions behind these interviews that I feel to be much more important and which are often ignored entirely by the average anthropologist.

SOMETHING WHICH IS 'UNSAID'

I have already claimed that there was something 'unsaid' within the interviews, something that was taken as implicit, as shared between myself and the interviewee. This 'something', I would argue, cannot be expressed solely in terms of linguistics or sociology. I came into this study as a full and active participant in the worship of the various churches, and was accepted as such by the members of those churches. I was therefore very wary of any attempt to reduce worship, or the understanding of worship, to a purely sociological or linguistic activity. At face value, however, this was exactly what the Baptists themselves were doing. The interviews focused almost entirely on the sociological factors in their worship; on other worshippers, on questions of language, of choice of hymns, of forms and structures within the worship, even on questions of space, seating and the decoration (or lack of it) of the worship space. The various members of the Baptist congregation very rarely mentioned God in any of their answers to my question. When asked directly, however, 'Doesn't God have something to do with this?', they would always reply, 'Oh yes, but of course'. God was assumed. What is perhaps even more significant was that if I went one step further and asked, 'What does God have to do with worship?', the answers were all, and always, of the same kind: 'I don't know', 'I'm not really sure'. I knew immediately what was meant. I knew that God was important to their understanding of worship but I also knew that it was impossible for them, or for me, to put that importance into words.

95

This realisation has made me challenge several of my own assumptions about God's role in worship and assumptions about our ability to express that role in concrete terms. I began to ask myself, for example, 'what place does God have within my own understanding of worship?'. I also needed to devise a way of encouraging the members of the Baptist congregation to say what God actually did mean for them within their understanding of worship. All the popular books on liturgy begin with some kind of definition of worship, all of which involve God: 'We worship God', 'We praise God', 'We proclaim God', 'We listen to God' (Burkhart 1979, Owen 1980, Kendrick 1984). God is undoubtedly important. We cannot get away from this. Is it possible, however, to go beyond such general statements and to say exactly what God does have to do with worship, based solely upon our own experience of worship Sunday by Sunday? The only answer that I was able to discover in relation to the Baptist congregation was that they did not know, or rather that they might 'know' but that they could not put that knowledge into words.

There is a long theological tradition behind this kind of answer. Mystical theologians, for example, talk about the 'mystery' of God and the 'darkness' of God; the inability to say anything concrete about God or even to 'know' God in any kind of completeness (Turner 1995). This tradition is best expressed within liturgical writing by Aidan Kavanagh's book *On Liturgical Theology* (1984). In this book Kavanagh reflects on the question, 'What has God got to do with worship?'. Kavanagh is reflecting on that question from within his own tradition as a Benedictine monk, and yet he comes to very much the same conclusion as the Baptists I was interviewing. He claims that we cannot say, or perhaps to put it more strongly, that we *must* not say, exactly what role God plays. There is something happening in worship that is beyond our understanding, that goes beyond the simple sociological construction of the ritual itself. There is something that takes us, in Kavanagh's words, 'to the edge of chaos' (1984: 169–70) and there transforms our very beings. It would perhaps be easy for us to dismiss this as speculative and subjective theology, and yet there is something that rings true in Kavanagh's almost poetical comments. Behind our worship there *is* something that must be affirmed but which cannot be fully grasped. What is more, that 'something' can never be turned into 'data'.

If this is so then it makes my job, as an anthropologist, very difficult indeed. If there is no 'concrete data', then presumably there is nothing that can be analysed. However, far from closing off the doors for study, this insight could begin to open up exciting new avenues that get us beyond simplistic theology and superficial sociology to something much deeper, much more essential to the 'experience' of worship. It was this insight that first alerted me to these new possibilities. It was the analysis of the unknowable that I felt could lead to a greater understanding of worship. It was at this point that I had to stand back and try to find another way of getting at the kind of information that I was after. If we cannot say what worship 'means' to any one individual then can we say anything about the way that meaning might be constructed or the forms in which they attempt to express it in ordinary conversation? In attempting to do this, I found myself reflecting on a sermon which the minister preached during my time at the chapel.

A SERMON

At the heart of all Baptist worship there was, without any doubt, the sermon. Every member of the congregation agreed on this point. Within the sermon, all the disparate parts of the service were drawn together. The more I listened to the sermons, taped them, and re-listened to them, the more I became aware of the centrality of the 'story' within their structure. In all the sermons the story was essential, be it a biblical story, an anecdote, or a quote from another author. These stories were told as stories and also woven into the arguments of the sermon, some of which were highly complex and subtle. When I asked people what they remembered of the previous week's sermon, many of them told me that they could not remember the argument, it was too intellectual or too clever, but they could remember the stories. Somehow, the story seemed to be important. The more I listened the more I realised that the story, in one form or another, sat at the heart of every act of worship at the Baptist chapel.

Of all the sermons that I heard during my six months with the Baptist church, one sticks in my mind. This is not because it was technically any better than the others, or because its message was particularly profound, but simply because it bore most directly upon my own project. The theme of the sermon was 'Christ the Teacher', and Matthew 5:1–12 (the Beatitudes) was the reading set for the day according to the Joint Liturgical Group Lectionary.

The Beatitudes, we were informed, intrigued the minister, not because of what they said, but rather because of what they did not say. The Beatitudes are all too familiar to us and we so easily think that we know exactly what they mean. However, the minister asked, have we ever stopped to read them carefully? Have we ever seen just how 'nonsensical' they actually are? 'Blessed are the poor in spirit for theirs is the kingdom of heaven.' 'Blessed are those who mourn for they shall be comforted.' 'Blessed are the pure in heart for they will see God.' 'Blessed are the peacemakers for they will be called the sons of God.' Not only are we left in some doubt as to who the 'poor in spirit' or the 'pure in heart' might be, but we are told, as a statement of fact, that 'theirs *is* the kingdom of heaven', and that 'they *will* see God'. There are no 'ifs' or 'buts', 'mights' or 'maybes' here.

So often, the minister told us, we assume that the Beatitudes, and the rest of the Sermon on the Mount, are a series of laws by which we must all try, as Christians, to lead our lives. We assume that Jesus is telling us, in effect, that we must be poor in spirit, pure in heart, peacemakers or whatever. However, the minister suggested, if we look closely this is not the case. Jesus, it seems, does not deal in rules and regulations, in 'laws'. Even some of the later sections ('You have heard it said, "Eye for an eye and tooth for a tooth". But I tell you, if someone strikes you on the right cheek turn to him the other also' (Matthew 5:38)) may look like commands, but in their context, in relation to The Law, they become extrapolations which seem, above all else, to make 'law' meaningless. How could we expect to maintain a legal code containing this kind of command? 'Love your enemies' overrides, in one statement, all possible forms of legality. Jesus may have come to fulfil the law and the prophets, but he certainly did not come to present us with a new Law. This, we were told, was not his way.

Jesus, the minister reminded us, taught with parables, with stories. These were stories that related to everyday life: about a woman who lost a coin; about a man who was attacked on the road to Jericho, and so on. These were stories that ordinary people could relate to. Even so, the people still did not seem to understand. The people of Jesus' day wanted commands. They wanted to be told what to do in every single situation, how to react to all possible circumstances. The pharisees of the day, it seems, fed this need. Jesus had a different way. Jesus was not in the business of easy answers. He simply told stories and those who had ears to hear would hear.

For two thousand years there has been a great deal of discussion and debate about these stories. Scholars and theologians have constantly attempted to give us an interpretation of the stories, to say what Jesus really meant. There has been a persistent effort to try to force these stories to give us the easy answers that Jesus himself would not give. The stories themselves remain ambiguous, and it is in their very ambiguity that their power lies. These stories are about 'real' people, 'real' happenings, events that the listener can empathise with, and even if at the time of hearing the ear is not open a time will come when the situation presents itself in which the story will suddenly make sense. At that point, we will all 'hear'. This, as the minister made clear, is not an uncommon occurrence restricted to saints and theologians. When any of us are faced with a difficult decision, a time of sadness, or even a time of great joy, a parable or a statement like those in the Beatitudes can suddenly ring true, not as a commandment, but as a statement of how things 'really' are: 'Blessed are they that mourn, for they *shall* be comforted.'

It is for this reason, the minister concluded, that we read and listen to these stories during worship: not to receive an immediate message from them, all the easy answers, but simply to keep them before us, to help us to learn them, not so much 'by heart' as 'in the heart'. In the constant telling and retelling of these stories, and many others like them, we collect a library of reference points within us. This means that when a crisis takes us unawares we do not have to turn to the Bible and search through for some relevant passage, the story is already there, welling up inside us to support us and to interpret our experience. Without the constant telling and listening to these stories we remain spiritually empty and, in a crisis, we could collapse, unsure of our own reference points. Jesus did not give us easy answers, commands that promise happiness if only we could follow them.

He knew human nature too well. Jesus gave us a store of stories, reference points, which can support and uphold us when things begin to get tough: 'Blessed are those who are persecuted for righteousness' sake for theirs *is* the kingdom of heaven.'

In this sermon I found laid out very clearly and succinctly how, at least in the minister's view, the story could function within the worship and in the lives of the people listening to it. This rang true for me. I could acknowledge in my own experience the kind of situation that had been described. Stories, according to this view, are not symbolic structures that need interpreting. They do not even have to be understood in any direct sense at the time of hearing. They are ambiguous, and deliberately so. They ring chords in the individual's experience, either at the time of hearing or later, and they lift that experience out of the everyday, giving it new and vital significance. Stories seen in this way can be said to bypass understanding and formal thought altogether and to relate directly to experience.

REFLECTING ON THE 'STORY'

The 'story', therefore, has a central place in Baptist worship. But what exactly is a 'story' and how does an understanding of the story help us to grasp that which is 'unknowable' within the Baptists' understanding of worship? If we begin with the sermon, we find that the 'story', or anecdote, is often referred to as 'illustrative'. What can this tell us? Firstly, it defines the story as reinforcing a message that has already been expressed in a different form. Secondly, it implies that the story will be 'remembered' where the raw message may not. This assumes that the recalling of the story will trigger the recalling of the message. Thirdly, it assumes that the story will relieve the tone of the sermon. The story brings the sermon 'down' from the level of academic discourse to the level of everyday speech. Why, then, is it that the story is thought to be so good at containing 'messages' and at being recalled, whereas academic discourse is not? Part of the answer must be that the story is so much a part of everyday speech. We are used to recalling and retelling stories. We do it all the time. This, however, only takes the question one step further back. Why is the story such a valuable part of everyday speech? One reason might be that the structure of the story is easy to remember. Compared to the vagaries and complexities of academic discourse this is often true. However, I would argue that what is more important than the structure is that the kind of 'message' that is contained within the story is itself more easily grasped. The story, I would suggest, engages with us, not intellectually, but empathetically. We respond to the story from within our own experiences and respond primarily to the 'experience' of the story.

We can see this point very clearly in the way that stories are exchanged after the service every Sunday morning and evening. At one level the speakers are, of course, transmitting factual statements: 'I did x, y or z this week'. However, the speaker actually wants to say more than that. To say simply that 'Mrs Jones hurt her leg last week' is to state a fact. To tell everybody how she hurt her leg, how she feels now and what she said when I went to visit her last Thursday is to expect sympathy (or not as the case may be). Such 'stories' ask the listener to match the experience recounted in the story with their own experience, to accept the factual information given but with an added depth of empathy. The same could be said, although in a much more general sense, of biblical stories. These do not set out to tell us simply what Jesus said or did as if our interest were mere academic curiosity. Biblical stories engage our empathy, they ask us to share in the recalling of an experience: 'Five thousand people met to hear the teacher, they were hungry and there was no food for them....'. We have probably never been in a crowd quite like this but our various experiences are enough to let us imagine, by extrapolation, what our own response would be: '.... and Jesus took the five loaves and the two small fishes, offered them up to God and broke them. All those present had enough to eat and twelve baskets of scraps were collected.' This seems incredible to us, not simply because it is scientifically impossible, but because it stretches our imagination, our empathy, to its limits.

If we now turn our attention to the various stories that were used during the interviews to recount each person's understanding of worship then we can, perhaps, take this discussion one step further. The interviewees could not tell me exactly how they understood worship, they did not have the analytic language to do this. Even those who did have access to suitable analytic language failed to use it. For those who took part in the worship week by week turning to such language would have reduced the whole experience of worship to gibberish. What the interviewee could do, however, was to tell me a story, to recount previous services that were important to them, to tell me about the significant events in their religious development and so on. These stories engaged me, not at the academic level, either of 'formulation' or of 'implicit knowledge', they engaged me on the empathetic level: 'The experience of worship is like this, you know, you were there also'. What this should tell us is that the understanding of worship is an understanding that fits in with the nature of the story. It is an understanding in the form of lived experience, an experience that cannot be classified analytically, but an experience that can be communicated empathetically through the medium of the story.

How, then, does the story work? What makes its role in worship so significant? Let me begin by presenting a simple model of how the story might function within the context of worship. I can then add further levels of sophistication as I develop my ideas.

THE INTERACTION OF STORIES

Consider our arrival at any one particular service. We each arrive at that service already possessing a personal narrative. This personal narrative consists of various presuppositions, some loose and general ideas, personal problems, a sense of what we expect from the worship, and so on. The list could be endless and its exact content is, at this point, irrelevant. What is important is the presence of the personal narrative in itself, the ongoing sense of being ourselves. Along with this specifically personal narrative, we may also be aware of various aspects of the wider cultural and historical narratives within which we all exist and which we will bring with us to the service. In most cases, these will be present in a 'personalised' form and hence they will be a part of the personal narrative itself.

Along with this ongoing 'narrative', however, we will also be carrying some specific problems, issues, or events. These will be in the front of our minds, bounded, closed, and hence, by my own definition, 'stories'.[3] As we sit through the worship, we will be presented with a general 'liturgical' narrative. We are unlikely, however, to take all of this in, even if we happen to be liturgists who are interested in studying what is going on. Within this general liturgical narrative, however, there will inevitably be a number of more specific 'stories'. At this point one of two things can happen. Either a story, or stories, from within the liturgy will interact in some way with a story that we have brought with us, or one that is drawn from a deeper level of our personal narrative. Or else the stories of the liturgy will simply be added to our personal narrative only to interact with the more specific personal stories at a later date, as the minister indicated in his sermon. Stories, therefore, will 'interact' but what exactly is happening at that moment of interaction?

One of the women from the Baptist chapel told me during an interview that whenever the hymn 'O Jesus I have promised' was sung she always recalled her own baptism. This hymn can be seen in this context as a 'story', a story that had previously interacted with her own personal narrative and one which therefore contained special significance for her. She mentioned this hymn specifically, however, because it had been used during the service on the previous Sunday. Here, she told me, the hymn, with its associations of baptism and assurance, had been sung at the end of the service after a particularly challenging sermon. This, the woman claimed, was a deliberate choice by the minister to set the hearts and minds of the congregation at rest after the unease created by the sermon.

In this illustration, I may seem to be stretching the definition of 'story' a little further than would, perhaps, be expected. How can a 'hymn', for example, be defined as a 'story', except in the very loosest sense? The first point of development for my model, therefore, must be for us to clarify exactly what is meant by the term 'story'.

The worship at the Baptist chapel showed many examples of what might be defined as stories. There are the readings and the sermon which I have already mentioned but there are also hymns, for example, which can be thought of as stories. In this particular chapel, all the hymns were carefully chosen to be clearly related to the readings, to comment upon them, to retell the story, or to take the story one step further. Hymns can, therefore, mirror Bible stories, they can relate these stories to our own personal stories, or they can lead us on to look at the greater narrative of 'faith'. Hymns in this context almost become stories in themselves, or at least triggers for the recalling of stories. Prayers and intercessions can do much the same thing. We are told, and asked to remember before God, the story of starving children in Africa. We are told, and asked to remember before God, the story of a building project at a local church. We are told, and asked to remember before God, the sick, each with their own individual story, often known only to God. In each case we offer the story to God and ask God to remember that story and to guide its outcome. In all this, in one form or another, the story is central, be it directly through readings and in the sermon, or at one step removed, through hymns and prayers.

In the majority of these cases it is not specific stories, told in full, that are being presented, but rather hints of stories, allusions to stories, even just the sense of a story. One line of a hymn has the potential to conjure up a whole series of biblical stories. Prayers only hint at numerous personal stories often unknown to the worshippers. However, I think that we have to go even further than this. We have to note, for example, that the hymn mentioned by the woman evoked not the story contained in the words of the hymn, but rather her own personal story of that hymn, a part of the larger story of her baptism. In another example, that of the sermon that I quoted earlier, it was not any one, specific, story within that sermon that caught my attention. Rather it was the 'story of the sermon' as a whole, the story about the way in which biblical stories might work in the lives of the worshippers, which attracted me. In other words the various 'stories' that each one of us 'hears' within the worship, and our own personal sense of the story, will be different from those of other members of the congregation. What is more the stories which have spoken to us will probably have more relation to the stories that we have personally brought with us than they have to those which were intended by the minister, although that may not always be the case.

This brings me to my second point of development. If it is our own personal narrative that is affecting the sense of the story that we hear in worship then how exactly are these 'new' stories that we are hearing interacting with those that we bring with us? Many people after a service commented that one or other element within the worship 'spoke' to them, that is they suddenly realised the relevance of a particular story to them personally. When a story that we sense in the worship 'speaks' to us, I would suggest, we find ourselves at a point in time in which two stories, our own and the liturgical, are instantaneously superimposed in such a way as to allow a flow of meaning or emotion between them. That moment, the moment of being 'spoken' to, creates a temporary bridge of significance between the two stories, inevitably transforming both stories in the process. The story that is sensed in the worship must have been triggered in some way by a personal story, or, alternatively, a story in the worship triggers the memory of a personal story. Either way, the process of interaction in the worship will transform both the personal story and the sense of the story which has spoken to us in the worship. The two stories are not only bridged at the moment of interaction but they become one, they merge, and the story that results, the story of the interaction, becomes a third, completely new story, one which is related to both the other two and yet different in form from either. The woman in my example could not hear the hymn without recalling her baptism and could not recall her baptism without remembering the hymn, but the significance of the merger at the point at which she 're-heard' the hymn and recalled the story was a new story about confidence after a challenging sermon. The interaction bridges, and so merges, two stories, creating in its turn a third and transforming the other two. None of the stories will ever be sensed in quite the same way again. However, it is still important to realise that the direction of the interaction can go either way, either from personal to liturgical during the worship itself, or, as the minister claimed in his sermon, from liturgical to personal at some later date.

EMPATHETIC MERGING AND THE UNKNOWABLE IN WORSHIP

I have talked about the sense of a story being determined by what members of the congregation bring into the worship. I have talked about the interaction of stories, transforming two original stories and creating in their turn new stories. But what is happening at the point of interaction that is so creative? Here we can only speculate.

Earlier in the chapter, I suggested that the essence of the story was its ability to engage our empathy. The response that the story demands is essentially an empathetic one. This must be significant to the way in which the stories interact. If the story is essentially empathetic then the moment of interaction must, in some way, be an 'empathetic moment', a point at which the emotions generated by the story sensed in the worship match, almost perfectly, those of the story we recall. The merging of these stories is a merging of empathy. In the future, therefore, both of these stories will engender the same, or at least very similar, empathetic responses. This is not an uncommon phenomenon. Empathetic merging happens all the time, when we read fiction, when watching films or plays, even in everyday experience. This is why we can 'relate' to other people's stories, because there is always that element of empathetic merging. There must, in our case, however, be something more significant. What is important, I think, is the liturgical setting itself, the aura of sacredness that surrounds the worship and hence the liturgical story. I have already said that each time a story 'speaks' to an individual, each time that two stories merge, a third is created out of this merger. It is this new story that takes on the charged emotional content of the context of the worship. This in turn relates the charge back to the two stories that came together, giving all three a new sense of significance. None of this could ever be expressed or transmitted in clear academic terms because the discourse is at all times that of experience and emotion, a discourse that can only be encapsulated in the story.

Having come down to the point of interaction, and speculated about what may be going on at this point, I think that it is important for us to widen our perspective once again and ask how this discussion of the story relates to my earlier discussion of the Baptists' inability to express that which was unknowable in worship. What I want to suggest is that at least something of this unknowable factor can be encompassed by the use of the story. I have already said that most people used stories, rather than academic or analytical discourse in response to my question concerning the meaning of worship. I have also suggested that this implies that part of their understanding of that meaning has to be concerned with that which stories can express particularly well, most notably the element of 'experience'. This relates directly to what Kavanagh has to say about that which is unknowable for him in relation to worship, that is the 'experience' of coming to the edge of chaos and returning (Kavanagh 1984). Whether this is exactly the kind of experience which the members of the Baptist congregation have during worship is unlikely and not particularly relevant. What is important is that the Baptists, in choosing the story as their preferred medium of discourse, are, like Kavanagh, saying that what is unknowable in worship is essentially experiential.

This is the point at which I wish to leave this particular discussion. I could go on to look at the different stories which were offered to me during the interviews and try to discover what kind of experience we are talking about in relation to the worship of the Baptist chapel. To do so, however, would probably be to move back into an analytic discourse and to distance the story from the experience and ourselves from both. I want to conclude this chapter simply by reinforcing the primary message that I felt that I gained from my time with the Baptists. This was that the essence of worship for the Baptists, as expressed through the medium of the story, is an experience of something which is beyond words, an experience which links the time of worship with everyday life and both with the larger experience of God.

NOTES

1   It is interesting to note how this situation reflects the theoretical thinking of Gerd Baumann (1996) who studied a multi-religious community in Southall and discovered that each member of each religious grouping could maintain a number of different, and often contradictory, discourses on their religion at the same time. The form of the discourse that was used in any one situation depended on who was talking to whom and the underlying assumptions of the context in which the discourse was being used. Baumann argues that individuals could switch between these discourses with ease, and often with little or no sense that they were doing so. What I was witnessing within the Baptist chapel therefore may well have been an example of what

Baumann defines as 'dual discursive competence'. There is clearly some truth in this but it does not invalidate the argument which I presented at the time and which is contained in the body of the text.

2   It has been pointed out that I actually had a great deal in common with this particular congregation, coming from a similar social background and being relatively literate theologically. Clearly in many cases I did share common views and understandings with certain members of the congregation, but I would also want to claim to have listened carefully and to have picked up and recognised those situations in which I did not share the view of the individual being interviewed. A common perspective was clearly not the only issue affecting my knowledge of what these people were going to say.

3   I am defining 'narrative' in this context as an ongoing process without a specific beginning or ending, while I am using 'story' to define that which is bounded. In these terms a narrative is clearly made up of a series of stories and the narrative relates to 'life' while the story relates to and reflects specific 'events'.

CHAPTER FIVE
THE ROMAN CATHOLIC
CHURCH

I always wanted to include a Roman Catholic church within this study but I was also keen to choose one that did not have a distinctive ethnic identity, be that Polish, Irish or other. It was also important that the church and the clergy would be open to the kind of study that I was interested in and give me wide access to people within the parish. I choose a church situated between a middle-class suburb and a fairly large council estate. The different congregations within the church were drawn about equally from both of these areas. When I approached the church the assistant priest, who had a diocesan youth post at the time, was very interested in the project and was very keen to offer his help. Unfortunately, however, he had moved on by the time that I began the study and the parish priest, who was left on his own to run the parish, was never quite as supportive.

There were five masses each weekend at the church (6.30pm Saturday, 8.00am, 9.15am, 11.00am and 5.30pm on Sunday) plus at least one mass each day, with extra masses for feasts, school masses and masses for other organisations within the congregation. The total congregation for each Sunday was approximately 1400 distributed fairly evenly over the four masses (with slightly fewer going to the 8.00am than the others). The age profile of each mass was slightly different (with the 8.00am and 9.15am congregations being significantly older than the others). However, there was always a mixture of middle- and working-class people at each mass, and only slightly more women than men, with a significant number of families (mother, father and children) attending the later masses. The congregation was entirely white and a high proportion of those from the council estate had Irish roots. There was a separate Ministry of the Word for children at the 11.00am mass that was run by a group of five families and attracted about twenty to thirty children each week. This mass was also the principal mass of the day and was celebrated with a choir, altar servers and full ceremonial. There were hymns at the two evening masses on Saturday and Sunday but none at the early morning celebrations. All the masses among those that I attended were celebrated by the parish priest with only a very few exceptions.

Apart from the masses there were a number of organisations within the parish and a church social club where forty to fifty men from the council estate, along with a few women, would meet most nights that it was open. I attended three meetings of the St Vincent de Paul society which met monthly and consisted mostly of older men, primarily from the council estate. I also attended a Justice and Peace group on a regular basis. This had seven regular members, all from the middle-class section of the parish and met weekly in member's homes. I did not attend the women's groups or other organisations within the parish (primarily because I was not always aware of their existence until I had been at the church for some time and had begun to talk to members of the congregation.).

I attended the Roman Catholic church from July to December 1985. I attended a different mass each Sunday, all the major festivals and a number of the weekday masses. I had great difficulty talking to members of the congregation about worship, as I explain below, and I kept no contact with the church following my period of study.

INTRODUCTION

Before I began to study the Roman Catholic congregation, my thoughts about Catholic worship could be summed up in two words: 'habit' and 'tradition'. I had a mental picture of Roman Catholics who went to mass out of 'habit', a religious duty that must be performed because that was what the Church had told them to do. 'Tradition', I assumed, with its overtones of authority and coercion, was that which bound these Catholics to their 'habit'. It took me a long time, well into the fourth month of my study of the Catholic congregation, for these underlying assumptions to surface and for me to begin to question the roots and implications of these assumptions. One reason for this was that both 'habit' and 'tradition' were words that the Catholics themselves used of their own approach to worship. For the Catholics, however, both these words had positive associations, and neither carried with them the negative baggage of my own Anglican upbringing.

'Habit', in the sense used by the members of the Roman Catholic church, can be summed up in one sentence: 'I have been to mass every week (or every day) of my life.' Many non-Catholic Christians could say something very similar. There would, however, be one fundamental distinction. The non-Catholic may say that they have been going to this or that particular church for as long as they can remember. The Catholic will say 'I have been to mass....'. The important word here is 'mass'. Unlike the more general 'church', or even a specifically named church, 'mass' is neither a place nor a community, it is an event. What is more, 'mass' is not dependent on any particular church. Wherever there are Roman Catholics, and a Roman Catholic priest, then 'mass' can be celebrated, and the particular church in which the mass takes place has very little relevance to the people concerned. 'Habit' for the Catholic congregation, therefore, is based primarily on attendance at 'mass'.

'The mass is always the same wherever and whenever it is celebrated.' This is one statement that everybody I talked to in the Catholic church stated as 'true'. In fact it is not 'true', and neither is it thought to be in any empirical sense. The mass is celebrated in many different ways in many different places. Most people know that. The mass has also changed considerably, especially over the lifetime of most of those I talked to. This statement, however, is always stated as being 'true' and by stating this 'truth' the members of the Roman Catholic church place themselves within a very particular mode of thought.

Another statement that the majority of Catholics I talked to claimed as being 'true' was that 'the mass is the most important event in my life'. This statement, or something very similar, is also an important element of sermons and the popular literature on the mass (Bernier 1981, Buono 1982, Gusmer 1989). As somebody who was not a member of the Roman Catholic Church I found this unquestioning acceptance of the 'official' line as 'fact' to be a little disturbing and, as a trained anthropologist, I wanted to question the nature and function of such a statement; how 'true' was it? This was one of the questions, along with the question of habit, which became central to my time with the church. Unfortunately the answer was not as easy to discover as it might seem. What, after all, is meant by 'fact' or even by the word 'true'? Before coming back to the question of 'truth' towards the end of this chapter, I wish to begin by looking more closely at the two concepts of 'habit' and 'tradition' in a little more detail. I want to unpack something of what the Catholics themselves might have meant when they used these terms.

UNDERSTANDING HABIT

What does the use of the word 'habit' suggest about the understanding of worship held by the Catholic congregation? First, 'habit' suggests repetition. This may sound obvious: 'I have been going to mass *every* week, or *every* day, of my life.' The mass is celebrated and attended over and over again, day in and day out, week in and week out, always the same, never missed, never changing. Attendance at mass, therefore, becomes a matter of 'habit'. There are very few rituals in the world which are never repeated, however long the time that elapses between each performance. The very act of repetition must, therefore, be important to the perception of the rite.

A second assumption that is made when non-Catholics use the word 'habit' is that individuals pay very little attention to what is going on within the worship. Members of the congregation, it is assumed, simply arrive, sit through whatever is happening, and then go, glad to have got the whole thing over for another week. This is certainly the impression that many outsiders would get of the Roman Catholic worship I attended. The majority of the congregation arrived within the last five minutes before the service began, they did not sing or respond very enthusiastically during the worship, and they left as soon as they could at the end, often during the final hymn. Such a response appears to make no sense of the second statement that I referred to in my first section; that the mass was said to be the

112

most important event in an individual's life. Surely the mass could not be all that important if they treated it so casually?

Whatever this kind of 'habitual' behaviour may or may not indicate in terms of the response of members of the congregation to worship, there was one particular way in which it had a very significant impact on my own work. Where it had been easy at the Baptist chapel to meet people informally, to talk to them at length and to get to know them as individuals, this was practically impossible within the context of the Catholic church. I did meet and get to know a few members of some small groups within the congregation, especially the Justice and Peace group which met fortnightly in different members' houses, and the Vincent de Paul Society which met monthly in the parish club. These groups, however, only represented a very small percentage of the congregation as a whole. It was also clear that the priest was reluctant to give me names and addresses, and felt that making appointments to see people in their own houses would not be a good idea. The priest therefore suggested, and eventually I was forced to accept, that the only way in which I could talk to members of the congregation was by catching them immediately after mass. I had to stand just outside the door and stop people as they were leaving, ask them if they would mind talking to me briefly about their responses to worship, and then carry on a short informal conversation.

The content of these conversations inevitably focused on the mass that we had both just attended. People had very little chance to think more widely or to offer a more reasoned response. This was a very serious practical problem for me as a researcher, but it was a problem that I had to work with. What resulted, however, was a twofold approach to discovering an understanding of what was happening within the worship. First I had to accept that what I was receiving were immediate responses to specific acts of worship. Secondly I had to focus much more carefully on my own personal responses to the worship and conduct a constant self-assessment of how I reacted to the worship over the six months that I was with the church.

As the six months went by I actually found myself adopting a very similar pattern to the rest of the congregation. I began to arrive very shortly before mass began. During mass I found my thoughts 'wandering'. I knew the words of the mass by heart and often, like most of the congregation, I never bothered to pick up one of the mass sheets that were left by the door. At the end of mass I would gladly have left as soon as it was over if this had not been the only time that I could actually talk to those who had attended. It was only when I realised at the end of four months that I was getting very little data from those members of the congregation that I was talking to that I stopped and asked myself what was happening. Outwardly I was beginning to be-have like a 'Catholic' but could my behaviour be described as 'habitual'? This was a difficult question to answer. All I can do is to try to explain exactly what that behaviour was and how it appeared to relate to what the other members of the congrega-tion were doing and saying.

Each mass, as we approached it, was very much like any oth-er. Everybody knew in principle what was going to happen. We knew what we were expected to do and we knew what other people would be doing. At each mass, however, there were al-ways a number of different things going on, and different peo-ple highlighted different elements in what they said to me dur-ing our conversations. Some mentioned the activity of the priest and the altar boys at the altar. Others referred to words that could be followed on the mass sheet. Occasionally people would focus on the congregational responses or on hymns. Often there were two or three things happening at the same time: the collec-tion, for example, was always taken while a hymn was being sung and while the bread and wine were being taken to the altar. At the same time the altar boys were preparing the altar and the priest was muttering various prayers over the gifts, all of which were written on the mass sheet if members of the congre-gation wished to follow them. While each of these activities might be mentioned by some members of the congregations nobody ever gave a full account of everything that was going on at this, or at any other, point in the service. Each individual clearly knew what was expected of them and what they were supposed to be doing and each individual was able to do their own thing with-out any obvious reference to anybody else.

One mass in particular made this situation clear. On this par-ticular Sunday we had an extremely moving homily about the persecution of the church in Guyana from a visiting preacher. Later in the mass the celebrant, before beginning the eucharistic prayer, suggested that as he offered the bread and wine in prayer upon the altar we, the congregation, might like to offer the situation of the church in Guyana to God within our own prayers. Two distinct levels of engagement were being set up by the celebrant, two very different things were going to be happening at the same time. The result, however, was a particularly moving experience. There was a clear sense of 'togetherness' at this mass that was distinctly lacking from practically all the other masses that I attended. This was also commented on by many of those I talked to following the worship.

This 'sense of togetherness' was something that I had come to expect in the Baptist chapel. It was also something that many Roman Catholic commentators on the liturgy present as an 'ideal' in modern liturgy (Gelineau 1978: 34–57, Moloney 1995: 195–206). But what exactly is it, and why was it so often lacking on a normal Sunday? In simple terms it appears that most of the members of the congregation knew that those individuals with specific tasks to perform within the mass would get on with their job irrespective of what anybody else was doing. Each of these tasks was distinct and there was usually only one person performing each task at any one time. If that person did not perform their task then there were only a very few other people who could stand in for them. The 'congregation', however, was very different. As a body it did not appear to have any clearly defined 'task'. The congregation was certainly needed to sing or to respond, to pray or simply to be there, but if any one member of that congregation opted out then there were always others who would continue to perform the necessary tasks. There were always some that would sing or make the responses, but there were always some that did not. It was only when all the members of the congregation were given a particular task, when they were specifically asked to pray together for the church in Guyana, that there was any sense of togetherness, any sense of all the people doing the same thing, at the same time.

The more normal situation clearly opened up for the average member of the congregation a number of different options, a variety of what I would want to call 'levels of engagement'. Certain individuals, for example, particularly older women, could be completely detached from their surroundings. They said their rosary or followed other prayers in an old mass book.

115

Others followed the mass sheet closely, and noted where the readings came from and which confession, which eucharistic prayer, which offertory prayers etc. were being used at any particular mass. Others referred to the mass sheet and told me that they preferred to meditate on the readings or reflect on the content of the sermon rather than concentrating on the actions of the mass itself. Others ignored the mass sheet altogether and watched what the celebrant, the altar boys, or, more normally, what other members of the congregation were up to. A few actually listened to what was being said by the celebrant or the readers and could report this to me fairly accurately. Some said that they sang when they happened to like the songs but did not when they disliked them or did not know them. Members of the congregation could, if they did nothing else, simply sit, kneel or stand quietly and let the mass proceed around them. Each of these 'levels of engagement' was open to each and every member of the congregation and each person could choose the level that suited their mood at any one particular mass.

When looked at in this way, one very significant factor becomes clear. This is the possibility that even if individual members of the congregation did not fully engage with each rite every time they attended, it is plausible to assume that over time they would touch upon many different levels of engagement within a whole series of rites. Perhaps some intense levels will only be touched on once or twice within a lifetime but that is enough to provide a wider context than that which can be derived from the limited experience, or partial awareness, of any one mass. The congregation's appreciation of the rite must, therefore, be fluid with time. Given a long enough time span, and a regular, habitual, attendance at worship, an individual's total 'understanding' could potentially become extremely complex.

It is one thing to talk about levels of engagement, however, and the distinct elements that individuals notice and talk about in relation to specific acts of worship. It is another to consider how these might relate to each other over time. Here the kind of evidence that I was able to collect at the church door was not a great help and so I needed to look elsewhere to find some kind of theoretical position which might offer me some help. Given the similarity between the kinds of elements which were being referred to in the conversations after mass, and Victor

Turner's definition of the symbol (the most fundamental element of any ritual (Turner 1967a: 20)) I chose to look towards the literature on symbolism to see whether this could shed any light on the problem.

HABIT, LEVELS OF ENGAGEMENT AND THE JUXTAPOSITION OF SYMBOLS

In an essay written for a collection of papers, *Symbolism and the Liturgy* (1981), Stephen Platten states that the various references to 'bread' in the text of the Church of England 'Rite A' Eucharist are drawn from different parts of the New Testament and hence offer different and, it is assumed, conflicting imagery. The Institution Narrative, for example, is a conflation of Pauline and synoptic material, each of which has its own series of associations for the word 'bread'. At another point the allusions become Johannine, with references to 'The Bread of Life', so adding another series of associations. Platten seems to assume that such a variety of references and associations is going to be confusing to any person who might be attending the worship and that this is a bad example of the way in which biblical imagery should be used within the liturgy.

In the light of anthropological material on symbolism, however, this kind of analysis, with its overtones of confusion and inconsistency, seems highly pedantic. It is, I would suggest, in the very ambiguity and richness of cross-references associated with symbols such as 'bread', that anthropologists would see their essential strength. Victor Turner, for example, uses the word 'multi-vocality' to express this kind of principle (1967a: 50). According to Turner the very essence of a symbol is its ability to bring together many diverse referents and to juxtapose them in a creative tension. Edmund Leach, on the other hand, might offer a structuralist analysis of the biblical (or liturgical) uses of the word 'bread'. This would take great delight in finding multiple references with multiple meanings and superimposing them to show how the various meanings interacted in terms of bipolar oppositions or otherwise (Leach & Aycock 1983). In both these cases the interest is not so much in consistency and coherence as on the creativity that is possible because of the very inconsistency of multiple meanings.

Inconsistency, multi-vocality, ambiguity; these seem to be the essence of symbolism for anthropologists. It is strange, therefore, that Platten should feel the need to object to such a rich diversity of references to 'bread' in the liturgy. There is, however, another question which could be asked of Platten's analysis: How many of those who actually attend the worship are aware of the biblical sources of the various allusions to 'bread' within the rite, and hence aware of the inconsistency and confusion which is supposed to underlie them? The same question could also be asked of Turner and of Leach. If, for example, the congregation never even notices that there are various different references to bread within the liturgy, they could never become confused by them nor, incidentally, draw them together and juxtapose them in the way that either Turner or Leach suggests. If this is what is actually happening, therefore, how far could any analysis of symbolism that is dependent of the multiple meaning of symbols make any sense at all? To begin to answer this question I want to go back and look more closely at some of the short answers given to my questions about the mass after each service and to my own experience of six months at the Catholic church.

I came to the church thinking that I possessed quite a considerable technical knowledge of Catholic worship, and therefore having a fairly clear idea of those things that would be of interest to me during the service. I was also aware of the writings of Turner and Leach and was interested in the nature of symbolism and the way in which it was being used within the rite. Or at least I thought I was. Whenever I was actually attending mass, however, the issue of symbolism never consciously occurred to me. Even when I came to look back from an academic distance on the service I always found it extremely difficult to come to terms with ideas of symbolism within the mass. Was the bread really a symbol or was it the word 'bread' that was being used symbolically? In either case what did this symbol of 'bread' actually 'mean'? Did it 'mean' anything or was it simply bread? It was only in reflection, away from the context of the rite itself, that I was able to make even partial sense of these kinds of question. During the mass we just got on with it.

However, over the six months, as I became used to what was going on, and as the service itself was becoming more of a 'habit' for me, I began to notice different aspects of the service and unusual elements in its presentation. One week, for example, I noticed that the altar servers had forgotten the bowl used to wash the priest's hands. During another, two sections of the mass came together in an unexpected way because of the way they were laid out on the mass sheet. I suddenly realised that one section of the mass was, in fact, a biblical quotation, which had not occurred to me before. Even a notice that was given out about a meeting of communion ministers later in the week raised new and interesting questions. A list of such examples could, in fact, be endless.

All these points are clearly significant. All of them raise fascinating questions about the mass and its significance that could fill page after page of a book such as this. Space, however, does not allow me to do this. What is important is that it was not only me, the 'trained' ethnographer or liturgical observer, who noticed such things. Conversations with different members of the congregation after the mass showed that they were also aware of, and reflected upon, many of these very same points.

In most of my conversations with ordinary members of the congregation it was noticeable that many of the items that were discussed had a personal significance for the person talking. When, for example, an older visiting priest insisted on communicating people on the tongue one member of the congregation refused. All kinds of questions were discussed after this mass, from the nature of change in the church to the possible theological significance of how communion is received. More specifically, there was one lady who talked at length about what the servers had been doing when I talked to her after one particular mass. It was only later that she informed me that one of the boys had been her own son and that this had been his first mass as an altar server. References to 'the sick' mentioned by name during the intercessions, or to the anniversary of a death, have an obvious significance for those individuals who are involved. Such individuals often associated their memory of these references with particular hymns, with Bible readings, or with prayers that had meant something specific to them on that occasion. As with my own series of associations the number and content of such juxtapositions is endless. In each case, however, some factor in the performance of a particular mass, and the meaning that becomes attached to it, allows the individual, or perhaps the whole congregation, to discover a new significance in some other aspect of the rite, or in the mass as a whole.

What we can see here is a process that is very similar to that described by Frederick Barth for the Baktaman of New Guinea (1975). Certain key 'symbols' are transformed by continual association and disassociation with others to generate a constantly shifting field of 'meaning'. One series of key elements are given significance at one point and others are illuminated at another, such that the cumulative effect is one of a gradual deepening and personalising of understandings over many years. This is something that is felt, rather than expressed explicitly, when talking to an older member of the congregation, somebody with a whole lifetime's attendance at mass behind them. There is a sense of depth in such an older person's report, a sense that they are aware of much more within the rite, and yet can put their finger on much less. The specific details begin to lose their relevance as the multiple associations of a lifetime's attendance begin to come into play. At this level the mass, any mass, becomes a real 'anamnesis', a 'recalling' as much of the details and associations of an individual's own life as of the life, death and resurrection of Christ.

It is arguments of this kind, with a similar root in repetition and personalisation, that anthropologists and sociologists such as Mary Douglas and David Martin have turned to in order to condemn liturgical revision (Douglas 1973, Martin 1980). There is some evidence to support such a view. The constant repetition of the liturgy does endow a particular rite with a special significance that is drawn from many years of cumulative meaning. However, there is another side to this argument that comes back to my critique of Platten. The 'new' or the 'different' need not necessarily contradict, confuse or wipe out the 'old', but can be added to it and supplement it, if given long enough in itself to become known and familiar. This was a view supported by a number of the older members of the Catholic congregation in my conversations with them. Having worshipped in English for the last twenty years or so, they would tell me, like one older lady, that 'having the mass in English allows me to see what has been said all these years, and gives me a new view on what I've always done'. The new does not have to wipe out the old, rather it can add to it and enrich it.

THE CREATION OF CUMULATIVE MEANING

If 'cumulative meanings' take the form that I have just suggested
then we must ask what is happening at any one mass to generate
the elements that come together to create such cumulative meaning. As with the discussion of the story in the previous chapter it
would be impossible for me to be specific on this point. Many
things are happening, and different things are happening for
different people at different times. The concept of 'levels of engagement' should make this clear. Despite this, however, I think
that one or two more specific points can be made which deal
not so much with the generalities of content but rather with the
details of processes.

Let me return, therefore, to the work of Turner and Leach.
As an analysis of the 'meaning' of symbols within the mass neither of these theories proved to be very helpful. However, as an
analysis of the process by which some kind of meaning can be
generated, I think that both have something important to say. At
the risk of simplification, the principle distinction between the
two theories is that Turner claims that 'meanings' can be juxtaposed within 'symbols' while Leach and other structuralists argue that the juxtaposition of 'symbols' creates 'meaning'. Turner suggests that various meanings are juxtaposed within any one
symbol. In other words, there are specific moments when two
or more levels of significance meet in a single word, a phrase, a
person, a particular object or a specific event. Leach on the
other hand claims that it is the juxtaposition of symbols that
creates, or reveals, meaning. This is probably more common in
practice. At one service, for example, there was some confusion
at the lectern as the celebrant arrived to read the Gospel before
the alleluia had been sung, and the lay lector was still there.
This drew attention to the fact that while a lay person reads the
first two lessons, the responsorial psalm and the alleluia, only
the priest was able to read the Gospel. The congregation knew
that this was the case and most probably knew why. However,
one small 'mistake' highlighted the point and raised the issue
within the minds of the congregation. During conversations after the service the more conservative element in the congregation asked whether there should be lay lectors at all, while the
more radical elements asked why lay people should not be allowed to read the Gospel. Very often it was mistakes of this kind

that highlighted such important questions, and these were discussed at length in the conversations that I held after the mass.

Whether it is the juxtaposition of meaning in one symbol, or the juxtaposition of symbols creating meaning, it is insights of this kind, sparked off within the worship, that create specific responses, or meanings, for individual members of the congregation. What is more, it is these meanings, added to the cumulative total of meaning from previous masses, that creates the highly personal cumulative understanding and appreciation of the mass that each member of the congregation holds.

Turner and Leach, in their different ways, both wanted to understand the meaning, nature, function or significance of specific rites. Each assumed that it was possible to come to some kind of final conclusion, to say conclusively that the rite means 'this' or 'that' or that the rite does 'this' or 'that'. What I have been suggesting, however, seems to turn this on its head by arguing that through a similar series of symbolic processes each individual creates their own very personal understanding of the rite which may be very different from that of others at the same event. What is more, I am suggesting that this personal understanding is derived as much from factors outside the official rite, from mistakes within the rite, or from chance associations between the two, as from the basic content of the formal text. One criticism that is often levelled at writers such as Leach and Turner is that the 'meaning' generated by the analyst from any given rite is determined as much by the analyst's own assumptions about the kind of meanings that are being looked for, as by the content of the rite itself. This implies that the specific text of the rite is irrelevant. A similar critique could also be made of my own argument. If meaning is generated through personal reflections on mistakes within the ritual performance, rather than being contained within the formal text of the rite, then surely the formal text has little or no real significance.

I would go some way in agreeing with this critique, but to go all the way would, of course, be nonsense and would go against the empirical facts. By way of a conclusion to this discussion of habit, therefore, I want to pursue a little further the possibility that the formal text may be of only secondary importance within the analysis of the rite. In so doing, I want to make a few observations that many liturgists and anthropologists have tended to overlook.

Let me assume, just for the moment, that I know an Ndembu anthropologist who cannot read English very well. If I were to take this anthropologist to a Roman Catholic mass so that she could record what happened, what kind of description would she produce? The result I am sure would not look anything like the official text. Very little distinction is likely to be made between that which is written and unchanging, the 'formal text', and that which changes from mass to mass, the 'informal text'. These would all merge into one specific 'text' for that particular mass. What is more the Ndembu anthropologist, like myself at times, would have no way of knowing what was 'mistake' and what was not. If this anthropologist were to go away and analyse her results what, I wonder, would be the conclusions? They would certainly be interesting.

Reflections of this kind, and the implications that they generate, are often presented to anthropologists when they enter an alien society. How far, for example, did Turner know what was 'official' and what was 'mistake' within the various rites of the Ndembu? Perhaps 'official' and 'mistake', 'formal' and 'informal', are terms that are meaningless in the context of Ndembu ritual. That is certainly possible and so the issue as I have presented it would not arise. All this should, however, highlight an important question for the ethnographer of worship: What is it that constitutes the 'worship', or, more specifically, the liturgical performance? Can we say that a liturgical performance is defined by the formal text or must we also include the informal text and even mistakes? We cannot simply ignore these factors, just as the people sitting in the congregation cannot ignore them. It is precisely the fact that some incidents are defined as 'mistakes', that they are unexpected and so cannot be ignored, that makes them so significant.

As academics perhaps we can ignore mistakes and so separate the formal from the informal texts. As participants I do not think that we can. This is not to say that the participants cannot acknowledge a mistake as a mistake – they can and they do – but that having acknowledged a mistake as a 'mistake' it will then take on a significance within the rite that triggers a line of thought which cannot be ignored. For any one rite, any one performance, the mistake is a vital, if not a desirable, element. Over time, and I have constantly stressed the value of time within this chapter, we may find that 'mistakes' or 'informal texts' take on a new significance in themselves and eventually lead to permanent changes in the formal text. The notion of the arbitrary nature of liturgical development is an appealing one. If, however, we want to claim that most liturgical change is a product of 'mistakes' or local 'idiosyncrasies' then what does this say about the nature of the text as an officially sanctioned item? It is at this point that I would suggest that we should turn to my second 'word' from my time with the Catholic church: that is, 'tradition'.[1]

UNDERSTANDING TRADITION

In turning to tradition I want to go back to the second statement which I quoted from my conversations with individual Catholics after mass, and which the vast majority claimed as being 'true', that is, that 'the mass is the most important event in my life'. While stating this assertion as 'true', however, the empirical evidence, so far as I could understand it, seemed to imply a very different situation. It appeared that many other things, from family to football, or a night out at the social club, were clearly far more important in an individual's life than going to mass. What, therefore, do such observations signify? I know a number of Roman Catholic clergy who would cite similar observations as evidence that Catholics today do not treat the mass with the respect or sanctity that it deserves. This may be true, but whenever I asked the members of the Roman Catholic congregation about the mass, the vast majority offered the statement that the mass was the most important event in their lives as the starting point for their answer to my question. What is more I am sure that if I were to ask any Roman Catholic (or almost any) if they accepted such a statement as 'true' they would almost certainly answer 'yes'. Is such a response simply a function of the way the question is asked? To some extent it must be. However I did not need to be a member of the Roman Catholic community for long to realise that the statement, as it was presented to me, was in fact 'true', and that it was 'true' for all those present, despite any apparent evidence to the contrary.

This kind of discussion relates directly to the kind of question that we have just been discussing. That is the relationship between the 'official' meaning of the rite, as laid down by the Church in the *Constitution on the Sacred Liturgy* (Flannery 1975: 1–282), the *General Instruction on the Missal* (Walsh 1979: 72–145) and other documents, and the 'individual' meanings of the various people who attend the mass. This is also a question that concerns many of the popular writings on the mass from Roman Catholic authors (Gelineau 1978: 67–74, Kavanagh 1978). The most important task for the Church, as presented in the popular literature, is that of trying to bring these two 'meanings', acknowledged to be divergent in the context of the old Latin mass, into some kind of harmony. What, however, is the nature of the relationship between 'official' and 'individual' meanings and does it really matter?

Since the Second Vatican Council there has been a great deal of writing within the Roman Catholic Church, both scholarly and popular, attempting to come to terms with, and to interpret, what the Council had to say about the liturgy. One thing that stands out within the whole of this literature is the uniformity of the stance that has been taken. The principal starting point for all that is written is the *Constitution on the Sacred Liturgy*. This is often quoted, within the first few pages of any book, as the basis for all that is to follow. Quotations from the Constitution are very rarely challenged and the points that they raise are very rarely argued through satisfactorily (Buono 1982: 3–4, Gelineau 1978: 13). Just as significant is the emphasis that is always placed on the statement that the Fathers of the Council made a fundamental break with 'tradition'. The new Church, we are told, is now free from the shackles of the old tradition. We are encouraged to look to the people for the future of the Church and no longer to the hierarchy. It is as if all that has gone before is to be thrown out. In the minds of the particular congregation that I studied, however, this was not case. 'Tradition' was a word that was still used regularly and for many it was the very continuation of 'tradition', despite Vatican II, that was of central importance.

'Tradition', like 'habit', is something that those outside the Roman Catholic Church immediately associate with Catholicism.

Like 'habit' it often has misleading connotations. Tradition, for example, is often linked with conservatism, with a lack of change, with authoritarianism, and so on. It is possible, however, to unpack the concept of 'tradition' in the same way that I have already unpacked 'habit' to show its central and positive role in Roman Catholic thinking. It is generally accepted that the Roman Catholic Church is seen as 'traditional'. The Church, for example, sees itself as being founded by Christ in his call to Peter to be the rock upon which the Church is to be built (Matthew 16: 18). The Church will also emphasise the great weight of tradition that has been built up over the centuries primarily around the Pope and the Vatican. However, even within a local church and its own celebration of mass, there is also a sense of this continuing tradition at work. At one time the tradition was clearly considered to be an immovable millstone. Now, since Vatican II, all that has been shrugged off and a new, more vibrant, but no less 'traditional' church is said to have emerged.

'Tradition' was a word that nearly all the Catholics I spoke to used of the mass, even those with more radical ideas. The mass was seen to be 'traditional', that is, it had been handed down within the Church from Christ's first institution at the Last Supper to the present day. This line of tradition is thought of as being unbroken and direct. Very few people would have gone so far as one person within the congregation, however, who dated the tradition back to Cain and Abel. This is not beyond the sense of Catholic understanding. The First Eucharistic Prayer in the Missal, for example, links the action of the mass directly with the sacrifice of Abel and with that of Melchizideck and other Old Testament figures (Winstone 1975: 36). There is, however, another point in taking the tradition back beyond Christ. I am told that if I had asked ordinary members of the congregation about the mass before Vatican II they would have told me that the mass had not changed since Christ had instituted it at the Last Supper. Whether people did 'believe' this or just refused to question it, I cannot say. However, if the tradition is taken back beyond the Last Supper to Cain and Abel then it is clear that the sacrifice, and subsequently the mass, must have changed, both in form and in significance over the years. Its essence, however, has, by implication, remained the same. The tradition, therefore, is seen to continue despite some changes in form. This was a position that was held by the majority of those I was able to talk to. Not to do so would be to deny the 'validity' of Vatican II and that would have challenged other, equally significant, elements of the 'tradition'.

A number of the older members of the congregation seemed to assume, without question, that the rite they now used was simply a translation of the rite they have always used. They were, on the whole, pleased to have it in English, but for them the rite itself has not changed. This is not, of course, to deny the significance of Vatican II and the very sweeping, and often disturbing, changes that followed in its wake. It is simply to acknowledge the power that tradition holds over and above any change in outward appearances. The tradition must, and will, continue. Tradition in this sense does not only look backwards to the foundations of the rite, monolithic and immovable, but rather it is a 'living tradition', one that looks both backwards and forwards, constantly changing and yet essentially the same.

TRADITION, MEANING AND 'PROOF'

Tradition could be seen to encompass the 'official' meaning of the mass, or at least to present us with the knowledge that an 'official' meaning does exist, a statement that all those people I talked to were prepared to acknowledge. On the other side of the equation are 'individual' meanings. These are not always acknowledged so specifically but it is clear that they also exist as we have already seen. Before going any further, however, we also need to ask the more fundamental question of what we mean by the word 'meaning'? In looking at this I would like to turn back to the anthropological discussion of symbolism and to the work of Dan Sperber who claims that 'symbols do not mean' (1975: 85). Such a statement seems to go against the whole of anthropological thought on the subject of symbolism, the main aim of which, as we have seen, has been to discover 'meanings'. Sperber begins his argument by criticising Turner and other anthropologists for taking too much notice of what the people themselves say about the meaning of their symbols. Sperber suggests that any 'native exegesis' of the symbol should itself be treated as an extension of that symbol and therefore should demand an explanation in its own right. In other words, when a

Roman Catholic talks about 'transubstantiation' and claims that the bread becomes the body of Christ, this cannot in any way help to explain what the symbol of 'bread' actually 'means'. Such statements can only take the problem one stage further such that the statement itself, the relationship between a symbol and its meaning, demands an explanation (1975: 34).

The best way of approaching this is through the statement which I quoted earlier: 'The mass is the most important event in a person's life'. We noted that this statement created all kinds of problems concerning the kind of 'truth' that should be associated with it. At an empirical level, through observations of the way people behave, the statement is not 'true', and yet everybody I talked to claimed, very insistently, that it was 'true'. What kinds of 'truth' are these? Is there more than one kind of truth and is one kind of truth more significant than the others? Sperber draws a distinction between two kinds of 'truth' in his analysis. He claims that certain statements – the example he uses from his own field-work is 'The leopard is a Christian animal' (1975: 93) – do not need to be empirically 'true'. However, for the people concerned, when they affirm the 'truth' of the statement, what is 'true' is the related statement that '"The leopard is a Christian animal" is true'. This may sound to be a rather pedantic distinction but once we grasp what Sperber is saying I think that it will prove to be very useful. The point at issue is not the empirical truth of the statement itself but the fact that people are willing to accept such a statement as 'true' without actually questioning its empirical status. This is what Sperber calls putting the statement in parenthesis (1975: 100), setting it apart from ordinary discourse. This is exactly what the Roman Catholics are doing with the statement 'the mass is the most important event in a person's life'. This is only 'true' because it is said to be 'true', although the exact nature of that 'truth' should not be, and on the whole is not, questioned.

The same can also be said for much of the religious discourse of the Catholic congregation. All the statements that make up the 'official' meaning of the liturgy, so far as these are written down and codified, are 'true' only in this Sperberian sense. Where I might differ from Sperber, however, is over the empirical truth of such statements. Sperber takes it for granted that these statements, 'all leopards are Christians', 'the mass is the most important event in a person's life', 'the bread is the Body of Christ' are not empirically true. That, according to Sperber, is the way in which we can distinguish a 'symbolic' statement from any other kind of statement (1975: 107). It is only within a certain western 'scientific' discourse, however, one that defines the word 'empirical' as Sperber uses it, that such statements have no truth. There is, by all known methods of proof, no way of knowing whether leopards are Christians or not. What Sperber should perhaps be saying is that the empirical truth of the statement is irrelevant, that this is not an issue that anybody would normally dream of raising. The same is basically true for Catholics in relation to the mass. The statement that the 'bread, after consecration, is the Body of Christ' is 'true' by definition. It cannot be 'proved' and nor would anybody really want to 'prove' it (despite the attempts of certain theologians). For the ordinary Catholic the truth of such statements is simply taken for granted.

I was asked during a seminar that I presented on my material from the Roman Catholic church, how far the liturgy 'proved' the existence of God. This struck me at the time as a very strange question. The implication behind such a question was that normal rational people could not possibly accept such nonsensical notions as the existence of God and that it was only those who go to church who held such strange, irrational ideas. Somehow, therefore, what goes on in church must 'prove' the notion beyond doubt. My response would be that this presents completely the wrong picture and begins from the wrong end of the argument. This is best illustrated by a short passage from Martin Southwold's book *Buddhism in Life* (1983) in which he talks about the creation story in Genesis (1983: 76). Southwold comments that this story, whether taken literally or not, is usually seen as saying something about God, about God's creativity, or God's love, or at the extreme, following one line of argument, about God's very existence. Southwold, however, suggests that this is not the point of the story at all. If we expect such stories to tell us of God then we are looking at them from the wrong angle. 'God' in such stories, Southwold argues, should be taken as a basic assumption, an unquestioned 'truth', as should God's goodness, God's love and so on. What the story is saying, Southwold suggests, is that if God is 'good', and we accept that without question, and if God created the world, as the story tells us, then the world itself must be good. It is assumptions that we make about God that give significance to the world, and not the other way round. Southwold goes on to say much the same about the doctrine of the incarnation. This is not an erudite philosophical argument about the nature of God, but rather that if God, whom we know to be good, takes on human form then humanity must in consequence be 'blessed', be special, or even be divine. The discourse is not one about the nature of God, but one about the world, about humanity, about us and our everyday lives that takes the existence and nature of God as a given.

Much the same, therefore, can be said about the mass, but in a rather more complex fashion. The mass can no more prove the existence of God than can the first four chapters of Genesis. The mass is played out within a framework of basic statements about God, about Jesus and about the bread being the Body of Christ. The truth of each of these statements is not to be questioned, and it is these statements, held and known as 'true', that give significance to the mass. The mass cannot prove that the bread becomes the Body of Christ, but the knowledge of that 'truth' gives the mass its significance, and by implication gives anything else that is brought into that mass, from an individual's personal life or elsewhere, the same kind of significance. The question still remains, however, of where the source of these basic 'true' statements is to be found, and why people are so willing, in fact eager, to hold them as 'true' despite an environment beyond, and sometimes within, the Church that claims, like Sperber, that they must be false. As Sperber says, the acceptance of the explanation must itself be explained.

TRADITION AND AUTHORITY

This brings me back to the concept of 'tradition' and the official meanings of the rite. One aspect of tradition, as we saw from my discussions above, is that of time and continuity. Another aspect is that of authority. There is always a sense in which 'tradition' and 'authority' are connected, be it 'traditional authority' or the 'authority of tradition', and this is especially true in the view of the Roman Catholic Church. However, it is very difficult for us to pinpoint exactly what this connection might be. I have al-

ready referred to Vatican II and the seeming contradiction between those who claim that the Council was a clear break with
'tradition' and the members of the congregation I studied who
acknowledged no such break, simply a change of emphasis within a single continuing 'tradition'. The 'tradition', however, in
both these views, is more than just the liturgical tradition. That
which is traditional is more than just the mass. The whole Roman Catholic Church, from the Pope to the people, and all the
power structures within it, are themselves understood as being
'traditional'.

To establish the Council Pope John XXIII had to work within
the 'tradition'; he had to follow precedent. The Council, therefore, was itself a part of the tradition, carrying all the weight and
authority that Councils traditionally held within the Church. One
of the most ironic features of the Council, especially to an outsider, was the way in which it was able to implement such sweeping changes, directed mainly at challenging the 'traditional authority' of the Church and putting the emphasis on the voice of
the 'people', using the very model of traditional centralised authority that it was aiming to challenge. This is a contradiction
that is still felt within the Roman Catholic Church today. As the
various changes to the liturgy and the concept of 'popular participation' that they implied were ordered by the hierarchy, the
people themselves, who accepted this traditional form of authority, never questioned it. They accepted the shift in the 'tradition' of the mass but never acknowledged (because in practice it
did not seem to be there) any equivalent break in the 'tradition'
of authority.

Even at the time of my study, twenty or so years after the
Council, when ideas of the communal and popular nature of
the liturgy had managed to filter down to the people (and many
people mentioned this 'official' line as part of their own conversations on the liturgy), the actual practice of authority within the
liturgy seems to have undergone very little change. There is, of
course, more participation in the rite itself, and a 'liturgical com-
mittee' sometimes undertakes a certain amount of liturgical planning. Fundamentally, however, very little has changed.

I was guided to the particular church that I chose to study
because it had a reputation for 'progressive' thinking on the
liturgy. I found that it had certainly made more progress than

most. A number of parents got together to organise a special Ministry of the Word for families in the parish hall during the 11.00am mass, after which they joined the rest of the congregation for the Ministry of the Sacrament. However despite this (and in practical terms only a handful of people were ever involved) when it came to 'important' issues the 'traditional' channels of authority were still in use.

This was seen very clearly in one particular series of sermons given by the parish priest over four successive Sundays. The reason for these sermons, we were told, was that the Bishop's Conference of England and Wales had decided that all churches should introduce communion from the cup as well as from the host for the congregation. These sermons were therefore designed to 'instruct' the people on this change and its implications. The first two sermons were 'theological', explaining the significance of the cup and the importance of receiving in both kinds, whilst being careful to stress that the receiving of the host alone was in no way 'invalid' and could be continued by those who so wished. Reception in both kinds, however, whilst not being 'better' was 'desirable'. The last two sermons were then practical. The first was a request for more communion ministers, who would now be needed, and the details of the training that would be involved. The second was a detailed account of how the process of reception itself was to be organised and what the congregation were expected to do 'to keep the system moving and to prevent traffic jams'. In this situation it is obvious that a request came from a higher authority and was presented to the congregation via the priest, that is through the traditional route of authority. This was far from being a popular local innovation.

What is ultimately traditional, therefore, within the Roman Catholic Church is not so much the mass, or any kind of outward appearance of the Church, but the structure of authority that keeps it all together. This however raises the question of whether the Church has authority because it is traditional, or whether the tradition is maintained by the authority of the Church? This is a fascinating ecclesiological question and one that I think would prove very difficult to answer. From the viewpoint of the individual member of a Roman Catholic congregation, however, tradition and authority are one, they cannot be separated. Tradition is not seen as some monolithic form that overshadows the individual and has total control over them. Each individual is a part of the tradition. The tradition is contained, held and passed on by individuals. Any individual can choose to move into that tradition and once in they would be swept along with it, as a vital and necessary part of it. Yet nobody, not even the Pope, could ultimately stop the flow of tradition; it is the flow of the Catholic Church itself, the work of the whole People of God.

CONCLUSION

In conclusion let me backtrack a little and see if I can draw some of what I have been saying in this chapter together. Within this chapter I have raised a number of questions which could easily be rephrased as paradoxes. I have just asked, in the previous section, about the relationship between authority and tradition and framed the question in the following form: if 'authority' is a part of the 'tradition', what is it that gives 'tradition' its 'authority'? In a previous section I talked about 'truth' and linked this to people's perceptions through a discussion of 'habit', levels of engagement, and the given truths which provide significance for that 'habit'. I could therefore construct this problem in much the same way as I did for 'authority' and 'tradition': if 'truths' give significance to 'habit', what significance might we want to give to the 'habit' of 'truth'? In both cases the relationship between the ideas appears to be circular. I do not think that this is coincidental as any of these four terms can, I think, be related to each of the others in a similar fashion, although each of the resulting questions is very different. To finish the cycle, therefore, I could ask: 'if 'tradition' is built up out of 'truths', where do we find the 'truth' that defines 'tradition'?'; 'if 'habit' reinforces the significance of the 'tradition', what is the place of 'habit' within that 'tradition'?'; 'if 'authority' provides support for 'truths', by what 'truth' is 'authority' maintained?'; 'if 'habit' is justified by 'authority', what is the 'habit' of 'authority' and how is that justified?'

All four of these concepts are obviously interrelated and in a sense it does not matter where we start, we will almost certainly come round to the same point at the end. All the questions and the arguments that underlie them are essentially circular. This should not really surprise us. All the arguments are based upon a 'truth', a 'tradition', an 'authority', and even a 'habit', that are, in themselves, unquestioned. Each term justifies each of the others at every point in the circle. This creates a closed system that cannot be broken apart, unless we wish to demolish it completely. It is for this reason that so much of what we take for truths, authority, tradition or habit only makes sense within the context of the mass. It is only within that context that we, as individuals, can sit fully within the closed system, free from all outside interference. At any other point the system itself must be questioned and, to a certain extent, be compromised.

In an article titled 'Is Symbolic Thought Prerational?' (1982), Sperber develops some of his ideas on symbolism which I have already outlined. He re-emphasises the point that symbols do not 'mean' and claims that these symbols can help us to manipulate ideas that the rational part of our mind cannot cope with. The question that Sperber asks is that if symbols do not 'mean', in the normal sense of the word, then what is it that they do? For Sperber what symbols do is to 'evoke', but he is never entirely clear what it is that is being evoked. At one level what is being evoked is an emotional response that has no rational basis. At another level it is some kind of interconnection between ideas such that the idea of bread, for example, will always be related to the concept of the Body of Christ. Sperber, however, rejects both these suggestions as being too simplistic and claims that what is evoked is neither an emotion, nor a connection of ideas, but rather a system of thought in which the associations that are presented make sense. In other words, bread does not in itself evoke the idea of the Body of Christ, or anything else, but rather the equation of 'bread equals body' evokes the system of thought in which this equation makes sense, that is the 'tradition' of the Roman Catholic Church.

It is perhaps this point that I was trying to express earlier when I said that the individual must place themselves within the tradition. 'Tradition' provides an all-embracing momentum that will proceed perfectly well without the intervention of specific individuals and which will only affect particular individuals when those individuals choose to commit themselves wholeheartedly to that tradition. Tradition, along with the related issues of authority, truth and experience, form a closed system into which individuals need to place themselves. If this is so, and it certainly seems to be the case, then how is it that outsiders can ever hope to investigate the system except from within the system itself? The analyst could, of course, pursue a kind of structuralism that simply looks for the logic by which the system works, while acknowledging that it holds no meaning outside of its own context. It only holds meaning within that context because the people who use it refuse to question it. However, if the system is so unpenetrable then how was it that I, as a researcher, was able to 'break in'? More importantly how could other people 'break out'? How could the Roman Catholics themselves look beyond the system and draw other areas of their life, issues of justice and peace, ecumenism and morality, and so on into their tradition?

It seems, therefore, at least in part, that I may have been ✓ asking the wrong questions. What I have done is to proceed along fairly established academic lines; I have chosen suitable terms, I have defined concepts and I have proceeded to show, so as far as it is possible, how these terms and the associated concepts are related. What I have failed to do, as most 'academic' thought fails to do, is to question the nature, or the existence, of the concepts in themselves. I have treated them in exactly the same way as I have suggested that the Roman Catholics treat their 'truths', simply as given.

I have, for example, talked about 'tradition'. I have defined it, based upon hints given by the members of the Roman Catholic congregation, as something that has a reality apart from the individual; that is, as something that is continuous despite the changes in its outward appearance; as something that is transcendent and all embracing; as something that is circular and closed. My definition sounded very much like the anthropological definition of 'culture' and not dissimilar to the Christian understanding of 'God' (although tradition and culture are impersonal while God is always seen as a 'person'). The question I ought to have been asking, therefore, following the contributor to my seminar and in opposition to Southwold, is 'does tradition exist?'. That, however, would have challenged the whole basis of the exercise and would have meant my standing at some position outside of the discourse that I had been studying. 'Tradition', 'culture' and 'God' are all unquestioned assumptions that allow the analyst to interpret experience in different ways and within different modes of discourse. Their objective existence should not, in itself, be questioned. However, as I hope to have shown, once the first assumption has been made then others are built upon it. If we assume that tradition does exist, for example, then we can ask how authority, or truth, or habit relates to that tradition. However if 'tradition' itself has no objective existence outside of the minds of the Roman Catholic worshippers then we have to ask whether it is possible to say anything at all about the way in which they understand their worship.

It is not surprising that if we build a theory upon an unquestioned assumption, such as tradition, it will eventually become circular, leading to a questioning of the basic assumption that we started with. As Southwold reminds us, philosophers have always found this to be the case when they come to talk about God (1983: 150). If they assumed that God exists they could prove that existence by what they assumed to be God's attributes, and so on. All such arguments are essentially circular. However in the case of my own argument, the circularity contained within this chapter, can we say that the argument itself, built upon the assumption of the existence of tradition, is itself a closed system, or is it only the system that we have described which is closed? Can any distinction be made between these two systems and does it really matter? I think that it does matter and I shall be coming back to questions of this kind towards the end of the book. However it was with questions of this kind lodged firmly in my own mind that I left the Roman Catholic church and moved on to study the Independent Christian Fellowship, a very different experience of worship but one which still worked very much within a closed system of thought.

NOTES

1 It is interesting to compare my own reflections on the importance or value of mistakes within the liturgy from the perspective of the congregation with Keiren Flanagan's discussion of mistakes from the perspective of the performers of the rite (Flanagan 1991). Mistakes for Flanagan are dangerous, subversive elements of the rite which need to be avoided; from the per-

spective of the congregation however, they have, as I have hoped to show, the potential to be creative and the primary carriers of meaning for those who recognise them. Bidget Nichols, on the other hand, in a 'hermeneutic' study of liturgy, dismisses mistakes as deviations from the ideal rite, despite the fact that, even in her own terms, the performance of the mistake would change the hermeneutic meaning of the rite (1996).

CHAPTER SIX
THE INDEPENDENT
CHRISTIAN FELLOWSHIP

The Independent Christian Fellowship was a very unusual church by any standards. I had wanted to study a church that came from an independent, evangelical or charismatic tradition and I heard about this house-church from people I knew around the university. The church was founded by the current pastor about four years before I began my study. At the time of my study a second congregation was in the process of being founded in another part of the city. The church was entirely independent, rejecting both 'evangelical' and 'charismatic' as labels, although the pastor did have colleagues and friends with responsibility for other congregations in other parts of the country and visitors from these congregations did visit the Fellowship on occasion.

The Fellowship owned two large semi-detached houses that had been knocked into one. The ground floor formed a large worship area and the cellars were used for communal eating. The top two floors had been converted into flats for the pastor and his wife, two other couples and a group of three young men who shared the fourth flat. This group formed the core of the congregation and lived an essentially communal lifestyle within the house. The total congregation consisted of about seventy individuals, most of whom were under thirty and either single or part of couples within the congregation. There were about ten children, all of church members. The congregation was entirely white, and equally divided as to men and women. Many of the members of the congregation worked for other members as one of the elders owned a small printing works which employed a number of the younger members of the group. Of those who worked elsewhere most were manual or clerical.

The life of the Fellowship clearly dominated the whole of the lives of the individual members. Worship took place twice on Sunday, lasting just over two hours each time. Most members attended both sessions, staying for a communal meal after the first and not going home until late into the evening. There were other events every night of the week: prayer meetings, Bible classes, women's meetings, men's meetings and, most importantly, 'confessional' groups. Every full member of the congregation belonged to a confessional group and these met once a week led by the pastor or one of the four elders of the church (all men in their forties or fifties). The group meeting consisted of worship and a time to talk about issues that were worrying individual members. Although I was treated with a great deal of suspicion when I first began to study the congregation I was, after four months, accepted fully enough to be invited to join one of these groups, which I attended sporadically for the rest of my time with the Fellowship.

I will say more about the form and content of the worship below. I had difficulties gaining permission to study this congregation. I had to agree not to take notes, not to quote any member of the congregation without first asking the pastor's permission, and to accept that I might, having been with the congregation for six months, not wish to leave. I accepted all these conditions, deciding not to quote any individual rather than seeking the pastor's permission. I worshipped with the congregation from January to June 1986. At the end of my time I was very relieved to leave and never made any further contact with the church.

INTRODUCTION

My move from the Catholic church to the Independent Christian Fellowship marked the half way point in my research and right from the start of my time with the Fellowship I found myself having to ask new and difficult questions.

My initial problem came from the fact that I could very rarely remember what had happened during any one act of worship. One reason for this was that remembering two hours of worship with no fixed text would stretch the powers of any person's memory. When I began to study the Independent Christian Fellowship I went to see the pastor, as I had with all the other churches, and asked for his permission to study the church. This permission was granted on certain conditions. The first of these was that I should not use a tape recorder or take notes during a service. If I was to attend worship at this church then I should come as a full participant member and not simply as an observer, or even in the more ambiguous role of 'participant-observer'. So, not only could I not remember what had happened, as a full participant I had no other record, written or taped. There was, however, another reason why I could very rarely remember the details of what had occurred. This was related to the 'feeling' that I had as I left the church after worship. It was only with the Independent Christian Fellowship that I could ever say conclusively that there was a specific 'feeling' on leaving the church. With the Baptists, the Roman Catholics and the Anglicans my mood after any one service varied from week to week, from boredom, through intellectual excitement, to a clear 'religious' commitment. With the Independent Christian Fellowship, however, I invariably felt exactly the same after each service. It is probably important, therefore, for me to try and capture that feeling on paper, and to understand what lay behind it, as I am sure that this is related to why I could remember so little about what was going on.

A number of words spring to mind as I think about this experience: 'relief', 'lightness', 'joy', 'commitment', 'praise'. I would invariably leave the house that served as a worship space whistling the tune of one of the choruses. There was a lightness in my step. There was a sense of the beauty and joy in my surroundings: the trees, the bird song, even the rain. I wanted to praise God and, in my heart, I did. I felt uplifted. I felt that I did not have to worry. God was in control of my life. I was bursting to tell others all about the service when I got home. Invariably I felt a commitment within me to do something concrete in response to what I had heard and experienced. The faith that was preached was so simple.... Why didn't everybody see this? There was a sense of wonder on leaving that act of worship, not just once or twice, but almost every week for the full six months. There was also a very clear sense of unease that somehow, underneath the wonder and the joy, it was all too simple, that I might have been lulled into a false security by the way the worship had been handled, that something very important was missing. I found my time at the Independent Christian Fellowship perhaps the most difficult of the four periods of study. Every time I set out to go on a Sunday morning or evening I wanted to turn back, I felt as though I was fighting something within myself. I knew that I was being challenged by that worship and I did not like it.

Is there any wonder, therefore, underneath this very personal response to the worship, that I could never remember what was actually happening? I suppose that I was more personally involved in this worship than in any other. I was drawn into it. I was participating in the way that had been requested by the pastor. It was only later that I was able to stand back and analyse what had been going on. It was not the worship itself that I was able to analyse, however. I have largely had to reconstruct that from the vague memories that I do have. It was the impact that the worship had on me and the forcefulness, and perhaps the ambiguity, of my own response that I had to analyse.

ORDER, SEQUENCE, STRUCTURE

The pastor's request that I participate fully in the worship makes any attempt to discuss the formal nature of the worship of the Independent Christian Fellowship very difficult. It is one thing to say that there is no formal text, so long as there is some kind of 'text' to work with. At least with the Baptist church I was able to tape and transcribe the informal text and treat that, to some degree at least, given the qualifications that I have already dealt with, as a 'text', much like any other liturgical text. However, if I was not allowed to tape or even to take notes, what kind of 'text' could I possibly create and analyse for the Independent Christian Fellowship? Such a 'text' cannot easily exist in any form.

On a number of occasions I did try to keep a list of items running in my mind: hymn, chorus, chorus, prayer, chorus, word, hymn, testimony ... and so on. I soon got lost and somehow it never really seemed to matter. Each item, with the possible exception of the sermon, was short and appeared to be independent of any other item. Items in the worship would be contributed by a different person each time and their place within the whole was ambiguous. What is more, if I could not remember the specific order of items in any one act of worship, still less could I remember exactly which hymns and which choruses were used. Nor could I recall the content of the prayers, the passages chosen for the sermon and so on. So much of this detailed information seemed to pass me by; it was irrelevant to the whole, or so it seemed at the time.

Perhaps the most obvious issue that I faced when dealing with worship in the Independent Christian Fellowship, therefore, was the problem of 'order' or 'structure'. According to the members of the congregation that I spoke to, any act of worship, which can last anything up to two hours, is guided solely by the Spirit and has no inherent 'order' as such. Each person present in the worshipping community can be led to contribute whatever is needed at any one time for the benefit of themselves personally or for the benefit of the whole congregation. Every act of worship was introduced by the pastor and would begin with a hymn. From that point on there was no way of determining the 'order' or the 'sequence' of the worship. After about an hour the children would leave to attend some form of instruction and the main body of worshippers would continue much as before. Invariably the service ended either with a sermon from the pastor, or with the sharing of bread and wine. This is, at best, a very loose framework, and within the Fellowship itself there was not even the sense that this was fixed in any way. Within such a framework the 'worship' happened, and at first sight there was very little to grasp hold of.

Such an apparent lack of 'order' is something that anthropologists have commented on in other societies, most especially those which practise rites that are normally classified as 'ecstatic' in one form or another (Lewis 1989). Invariably anthropologists see their role, when analysing 'ecstatic' rituals, as that of the 'interpreter' whose job it is to show that there really is some kind of underlying structure after all. It is assumed that there must be 'order' even if this is not apparent to the participants or immediately obvious to the outsider. It is also assumed that there must be some level of constraint or else the rite would disintegrate into a general free-for-all, which, on the whole, very rarely happens.

In the context of the worship of the Independent Christian Fellowship, for instance, despite the lack of any obvious 'structure', the worship always gave the impression of being very 'orderly'. Nothing in the service was out of control. Only on a couple of occasions did one or more of the elders have to 'impose' on the proceedings to bring them back into line: once when an individual was obviously 'unbalanced' and once when the whole worshipping body began to get a little too 'excited'. On the whole the worship in this particular church was not what might be called 'ecstatic'. Very rarely in the whole of my six months study did I hear tongues being used at a public level, although many people mumbled in tongues under their breath. When tongues were used openly they were always quiet and restrained and were followed by a clear interpretation. The overall sense of the service was one of peace and quietness. Any restraint that was being shown was shown by each individual at a personal level.

When anthropologists talk about the issue of order or disorder in worship, or in any kind of ritual, they immediately run up against a problem of terminology. One of the problems is that there are two related issues involved in this discussion, which often get confused. First there is the idea of 'sequence', that is the precise order of subsequent events during the rite: A follows B follows C etc. 'Sequence' in this form is also related to 'structure'. Secondly there is the question of 'order', the level of control that is imposed, the freedom that any individual may or may not have to do their own thing. What the Independent Christian Fellowship shows, I think, is a situation in which 'sequence' and 'order' are not in any sense related. In a Roman Catholic mass, for example, there is a well-established 'sequence', it is written down for everybody to see and to follow. The mass is also, and some would say consequentially so, 'ordered'. Everybody knows what is expected of them and what their own particular role within the totality of the worship is. Very rarely does a Roman Catholic ritual get out of hand. In various forms of Pentecostal worship that I have experienced outside of my research, however, the opposite seems to be the case, especially during those moments that are often referred to as 'Singing in the Spirit'. Here there is neither sequence nor order and the overall effect is one of 'chaos'. This sense of 'chaos', however, is often illusory, especially when we consider the restraints on any one individual that limit the range of responses that can be made. Also we must realise that moments of this kind often fall within a wider act of worship which shows a much greater sense of order and sequence, even if the specific responses of individuals during that worship are often left open.

It is this last situation, the wider arena of Pentecostal worship, which often gets labelled as 'free' worship or as worship 'in the Spirit'. The assumption behind this is that the personal abandonment to the flow of the sequence, very often controlled by the leader, is what makes this worship 'free'. When anthropologists have come to study 'ecstatic' rituals in other societies it is this kind of 'freedom' and 'disorder' that they have found, disorder as perceived by the participant. It should not surprise us therefore that they often come away telling us that the whole rite is really very 'ordered' or even 'structured' after all. Much of this kind of worship does have a very clear, fixed, and often traditional, 'sequence' (Lewis 1989: 110–13).

This, however, was not the case with the Independent Christian Fellowship. Here everything was very orderly, very 'ordered' in many ways. Ecstatic abandon played only a very small role, and was usually disapproved of within the everyday worship of the church. What I found lacking, however, was any clear sense of 'sequence'. There was certainly only a limited range of 'responses' that any one individual could make: a general low murmur of prayer, or a specific contribution in the form of one of five different types of item, each with its own specific style and rules of content. Despite this, however, there was no way that the outsider could ever 'predict' the sequence in which these elements would appear.

THE CONSTRAINTS ON WORSHIP

What happened within the worship of the Independent Christian Fellowship could not simply be called 'disordered'. There were certain constraints upon the worship, and on the worshippers but it was often difficult to see what these might be. When I have been talking about this worship to other people I am often asked 'Who controls the worship?', 'Who is the leader?' 'Surely,' I am told, 'only a few people can actually take part, those who are considered to be "sound"'. This kind of comment is made by those with a basic knowledge of Pentecostal worship, where a firm and obvious leadership is imposed, controlling who takes part and what they can contribute. In this kind of church the leader, and perhaps the elders, sit at the front and the congregation sits in rows facing them, much like any ordinary, traditional, church. In the Independent Christian Fellowship, however, that was not the case: the layout and ordering of the worship space were very different. The worship space was constructed out of two rooms of the large old house that formed the base for the church. This created an 'L-shaped' space. The congregation, therefore, sat within the two long arms of the L and also in the corner space, forming three, basically facing, blocks. The piano was situated in the window and if there was any focus then it was a small table containing a vase of flowers, a basket of bread and a jug of grape juice. This provided a much more informal setting than a traditional church. It also provided one that had no obvious focus for leadership.

The worship leader at the Fellowship, often the pastor but frequently one of the elders, stood to open the service and then sat down on one of the front rows, as any ordinary member of the congregation. Only at the sermon, if the leader were giving this, would he stand again to face the group. The other elders were scattered amongst the congregation, often with their families, and although members of the congregation seemed to have their own favourite spots, as is common in most churches, these were not determined formally. This kind of arrangement obviously placed considerable constraints upon the leaders. It would have been much more difficult for them to impose any kind of order on the proceedings when they were a part of the group in this way rather than standing in front of it. On only a few occasions, therefore, was formal leadership apparent. These were times when there was nothing very much happening within the worship and it was obvious that the leader or one of the elders was trying to instil some sort of movement into the proceedings, or at times when the opposite, restraining function, was needed.

Such an arrangement also placed some kind of constraint on the congregation. Practically everybody was visible in one way or another. Most people seemed to be occupied within themselves for most of the time and uninterested in what their neighbours were doing, but the sense of vulnerability was always present. The obverse of this was that any one member of the congregation was automatically one of the crowd, a part of the worshipping group. The church itself was always full. In this sense individuals could be carried along by the general movement of the worship. It is the combination of these two factors, I would suggest, that led to the fact that the vast majority of people present at any one act of worship would, at some time during the two hours, contribute something to the whole.

Personally, I found this level of participation strange. Even in the various Pentecostal churches that I know spontaneous contributions to the worship only came from a few well-known people, unless specifically asked for by the leader. Within the Independent Christian Fellowship, however, there seemed to be no such restriction and any person could, and most did, contribute something. There were clearly some people who would contribute more than others. One lady obviously enjoyed singing and would invariably offer a number of choruses at each meeting. On the other hand only two or three people ever offered 'words'. Despite this, however, there was considerable freedom. The only 'constraint' in the literal sense of the word, was that no two things could happen at the same time. When situations arose in which two items were suggested simultaneously, one or the other would soon back down, or it was agreed to allow one to follow the other.

The only other kind of constraint on the worship was one of content and of style. Any member of the congregation was able to offer some kind of contribution to the whole but the nature of that contribution was very clearly limited. In practice there were only ever five kinds of contribution that could be offered and each of these had a clear style and was limited in terms of content. If any member of the congregation were asked to list these possible contributions, I am sure that most would not have been able to do so. For members of the congregation there were no known limitations. The five possible contributions, however, were hymn, chorus, prayer, word, and testimony.

Hymns and choruses are best taken together as they can only be understood and distinguished in terms of their differences. Any item that was sung must have been either a hymn or a chorus. A hymn was easily distinguished because hymns were written out in one of the two hymnbooks that were found on every seat. Generally, once a hymn was announced the whole congregation would stand and everybody was expected to join in. The hymns that were found in the hymnbooks were on the whole traditional and dealt with aspects of faith or were related to Bible passages. Most of those sung by the Fellowship were by Charles Wesley. Anything else that was sung, therefore, must have been a chorus. Choruses, however, also had a style of their own. They were usually short, sung from memory and related to a biblical passage or a simple statement of faith. Choruses were always sung sitting down, or more precisely in the position in which any one individual might find themselves, as people stood and sat at irregular intervals during the service. It was also noticeable that once one chorus had been sung, usually more than once in itself, a number of others would follow on a similar theme. Occasionally one chorus was sung for ten or more minutes, over and over again, in a meditative fashion. Lastly, the turnover of choruses was very high, new ones were always being sung and, whilst there were some obvious favourites, we only sang most of the choruses that I heard once or twice over the whole six months of the study.

If I define hymns and choruses by the fact that they were sung then, obviously, anything that was not sung must have been a word, a prayer or a testimony. These can be distinguished from each other first by the fact that prayers and words were always delivered from an individual's own seat, and generally over the constant murmuring of others, while the testimony was delivered from the front when everybody else was listening. At first sight it was not always obvious what was a prayer and what was a word, but there were very clear stylistic differences between them and their functions within the worship were very different. The prayer was always addressed by one individual to God. Others might have linked themselves with the prayer, by adding 'Alleluias' or 'Amens' at suitable breaks, but the prayer was essentially a private statement expressed aloud. Such prayers were nearly always prayers of thanksgiving or of praise, most often of both: thanksgiving for the fact that the individual had come to salvation: praise of God, or of Jesus, who had achieved that salvation. In only two cases over the six months were prayers given any specific reference; once for a member of the congregation who was ill and once for a family from the Fellowship who were going out to Nepal as missionaries.

Prayers, therefore, were spoken by individuals and addressed to God. Words, on the other hand, were spoken as if by God through the individual. Words were spoken in the first person, and were addressed to the congregation, or perhaps to one, unnamed, member of that congregation. Words were almost always reassuring and encouraging, and they often involved an elaborate and poetic use of biblical imagery. As I have already said, the number of people who actually spoke words were limited to the few who were known to have this gift. In this the word is unique amongst the items that I am listing. It should also be noted that speaking in tongues, at a public level, was only an extension of the word, as the tongues always needed interpretation and the content and style of that interpretation was always identical to that of the word.

Finally, therefore, we come to testimony. There is a sense in which this is a ragbag of items that do not fit into any of the other categories. I have already defined the testimony by the fact that an individual would come to the front to deliver it and the congregation was expected to sit and listen. At times, therefore, these would be traditional testimonies, accounts of how the individual 'came to the Lord'. More often they would be an account of how a reading from scripture had 'spoken' to an individual over the week or of some other event or 'blessing' that they wished to share with the Fellowship as a whole. It is also within this category of testimony that I would place the sermon. This might seem strange at first but the connections became clear one Sunday when a number of people gave a series of extended testimonies that almost turned into mini sermons and the pastor decided not to add a sermon of his own. The sermon also invariably began, like a testimony, by expounding some passage from scripture that had 'spoken' to the preacher over the last week. This immediately created a link with other testimonies; the only difference was one of length. Finally, the testimony was distinguished from all the other contributions by the fact that the contributor always asked permission of the pastor and the elders before coming to the front. However, nobody, whilst I was with the church, was ever refused.

These then are the five elements that made up the worship of this congregation. Each act of worship was built up out of some combination, according to no particular sequence, of these five elements. It was the lack of sequence, however, that is of specific interest to me. Before moving on to look at the implications of this lack of sequence, I must mention two other factors that complete this account of the worship itself. Firstly, I must mention the 'background noise'. There was, throughout the worship, a continuous low murmuring, out of which these various elements grew and into which they consequently subsided. This murmuring was made up of various members of the congregation, most of those present but by no means all, constantly repeating to themselves words such as 'Jesus', 'Lord', 'Alleluia', and short phrases of praise and thanksgiving. Some members of the congregation also muttered longer prayers to themselves under their breath or were even very quietly speaking in tongues. This provided a constant background against which the worship continued, broken only by hymns, for which everybody stood and sang, and testimonies for which everybody sat and listened.

Lastly, there was the sharing of bread and wine. I cannot say whether this happened every week at either the evening or the morning service. I was told, however, that there was no obligation for it to do so. I was also constantly being told that the sharing of bread and wine was becoming too formal and the congregation itself was invariably told that they should relax during the sharing and let the Spirit move them. Despite this, the sharing was perhaps the most formal element of any service. There was no accompanying prayer or scriptural warrant but at a particular point, usually towards the end of an act of worship, the basket of bread and a glass of grape juice would be handed along the rows of each block within the congregation, from one person to the next. As the bread or juice was passed each person would embrace their neighbour and offer some comment such as 'the Lord be with you'. The bread or juice was then taken, and passed on with a similar embrace and comment. All this was carried on to the constant sound of the muttering of individual prayers, or occasionally while choruses were being sung.

QUESTIONS OF SEQUENCE

At the beginning of this chapter I posed the problem of the worship of the Independent Christian Fellowship as one of trying to come to terms with an act of worship that, whilst being orderly, had no definable sequence. However, as I have just shown, the particular elements of the worship were very clearly defined and followed very specific rules in terms of their style, their content and their position within the worship. Surely the rules that govern each particular item must in some way relate to the whole and make some kind of impact on its sequence and its structure.

So far we have considered 'order', 'structure' or 'sequence' as holistic, all embracing, concepts. It is as if we were able stand back from the act of worship itself and say that this worship has order, structure, sequence, or whatever. However, this is not the only kind of order or structure that we can deal with. I would want to argue that by looking at the specific rules that are related to the various elements that make up the worship, we can suggest other ways of looking at the issues of order, not from an overall perspective but rather from within the act of worship itself. What I am suggesting is that even if we do not have some overall pattern which can predict how any one act of worship might turn out we will always, whilst we are actually within that worship be following a series of rules that, in themselves, will determine the outcome. The situation with the Christian Fellowship is one in which the few basic rules which govern the nature and placing of the various elements that make up the content of the worship can generate an infinite number of sequences. The resulting structures of each sequence, therefore, may end up having very little in common.

I can illustrate what I am saying by the use of an example. I have claimed that once one chorus has been sung then there are two choices, either (a) the chorus will be repeated or (b) another chorus with a similar theme will be sung. In this case the existence of one element, the chorus, will define the limits that determine what kind of element will follow. Similarly, it is assumed that only a certain number of choruses can follow each other at any one time, or, alternatively, only a certain number of testimonies can occur in any one service. If too many testimonies occur then there will be no sermon. These rules are not particularly formal, nor are they known consciously by the participants, but they do act in practice and this is what matters. From within the worship, therefore, certain constraints limit the next action in the sequence to a number of easily identifiable options, and it is this that generates the overall sequence for any one act of worship.

An extension of this basic concept of evolving sequences can be seen by the fact that as the worship progressed the thematic content of any one item was related to those that had gone before. There was, of course, no formal reason why any one member of the congregation could not introduce an element into the worship with any theme that they choose. Theoretically this was possible but such free choice was very rarely taken up. This thematic consistency was primarily a factor of the first kind of constraint that I mentioned above, the constraint of freedom. Because any person was able contribute to the worship, and because nobody would ever introduce an element, with the possible exception of a testimony, that had been prepared before the worship, the trigger that compelled a person to contribute an element of their own must have been contained within the elements that preceded it. This was largely a process triggered by the association of ideas. One result of this, that became very obvious to any observer who was actually attending the worship, was that, after about a quarter of an hour or so, a very clear theme began to emerge within the worship around which all the various elements revolved. This theme was not determined externally or even consciously, it simply occurred through the association of ideas as the worship itself proceeded.

From all this we can see that there was very obviously an internal logic to any one act of worship, something which drew it all together. And yet it was an internal logic that grew as the service itself was generated, it was organic and dynamic rather than static. Whether this can be called 'sequence', 'order', 'structure', or any other such term as I have defined them is difficult to say, but such a logic is most definitely there. Discussing this logic only becomes difficult if we wish to stand back, as I said earlier, and attempt to take in a number of services, trying to relate their various internal logics to each other as if they were static. Here we see again, as with my analysis of the Roman Catholic church the importance of time in the understanding of ritual. 'Time' in this particular case, however is internal to the rite and not external, over a series of rites.

WORSHIP AS MONTAGE

As a conclusion to this particular discussion I would like to introduce one final concept that I hope will draw together most of what I have been saying and perhaps tie up some of the loose ends. This is the concept of 'montage'. 'Montage' as a technique became very popular amongst radical artists in Berlin just before the Second World War. These artists tried to bring together aspects of the society around them, that they felt to be oppressing them, to break these images of the society apart and to reconstruct them in a different, often disturbing fashion. Montages within the visual medium were made out of popular newspaper images, with paint and through collage. A similar process was applied to the traditional structure of the play within the theatre, and Bertolt Brecht is probably the most famous of the playwrights at this time to use this method widely (Willett 1959). All Brecht's best-known plays are 'montages' in some form. They aim to rip apart our understandings of the dominant, capitalist, society and so to draw us into revolution against the regime. 'Montage' has recently been picked up again by both artists and academics, this time in relation to the post-modern, which has very different aims from those of the pre-war German Marxists.

One anthropologist who has brought together both the Marxist and the post-modern understandings of montage, and has applied these understandings specifically to ritual, is Michael Taussig. In his book on terror and healing in South America, *Shamanism, Colonialism and the Wild Man* (1987), Taussig describes a drug-induced healing rite in the Andes as 'montage' (1987: 435–46). He describes the effect of this rite upon the individual as being similar to the effect that Brecht would have liked his plays to have had on his audiences. Primary images of the world are broken up so generating 'disorder' that leads ultimately to revolution, healing, or perhaps even conversion. For Taussig the primary nature of montage is disorder. It is obvious from reading Taussig's book that the rites that he is describing are very disordered. They occur under the influence of hallucinatory drugs and, despite certain conventions relating to the way in which the ritual gets under way, practically anything might happen. Once the rite is under way, however, there is a constant 'interruptedness', people are coming and going all the time, the rite is full of disjointed images, broken narratives, sudden scene-changing, fragments of things, complete disorder. It is this disorder that, for Taussig, is the heart and soul of the rite (1987: 440).

We can see something of this, but perhaps not to such an extreme, within the worship of the Independent Christian Fellowship. In this case, however, the apparent disorder is not nearly so complete. The worship itself is, as we have seen, very 'orderly'. Something very similar could be said for the work of Brecht and the other montage artists of pre-war Berlin. A Brecht play is a very carefully structured performance; it only has an apparent disorder because of the way in which it breaks the norms of classical theatre (Willett 1959). A Brechtian play is typically made up of a series of very short scenes. Each one has a point to make within itself, but each one is also connected to all the others to create the overall structure which will only dawn on us slowly as the play progresses. This is very similar to the process I have described for the worship of the Christian Fellowship, with the distinction that there is no 'author' to the worship. With the act of worship, therefore, it is internal rules that determine the overall structure and not, as with Brecht, the overall structure that determines the internal relations.

I have indicated in the last section that one of the products of the montage nature of the worship was the way in which a theme invariably emerged out of each act of worship within the first quarter of an hour or so. These themes varied slightly from week to week. However, one factor that became more and more obvious to me, as my time with the Fellowship increased, was that in everything that emerged as a theme during the worship there was only one focus. This was the act of conversion that was expressed as coming to the Cross, dying to the world and rising to Christ. This was made explicit in a number of cases, as in testimonies or occasionally during the sermon. However, in almost all the other aspects of the worship, conversion, and the Cross, played a central role. Prayers would consist almost entirely of praise and thanksgiving for the act of conversion, or salvation. Intercession for others was very rarely heard. Hymns and choruses were chosen for their emphasis on God's saving power, the Cross and the implications of salvation in the life of the Christian. In the 'words' and the sermon there was a constant encouragement to come to the Cross, to die to the ways of the world and to rise in Christ.

Week in, week out, for two or more hours each Sunday this same, very simple, message was expressed, emphasised and encouraged. This cannot continue without having some impact on the individual worshipper. The focus of the worship was on conversion. The focus of the worshipper, therefore, was bound to be on conversion as well. This was certainly true for me. There was a simplicity about this message which I could not help noticing and beginning to work through. This central unifying focus, coming through the constant variety and uncertainty of the worship itself, was the aspect of worship at the Independent Christian Fellowship that struck me most forcefully.

Brecht saw the purpose of montage as being to break up the accepted images of bourgeois society in such a way that the working class could see the falseness of their security and would rise up and begin the revolution (Willett 1959). Unfortunately, or perhaps fortunately, Brecht was far too good a playwright ever to be able to achieve this. His plays are far too sophisticated to cause the mass outrage and revolution that he had hoped for. Taussig claimed something similar for the Andean healing rites that he was dealing with (1987). He saw the montage effect of the healing rites as being an attempt to break down the client's view of the world and to get within the cracks, to challenge that worldview and to reconstruct it. In both cases montage was seen to work through the dislocation of the individual and it demanded a very specific response to the world. Obviously something very similar was happening within the worship of the Independent Christian Fellowship. Put very crudely, the worship, with its dislocation and montage style, was breaking down the resistance of the individual. The constant emphasis of each element of the worship on the Cross and conversion was then forcing this new image, the new worldview, into the minds of the worshippers.

Put as bluntly as this the worship is made to sound suspiciously like 'brainwashing', which in a sense it probably was. I would certainly argue that both brainwashing and this kind of worship are based upon a similar process. However, I would distinguish the two on the grounds that brainwashing, as such, is premeditated, an attempt is made purposefully to force an individual to change their fundamental views. There was no such purposeful intention within this worship. What happened within the worship was a direct response to the experience of conversion. The fact that this response recreated the conditions in which conversion was likely to take place was not coincidental but neither was it premeditated. Another, similarly simplistic, understanding would claim that the recreation of the conditions of conversion allowed the people to keep the experience of conversion uppermost in their minds. That is to focus their attention on that to the detriment of everything else, leading to a situation where the authenticity and nature of that experience was never questioned. Again there is some truth in this. The main purpose of the Christian life as expressed by members of the congregation was to 'be right with the Lord' which meant basically to recall the experience of conversion and to make it a constant and present reality. Such scepticism, however, I would argue, is only half the story and fails to take account of what the people themselves said, and obviously felt, about the centrality of conversion in their lives.

STORIES OF CONVERSION

Conversion was the central point of reference in the lives of almost every member of the congregation at the Independent Christian Fellowship. Not only did every item of the worship focus back upon a moment of conversion, but much of the conversation that I had with members of the congregation after the worship also revolved around the same subject. After each morning service the congregation met for lunch in another room of the house. This provided a good chance for me to talk to individuals, and to listen to what people had to say. In this environment, however, I was not able to ask my standard questions about the meaning of worship, and on the whole there was no real need to. With this congregation, more than with any other, I found people more than willing to talk to me about their faith and primarily about their conversion to that faith. Over time it became more and more obvious that the content of each of these 'stories' of conversion was very nearly identical, give or take a few personal details. There was a similar structure to each story and the language used was common to every person. I began, therefore, to look at both the language and the story itself in much more detail.

A Christian, according to the members of the Fellowship, was one who had 'come to Christ', one who had 'accepted Jesus into their hearts', one who had 'died to sin and risen with Christ'. All these phrases are part of an accepted 'evangelical' or 'charismatic' language, so much so that it is possible for those outside the tradition to parody evangelical talk with remarkable accuracy. The whole of this language is riddled with clichés and stock phrases, although it is questionable whether they are seen as such by the individuals concerned. All the phrases that are used are biblical in origin and these phrases are learnt during worship, primarily during the sermon where the constant repetition of stock passages and phrases from Paul's Epistles was obvious. Short phrases of this kind were also a vital part of the individual's own understanding and expression of their faith. Such phrases came up over and over again during the various stories of conversion. When I was invited to respond with the story of my own 'conversion' I could use similar phrases and people would know immediately what it was that I was talking about. It was also obvious that the more peripheral the individual was to the central organisation of the church, the more emphasis was placed on these phrases and the less attention was given to specific details. Furthermore, such phrases also formed the basis of the prayers, words, testimonies and all other aspects of the worship. Such clichés and stock phrases were clearly central to the self-expression of all the members of this congregation.

One advantage of stock phrases and clichés of this kind was that they gave the ordinary members of the congregation a language in which to talk about their faith. Stock phrases and clichés presented the average member of the congregation with a vocabulary that could be used to talk about things that most Christians from other churches find very difficult to mention, let alone to express fluently. Over lunch on various Sunday mornings I had many conversations with people about their faith, about their commitment to Jesus, how they had come to know Jesus and accepted him into their hearts, and so on. Such conversations would have been impossible, or, at best, very embarrassing, in any other church. In the conversations at this church, however, we shared a language that we both knew, a form of discourse that allowed us to communicate about that which cannot normally be communicated. It would have been pointless for me to have asked any person what they meant by saying that they had 'accepted Jesus into their heart'. The phrase itself allowed a commonly understood meaning to stand between us. It is this that makes such language so important to a church whose primary objective, as they see it, is to tell others about their faith.

It was not just language, however, that was common to the various stories about conversion. There was also a common structure. The reasons for this are probably much the same as the reasons behind the common language. A common structure allows the individual to tell the story, and allows the story to be understood by others, without anybody having to stretch their powers of imagination or memory too far. This is a principle that is well known and commonly noted in studies of oral literature (Finnegan 1977). Such a story becomes a 'symbolic' statement, it is known even before it is stated and it allows the speaker to be identified as one of the 'in group', as a Christian. I would want to argue, however, that this common structure also had a far more subtle significance. Not only did the structure of the story allow an experience of conversion to be recalled and communicated, but, I would also want to argue, the structure itself was related to, even if it did not directly determine, the structure of the experience itself.

To explore this, however, we need to know what that structure was. Unfortunately I cannot recount a real story and extract the structure from it. Such stories were always expressed during informal conversation, and I was asked specifically not to quote individual members of the Fellowship.[1] However, I can lay out very simply what I see to be the basic structure and hopefully relate this to what might be called a 'typical' story.

All stories of conversion will begin with a state of unease. This may be a dramatic former life, as a drug addict, heavy drinker, manic depressive or whatever, or it may be a state of unease with the world generally, a sense of searching for something. From this initial state the first stage is a coming to awareness of 'sin', an understanding that the individual does not have

Jesus in their heart and a sense of emptiness that is associated with this. This invariably leads the individual to seek help, either through personal prayer, or by approaching an elder and asking for prayer to be said for them. Associated with this is an acceptance by the individual of the fact that they cannot do anything by or for themselves, that they are powerless, that they have to 'die' to self, to sin and to the world. It is at this point of total rejection, of death, that Jesus is said to enter and the Christian is able to share in Jesus' resurrection and the new life that he promises through that resurrection. This upsurge of joy within the individual is met by praise and thanksgiving and a commitment to a new life free from sin. Conversion is complete.

Before moving on I wish to make three small but very important points which I will come back to later. Firstly, it should be obvious that the dislocation that I was talking about earlier, as created by the worship, is an ideal way of bringing the individual to an acknowledgement of the state of unease in which they find themselves, thus making worship the most likely place for conversion to occur. Secondly, I want to stress that in this church the process of conversion is seen to be complete in itself. In other evangelical churches conversion would simply be the first step in a long process of growing into God. The pastor of this Fellowship, however, in a number of sermons, made it very clear that once converted the Christian is totally free from sin. There is no need for further movement, the individual stays at the foot of the Cross and praises God for the salvation that has been won once and for all. Thirdly, despite this insistence on the lack of movement, it is obvious that in the everyday life of the Christian this process of 'conversion' is repeated over and over again. One woman told me that she had got up one day feeling ill at ease, she was not 'right with the Lord'. She tried to avoid it and get on with her everyday life but this proved too much and eventually she came to a woman's meeting at church. Through that worship she found Jesus to be in her heart once again and so, once again, she was right with the Lord, ready to live anew her life as a Christian. The process of conversion, of response to Jesus, is continuous, even if conversion itself is seen to be complete within itself.

The language and structure of the stories relating to conversion are, therefore, common to all the members of the Fellow-

ship. I have suggested that this may be more than simply a means
of making communication easier between members about a subject that is very personal and often difficult to talk about directly.
I have suggested that the structure may bear some relation to
the actual structure of the event or experience of conversion.
Unfortunately this cannot be proved in any way. If we were to
argue, however, that the stories are often known to members of
the congregation before the event takes place we could, justifia-
bly, go on to claim that such stories have a determining effect on
that experience. That may well be the case but, as with so much
else relating to this church, it is probably too simplistic to stand
on its own. I think that there is much more to this than is obvious on the surface and it is this that I now wish to explore, primarily through the concept of 'experience'.

EXPERIENCE AND RESPONSE

One point that has become obvious in the preceding discussion
is the centrality of 'experience' within the understanding of the
worship in the Independent Christian Fellowship. I have claimed
that the act of worship creates both a sense of chaos and, through
this, a commitment to order. This is done primarily through the
medium of experience: the experience of chaos, the experience
of renewed order. Whether we see the story of conversion as
encapsulating the experience of conversion, evoking the experience of conversion or determining it, we have to say that the
experience itself lies at the heart of all thinking about worship
within the Fellowship. In the Independent Christian Fellowship
the experience of conversion, whatever that may be for the individual, is the experience that is constantly being evoked by the
worship and the experience that, through this constant evocation, colours all other experiences within worship. That conversion experience, expressed in the language of the laying down
of our own life in the death of Christ on the Cross and the taking up of the life of Christ in his resurrection, is the root experience of the whole church. It is constantly being recalled, over
and over again, in worship, so forming a cohering element to
what would, otherwise, be totally chaotic worship.

At this point I wish to move away from the Independent Christian Fellowship for a short while and go on to look at Gregory

Manly and Anneliese Reinhard's *The Art of Praying the Liturgy* (1984). This is a book written by two members of Catholic religious orders in Australia and is an attempt to put into words the essence of a course that they run for religious communities on prayer and the liturgy. To this extent it is a 'how to' book. It is not in itself, therefore, an analysis of the liturgy or of individual responses to it. However, despite this, I found that the basis of what was said equated very closely to the way that I had come to understand how ordinary people viewed worship. One chapter in particular, towards the middle of the book, summed up very clearly what I was trying to say. For that reason I will reproduce some of the main ideas of that chapter here. In doing this, however, I will work backwards, starting at the end of the chapter and working back to the beginning.

The chapter in question, chapter ten, is the central chapter of a section called 'Responding to Symbols'. The particular chapter is called '"See More" to Respond' and contains the heart of the authors' view on how we should respond to what we see around us in prayer (1984: 148–90). In laying out the process by which this response is made Reinhard, who writes this particular chapter, quotes an example from the life of Martin Luther King. The short story that she gives is of Luther King receiving a phone call that threatens his life, of his trying to work through how he can escape from this without losing face, of his acknowledging his own powerlessness, of his desperate prayer to God and, it is assumed, of the strength that is finally received to meet the challenge (1984: 169–71). Taking this as an example Reinhard suggests that our response in prayer should follow a number of set stages; (1) focusing on self, (2) gathering and accumulating, (3) choosing to stop, (4) becoming empty, (5) responding.

The words used at each stage are Reinhard's own and each numbered stage corresponds to a point in Luther King's own experience. The focusing on the self (1) is the telephone call, the trigger that demands that Luther King takes some immediate action. The gathering and accumulating (2) is the subsequent activity, the attempting to run away, to take control of his own life. That stops (3), Luther King realises that it is pointless, and then the becoming empty (4) is the opening up to the despair within himself and the possibility of response from God, which is the final stage (5). Reinhard presents all this as a way of indicating what it is that we have to do when we come to prayer if we are to get the most out of the praying experience. I, however, wish to turn the argument around and show that this might reflect what is happening at all worship to some extent or another.

It should be obvious that the structure of conversion that I outlined earlier can easily be fitted into Reinhard's model. Stage one is the sense of unease at life generally. Stage two is the bringing of this to awareness and the attempt by the individual to do something about it. Stage three is the acceptance that the individual is powerless. The 'dying' is stage four, leading into new life at stage five. Conversion is very clearly a situation of 're-sponse' in the way that Reinhard outlines it. This in itself should not surprise us; the story that was quoted from Martin Luther King is a story about conversion. Conversion is itself a form of response and so, therefore, it should follow the same structural pattern as other forms of response. Does this, however, apply to worship generally? How far can we say that this structure represents what is happening within worship? Surely every act of worship is not a conversion experience, despite the attempts of Reinhard to claim that it should be.

For the Independent Christian Fellowship the worship certainly reinforces and focuses on the conversion experience but does that make it a 'conversion' in its own right? Perhaps not, but let us look at this model of 'response' and ask how closely that can be related to what is going on in the worship. The first thing that we have to say is that a model such as this, designed to help others come to worship, is probably far too rigid to explain exactly what is going on for each individual in any one act of worship. I have already questioned whether the accounts of conversion actually match the experience of conversion. In one sense this is a pointless question. The accounts themselves are models, in much the same way as Reinhard's understanding of response is a model. As such they can only have limited value in trying to understand the experience itself. If, however, we also acknowledge that the experience in itself is unavailable to us, either for worship or for conversion, then we find that we only have the models to work with. In doing this, however, we must deprive them of their rigidity and ask what it might be that such models are trying to say about the experience of worship.

161

What we have seen in Reinhard's model is a 'dynamic' response to worship that demands as much from the one praying as it does from the worship, or whatever lies behind that worship. The worshipper sitting in the worship space is not simply a member of an audience watching a show, however much that might seem to be the case at times. The worshipper is one who is responding to all that is going on around them or within themselves, and through that response changing the way in which the world, or some small part of it, is viewed. Reinhard's model offers us a twofold movement. First, there is a bringing in to the worship space all the issues, cares and worries of the individual, a 'movement in', which would equate with stage two of the model. Secondly, there is a movement from the worship itself, a transforming of the cares and an acceptance by the person of what the worship is trying to say, a 'movement out', stage four of the model. Here again what I am saying is very simplistic so let me try to explore this in more detail.

One author who is very aware of the dynamic nature of liturgy as it relates to the individual is Aiden Kavanagh. In his work *On Liturgical Theology* (1984) Kavanagh talks about the worshipper being brought to the edge of chaos by the worship, being transformed by that experience and being sent out again into the world. This is very similar in content, and remarkably similar in structure, to both Reinhard's model and to the story of conversion as I have outlined it. When I first read this work, however, I felt very suspicious. As with all these models I felt that this view did not really express what was happening to most ordinary people in the liturgy. Kavanagh, however, would be the first to acknowledge this. He is very forthright in his condemnation of suburban Christianity where chaos is avoided at all costs and is certainly not experienced in liturgy. In dismissing this, however, I think that we are mistaking two things that should perhaps be kept apart. First we have the experience that we are discussing, the response to worship, the bringing to the edge of chaos, the dying to self and the rising in Christ, or however it is that we wish to express it. Secondly, we have the everyday, or more normally the 'every Sunday', experience of worship. What I am not saying is that worship is responded to in this dramatic way every Sunday. Rather I am suggesting that the experience of response, the being brought to the edge of chaos, perhaps only once or twice over a life time, perhaps more frequently, is able to colour and determine our everyday, our every Sunday, experience of worship.

Let me try to explain this with reference to the Independent Christian Fellowship. Here, as I have said, conversion is the root experience that sits at the heart of the understanding of worship. Conversion is, in a very literal sense, a bringing to the edge of chaos in the way in which Reinhard and Kavanagh have outlined. However this does not mean that every individual will come to that same point at every act of worship. Clearly I have suggested that the worship is ideally suited to achieve this, but could we not turn that argument round? What would happen if I suggested, for example, that the worship, being a free expression of what the individuals present wish to say, is a spontaneous 'reflection' of that experience of conversion, not in any way an attempt to 'recreate' it. The worship, like the story, becomes, in itself, a model for that experience. Within a free environment such as the Independent Christian Fellowship this is bound to reflect the experience much more directly than the more carefully constructed models of the Roman Catholic Church or other more formal churches. If this is the case then what I have said about the dynamic experience of conversion is of the utmost importance.

What I have failed to explain, however, is why this model is necessary and how the model itself actually works. Here I think that some of the earlier ideas from Reinhard's chapter are important. As a prerequisite to the process of response Reinhard introduces two concepts, that of 'seeing more' and that of 'framing' (1984: 148, 164). She claims that we have to become skilled in both these techniques before we can begin to respond to worship properly. As we are moving backwards through the chapter I wish to begin with framing. I have already claimed that certain members of the various congregations I have studied see the act of worship as a time set apart. The members of the Independent Christian Fellowship are no different in this. The worship begins clearly with a hymn and it is brought to a clear end by the singing of the grace before the communal meal downstairs. The worship time is therefore 'framed'. Reinhard sees the framing as an opportunity to concentrate on one specific idea or item, to cut out everything that is not relevant. Worship, therefore, or more specifically the corporate act of worship, allows us to 'frame' in Reinhard's sense. What we frame will depend on a number of factors. We will bring ideas and concerns that are worrying us and these will be framed. We will think about God, about life, and about the larger truths that we do not normally reflect on in our everyday life, these will also be framed. Finally, we will recall the experience of chaos, of conversion, and this will also be framed along with everything else. The frame of the liturgy allows us to bring a whole range of specific items together and see them in the same light. That light is, I would argue, the experience of response, and that is where Reinhard's second notion, the idea of 'seeing more' becomes important.

When Reinhard talks about 'seeing more' she is using a phrase that she has developed out of the practice of art and also through the thinking of Zen Buddhism (Manly & Reinhard 1984: 156). What she is basically saying is that we must see beyond the surface of things at what is 'really' there. This is a semi-mystical concept that can only really make sense if it is experienced. Reinhard makes this clear by offering exercises in 'seeing more' rather than by trying to explain what she means analytically. However it becomes clear that her understanding of 'seeing more' would link in very closely to the understanding of 'response' that we have been developing within this chapter. The response, the move into chaos, only becomes possible when the person sees beyond the everyday, when the person reaches out to that which is 'beyond'. The experience of response, the root experience of worship, is an experience of 'seeing more', of reaching out, of gaining greater insights. This gives the experience a great power and significance that can be transferred directly to any item or issue that is brought within the frame of worship. It is the power of the response to that which is beyond that gives us the incentive to respond again and again when the worship triggers that response within its own frame.

CONCLUSION

The argument that I have just presented certainly makes sense for me of my own experience of worship at the Independent Christian Fellowship. The whole of this argument, however, leaves us with the very tricky problem of verification. I have already asked whether the stylised account of conversion that is given by the members of the Independent Christian Fellowship can be equated with what they actually experience. We now have to go on to ask whether either of these, the account or the experience, is in any way related to the analysis of Reinhard or Kavanagh. We could easily be talking about a very wide range of different experiences. Obviously it is impossible to verify this entirely. There is no way in which I can say categorically what some other person has or has not experienced, especially if I am going to doubt their own account of that experience. I can only offer a few guidelines that I hope will help us. If we begin with the relationship between what the members of the Fellowship experience and what they say they experience. I have already indicated my own opinion that the experience itself is structured by the account of that experience and so the fit, if I am correct, should be fairly close. Having made that assumption let us go on to look at the other accounts and models.

For both of the books that I have referred to I think that the best kind of verification that I can offer is to lay out the 'qualifications' and background of each of the authors involved. In the case of Reinhard and Manly both authors have been working for some time on training programmes to renew the sense of liturgy in Roman Catholic religious communities in Australia (1984: 2–11). This particular book derives directly from that experience. Over the years they have presented their technique, checked it against the experiences of the people they are working with, and modified it accordingly. They have therefore found that the analysis they have been using reflects the experience of those with whom they have been working. Reinhard has also done a good deal of work in this field, and within the area of the appreciation of art, before she began to work specifically on the area of liturgical renewal. This other work has also helped her to see the value of the approach that they have used. Throughout the book the authors have constantly told stories that reflect the various experiences that they have talked about and have used these to justify their own approach. These stories are personal, starting with a short self-introduction towards the beginning of the book, and the stories of others, like that of Martin Luther King. I think, therefore that it is fair to say, from what the authors themselves tell us, that this analysis is of value in their work of encouraging and stimulating a response to liturgy. More than that, it does in some way reflect the experiences of the members of the various religious communities within which they work.

The case for Kavanagh is much the same. He is a priest and a Benedictine monk, who has worshipped in one form or another every day of his life, both communally and privately, within the bounds of the monastery and out in the parishes (1984: 3–11). What he tells us about liturgy is that which has grown within him whilst he has been worshipping and it is this that gives his analysis both its complexity and its seeming impenetrability. This also gives the work its conviction and sense of 'rightness'. Here is man who knows what worship is from his own experience and it is that personal experience that he is primarily trying to express in his analysis.

In the end, however, with both these authors, as with the Independent Christians there can only be one real source of verification, and that is our own experience. I have chosen to use the work of Manly and Reinhard and the work of Kavanagh primarily because this work made sense of my own personal experience of worship in the various churches. Other people may well have chosen other works and found that the ones I chose do not speak to their experience at all. If this is the case then they will no doubt find that what I have been writing in this chapter does not speak to their experience either, which would be unfortunate but unavoidable. I do not feel that this problem of verification at the level of experience can ever be overcome. What I have offered throughout this chapter is speculation. What I have written makes sense of my own experience and it makes sense of what others have told me of their experience; beyond that I can say nothing.

There is, however, another side to this. Even if we accept that analysis of the kind that I have offered in this chapter does make sense of the experience of the Independent Christian Fellowship, what can this say for the experiences of the Baptists or the Roman Catholics? Surely, we might ask, as they each have an act of worship that bears no real resemblance to that of the Independent Christian Fellowship, or even to each other, can we say that their particular experiences of worship are the same as that of the Independent Christian Fellowship? If we can not then what are they? Here again we run into exactly the same problem and one which in many ways I do not want to get too caught up in. There is, after all, ultimately, no answer.

What I do want to point out, however, are the similarities in what I have been saying in this chapter to the various forms of analysis that I have previously offered – the analysis of the story in Baptist worship and that of symbols and basic truths in Roman Catholic worship. With the Baptists I illustrated the way in which the story worked and showed how the story can help to superimpose two, recalled, experiences to create a third, new, experience with a greater significance in itself. This is not so different from the argument that I offered in relation to the basic truths of the Roman Catholics where symbols evoked the context in which such truths, and by implication the experiences that they contained, made sense. In what I have just written, I hope that I have simply offered another variation on a similar theme. In this chapter, however, the experience is contained within the clichés and stock phrases of evangelical language and is recalled much more directly within the worship. The same kind of movement, however, from self to the other and back to a self transformed, is still important. In all these cases, and arguably with the Anglican church that I will come on to in the following chapter, it is the experience of response, that I have outlined in this chapter, that sits at the heart of the worship, whether that is a response to a story, to a truth or to an experience of conversion. Response, in one way or another, I would argue, forms the root and the heart of all our experiences within worship.

NOTES

1   I was asked by the pastor, as one of his original conditions for the study, not to quote any member of the congregation without first asking his permission. I had no wish to ask for that permission and so I have chosen not to quote any member of any of the four congregations I studied.

CHAPTER SEVEN
THE ANGLICAN
CHURCH

When I came to look for an Anglican church to study I had to find a church which I was not already familiar with, and one which would be open to the aims and process of the study itself. The church I chose was located just east of the university in one of the more notorious of the inner-city areas of Manchester. The church consists of a relatively modern multi-purpose building, built at the same time as the flats surrounding it, and incorporating a worship space, halls and kitchens, meeting rooms and the parish priest's living area. The church replaced five separate Anglican churches which used to serve the area before the redevelopments of the 1960s and 1970s.

There was one main service each Sunday, plus regular midweek Eucharists. Morning and evening prayer was said daily. The building was widely used by community groups during the week but there were no other regular activities for members of the congregation. The Wednesday lunchtime Eucharist was, however, followed by coffee in the vestry and was attended by six or seven older white women. Throughout the year there were regular socials and festivals for members of the congregation. Holidays and pilgrimages were also arranged on an annual basis.

The congregation was made up of three fairly distinct groups. The largest group, about forty to fifty people, comprised the black members who lived in the flats surrounding the church. Many of these came as families, although there were far more women and children than men. These members came to worship very regularly and attended socials, festivals, etc. (where

they were often asked to provide food with a West Indian fla-
vour) but took very little active part in the rest of the life of the
church, including the parish council and other leadership functions. The second group consisted of about fifteen elderly wom-
en, and one or two older men, all white, who had lived in the
area as children and most of whom had moved out following
the redevelopments. This group came to Sunday worship and
the midweek Eucharist on Wednesday but had very little to do
with the rest of the church. A small number sat on the parish
council. The third group was made up of about ten younger
white people (in their twenties or thirties), mainly men, who
had been university students and were now community activists
or social workers of different kinds, and who lived in the flats
surrounding the church. This group attended the daily morning and evening prayers, were the principal members of the
parish council and performed most other leadership roles. There
was a strong ideology of co-operation and anti-discrimination
within the church but this was in practice a very divided congregation, primarily on lines of colour and age.

The church had a Catholic tradition and the worship reflected this with the use of vestments, ceremonial and incense. Being
in a modern building, however, this was not as fussy as in some
Anglo-Catholic contexts and the parish priest's own commitment
to bold, colourful, symbolic worship provided the primary focus for the celebrations. There was a great deal of innovation
within worship, with the use of dance, different kinds of music,
and an attempt to reflect the multi-cultural nature of the congregation and the community. The mid-week Eucharists and the
daily prayer had a very meditative, almost monastic, feel to them
and were generally held in a small side chapel.

I attended the church from July to November 1986 and again
from January to March 1987. I attended the Sunday Eucharist
and all festivals and was a regular member of the Wednesday
lunchtime communion group. I began to attend the morning
and evening prayer when I could during the early months of my
study but stopped doing this when I realised that the black members were associating me too closely with the third, younger,
leadership group within the congregation. I was constantly being encouraged to take a more active role in worship and leadership within the church but resisted this throughout. I contin-

ued to keep close contacts with the church for several years after
the end of my study.

INTRODUCTION

When I moved on to the Anglican church I moved back to the
tradition in which I had been brought up. The first thing that
struck me about this Anglican church, having spent the previous
eighteen months with other churches, was the discontinuity of
the worship. In each of the other churches the worship had always had some kind of unity, it had always seemed to be a complete whole. The Baptists, for instance, would always expect the
minister or leader to draw all the various aspects of the worship
together. The formal text of the Roman Catholics meant that
the liturgy had a kind of unity. The disorder, allied to a continuity of content, made sure that all the worship at the Independent
Christian Fellowship was much the same. The Anglicans, however, were different.

The impression of discontinuity was created primarily by the
fact that the Eucharist service on any Sunday morning consisted
of two distinct parts, sometimes three or more. First there was
the Ministry of the Word which was treated as a complete unit.
Then there was a clear break: the notices were read, the formality of the proceeding dropped momentarily, the children came
back from their Sunday school, the peace was shared and the
collection was taken. It was only after all this, and the entrance
of a second procession, with the gifts of bread and wine and the
offertory, that the Ministry of the Sacrament began. This second
section also had a sense of unity of its own. Superimposed upon
this basic pattern were a number of other items. These were
never really a part of the whole but were always added onto the
structure in some way. There would perhaps be a baptism or a
'thanksgiving after childbirth' following the Ministry of the Word,
or there might be a person or an object to bless at the end of the
service. People were blessed when they were leaving on a long
journey. Banners and other items presented to the church were
blessed. New members of the Mothers' Union were inaugurat-
ed and after one particular service a woman was blessed and
anointed after a long illness. All these items consisted of short

170

sub-liturgies and were slotted into the main service at appropriate points, adding to the disjointed nature of the whole.

This disjointedness, however, went further than the content of the worship. As I stayed in the church for a longer period I began to see that the different items which were added onto the worship meant that each week was slightly different. Added to this were a surprisingly large number of festivals. I was not at the church for either of the two major festivals of the year, Christmas or Easter. However, in the time that I was there, from June to March, we celebrated the Patronal Festival, Corpus Christi, the Feast of the Transfiguration, the Start of the New School Year, Harvest Festival, Creation Sunday, All Saints and All Souls, Remembrance Sunday, Advent Sunday, Candlemas and Ash Wednesday. This did not mean that every Sunday was a festival (I was there for a large section of the year, July and August, when very little seemed to happen at all, and a number of these festivals did not fall on a Sunday). Each festival, however, was celebrated with its own little additions to the rite and with great verve and sense of celebration.

When I came to talk to the members of the congregation, from September onwards, I also came to realise that the attitude of the Anglicans to belief followed, to some extent at least, their attitude to the liturgy. Belief was expressed in clear and specified chunks. I was never able to construct any coherent, all-embracing, system of belief that could underlie all that all the people of this church seemed to believe. With the Roman Catholics there had been the tradition and the teaching of the Church, which everybody at least claimed to acknowledge. With the Independent Christian Fellowship there had been the Bible and a fairly consistent interpretation of the Bible that everybody accepted. With the Baptists notions of belief had been far more difficult to pin down. A number of the members would have said that they did not 'believe' as such and the content of belief was certainly open to debate. On the whole, however, such a debate was not continued in the Anglican church and nothing very much was said about belief at all beyond the sermons. All the comments that I got on the 'meaning' of worship in the Anglican church related very specifically to the way that the service was performed or to the people who made up the congregation and performed the various roles within the liturgy. Some notion of belief was present, however, and where that belief was expressed it seemed to me to be very inconsistent.

One phenomenon that I noticed was that specific beliefs were introduced into conversation for specific purposes, and stated, as facts, during specific debates. These debates were most common when the discussion turned to churchmanship within the wider Anglican church. This church was a high, 'Catholic', Anglican church and this was defined and expressed by the people through the notion of 'beliefs': those beliefs which this church held as opposed to those of other traditions. Very rarely, however, were the beliefs in themselves discussed in depth, except perhaps in formal situations such as lay training groups. This led me to look much more closely at the way 'belief' was understood and the way 'beliefs' as such were being used.

As I sat and listened to conversations at various times when some matter of belief was being discussed I felt that the distinction I have already raised for the Catholic church, between official teaching and popular belief, would be very useful. There were a number of elderly women at the Anglican church who firmly believed in the power of the Saints and in the healing qualities of the host or of holy water. This, however, was not the official line of the 'church'. At times the priest might endorse such views – he certainly made no attempt to contradict them – but he was aware of the fact that they were not a vital and central part of Christian teaching. They were, in most people's view, 'superstitious'. The priest at this church, however, consciously went out of his way to appeal to the more 'superstitious' aspects of the ritual and of belief. This was something, he claimed, that the people of this inner-city neighbourhood could relate to. This was seen in worship through the use of the distinct elements of the rite that I have already mentioned, along with the way in which each element was to some extent exaggerated with flamboyant and easily seen gestures. It was almost as if the worship was deliberately constructed out of 'ritual statements', each of which was distinct and unique, in the same way as the beliefs of those I talked to appeared to be made up of 'belief statements' which were equally unique and distinct.

'Belief', as an issue, had fascinated me throughout my study but it was something that I always found very difficult to grasp.

This was partly because of the tendency within all four churches, with the possible exception of the Independent Christian Fellowship, to be reticent about the expression of beliefs in ordinary conversation. However, I became convinced that belief and ritual must be connected in some way, although perhaps not as simplistically as this short introduction might suggest. It is for this reason that I felt that it would be important to concentrate briefly on the understanding of belief, to see what anthropologists and others have had to say about the subject and to see how this is reflected in what was happening in the churches I had studied.

UNDERSTANDING BELIEF

'Belief' is an issue that anthropologists have, on the whole, been very reluctant to address (see Needham 1972, Gellner 1974, Stringer 1997b). W. Robertson Smith argued that what people say about their rituals should be seen as secondary to what is actually done (1907). Beliefs, Robertson Smith claimed, change over time and are often created 'post-hoc', whereas the ritual generally remains static. This has led anthropologists over the years to give most of their attention to what is actually 'done' during ritual, often with very little information on what the people themselves say about it. Another, more recent, tendency within anthropology has been to try to construct a system of beliefs, not unlike Catholic doctrine, that is both coherent and all embracing. The views of the Dogon in West Africa have perhaps been subjected most thoroughly to this technique (Griaule 1965). E.E. Evans-Pritchard, when he came to study the religion of the Nuer, fell into much the same trap (1956), although this is probably a reflection of Evans-Pritchard's own systematic imagination, strongly influenced by his recent conversion to Roman Catholicism, rather than a reflection of the 'beliefs' of the Nuer themselves.

More recently the concept of 'belief' itself has come in for criticism and I would like to begin my own review with J. Pouillon's essay 'Remarks on the Verb "To Believe"' (1982). Pouillon relies very heavily on the specifically French aspects of the verb and tackles the issue of belief in other cultures by asking whether other non Western European peoples do, in fact, understand 'believe' in the way that we suggest when we use this term. This leads Pouillon to look at the term and to divide its meanings, in French, in such a way that we can look more closely at what it is that we, and people of other cultures, might be saying.

Pouillon distinguishes three uses for the verb 'to believe' (1982: 2). These three uses are best translated into English as 'to trust in', 'to believe that' and 'to believe in'. At the root of this distinction is the assumption, made explicit by Pouillon, that when we say that we 'believe that' a particular statement is true then there must be a certain doubt about the truth of that statement. If we say, for example that we 'believe' that God exists then the statement, the concept of 'God', must be open to question. This sense of doubt, Pouillon argues, is central to the European understanding of the verb 'to believe'. Without that doubt, we do not claim that we 'believe that...', rather we say that we 'know that...': we know that God exists, that stones fall, or whatever. Other cultures, Pouillon argues, do not necessarily have this distinction, or rather they make it explicit by the use of distinct terms. I often heard members of the Independent Christian Fellowship making the same distinction: they did not claim to 'believe' that God existed, they 'knew' that God existed. When they did use the verb 'to believe' they used it in the first of Pouillon's senses, as a statement of trust, of commitment, or of faith. Pouillon claims that it is the very ambiguity of the term 'to believe' that gives such a term its usefulness and its power in European languages. This ambiguity, however, does not necessarily translate into other languages.

Martin Southwold picks up a very similar point in his own discussion of belief amongst the village Buddhists he studied (1983). For Southwold it is the distinction between 'belief that' and 'belief in' that is the vital one and he expresses this in relation to Christian theology and especially in relation to arguments about the existence of God (1983: 150). To say that we 'believe that God exists' is to make a statement similar in form to one that we would make were we to say that we know that a table or a friend exists. For Southwold, such a statement would, therefore, be untrue. However this is only half the story. Southwold argues that the understanding of the word 'exists' in both of these statements is acknowledged to be different, a view that I would probably wish to question. More importantly, however, Southwold claims that we very rarely hear people make a statement to the effect that they 'believe that' God exists, rather they are likely to say, as the Christian creeds do in fact say, that they 'believe in' God. For Southwold, to 'believe in' God is, as Pouillon also argues, to put one's trust in God, to have faith in God, not to make any special reference to God's existence or to the nature of that existence. To believe in God is to take God as an assumption, a starting point, and to begin to work as from that point.

I have introduced this argument before when I was talking about basic 'truths' in the Roman Catholic church, and the principles are identical (Chapter Five). We could go on, therefore, as I did before, to introduce Dan Sperber's work and talk about 'belief statements' rather than beliefs as such. A belief statement, as I illustrated in Chapter Five, is a statement that is set apart from ordinary discourse, and one whose truth is not questioned at an empirical level. This would match nicely with Pouillon's understanding of belief as implying at least some kind of doubt. The belief statement is of a different order from ordinary discourse. It is a symbolic statement, whose empirical truth is irrelevant. Sperber, however, argues that such statements evoke a system of thought, a total system of belief, very like the one which Evans-Pritchard constructed for the Nuer, in which such statements do, in fact, make sense (Sperber 1975, Evans-Pritchard 1956). It is here, I would claim, that the argument begins to fall down. Sperber's argument may well be correct for the Roman Catholics, but I would also want to question that. For the Anglicans, however, I would want to challenge Sperber's assumptions very carefully and look much more closely at the disjointed nature of their belief, which made very little reference to belief systems, and the inconsistency of their use of belief statements.

BELIEF AND SUPERSTITION

Sociologists have, on the whole, been much more willing than anthropologists to acknowledge the place of belief in their studies. This is probably because they are working within our own society where statements of belief do tend to have an importance that is not so obvious, or so easily available, in other parts of the world. One particular study that caught my attention was a study of a North Yorkshire fishing village by David Clark, *Be-*

tween Pulpit and Pew (1982). This is a study of an isolated, and in many ways old-fashioned, community. The village was almost entirely Methodist or Congregational in its church attendance with a small Roman Catholic church and a very marginal Anglican church. As the study progresses we learn a great deal about the community and the views of the members of the community, about the organisation of the chapels and the rivalry that exists between them.

The premise that Clark is working on is that there is a fundamental conflict between 'official' belief and 'folk' belief, 'popular' belief, or 'superstition' (1982: 35). It is clear to Clark that there must be a distinction between these two types of belief as it is said to be clear to the leaders of the various churches and chapels within the village. How clear this distinction is to the average member of the congregations, however, or even to ordinary villagers, is more uncertain. Clark gives an excellent analysis of the history of the area showing how the old superstitious beliefs of the fishermen were hardly touched by Christianity until the Methodist preachers arrived in the late eighteenth century. From that time on, however, whilst there was a constant tension between superstition and official belief in the eyes of the religious establishment, the people themselves seem to have managed to hold both while keeping the two very much apart. The official beliefs were for the chapel, while the superstitions of the fishing industry were for the coast and the fishermen. This all seems to make a great deal of sense. However, I would want to ask what the real nature of the distinction that Clark draws between official and popular beliefs actually is. Clark is seeing the village mainly from the point of view of the official religion, he even acknowledges this at times. How far, therefore, do the people themselves see these two forms of 'belief' as being in conflict? There is certainly enough evidence in Clark's very thorough study to raise the question and, I think, to offer an alternative answer.

The same question can, of course, be asked of the Anglican church that I studied. I have already suggested that some of the belief statements used by members of the congregation could be seen as 'superstitious' from the point of view of official doctrine. Obviously these superstitions were not as clear cut and complex as those relating to the fishing industry. However, I, and the priest at the church, still felt a need to make the distinction. I was, of course, aware of the 'official' doctrine and I knew that what was being talked about within the congregation was not always in line with that teaching. Does this mean, however, that for the people themselves there were two clear sets of belief? I would want to argue not.

In the article that follows Pouillon's discussion of belief in the book in which it appears there is a discussion of superstition and popular religion in Western societies by Nicole Belmont (1982). In this paper Belmont argues for a similar distinction between official and popular religion to that of Clark, and suggests that this must always be a part of Western, that is Christian, religion. The reason she gives for this is that the logical cohesion of the Christian doctrinal system is unable to take account of every aspect of an individual's life. Christianity's very systematic approach to belief makes this impossible. Therefore, Belmont argues, there have always been large areas of life that Christianity has failed to touch leaving the potential for the continuation of pagan practices as superstitions. This is almost exactly what Clark was trying to say in relation to his fishing village. Whilst Christianity failed to take the real dangers of the fishing industry seriously, for example, superstitions relating to these dangers would continue. This argument is very persuasive as an historical overview, and as such I would probably want to agree with it. Where I would wish to question it, however, is in the way that such issues are viewed from the other side. All the views that draw a distinction between official and popular belief – Clark's, the priest's at the Anglican church, Belmont's, even my own preconceived ideas – are looking at the situation from the top down. What I want to ask is what the same situation may look like if viewed from the bottom up. Is it, in fact, any different?

THE ECONOMY OF LOGIC

Another Frenchman, Pierre Bourdieu, raises a very similar issue, whilst discussing a very different field of anthropology, in his book *Outline of a Theory of Practice* (1977). Bourdieu comes eventually to look at the 'calendar' of the people he is studying and the way in which they think about time and relations between different aspects of time. He shows that this, like everything else in the society, is determined by certain basic underlying oppositions in the thought process of the people (1977: 97–113). He goes further than this, however, by showing that for each moment in time the kind of opposition that is relevant in understanding the place of that moment within the calendrical system changes. At one point on the calendar the distinction between work and leisure in terms of agriculture might be important, at another the distinction might be between hoeing and harvesting, that is between two different kinds of work. At each point some kind of opposition is vital, but exactly what that opposition is will be determined, not by underlying rules as such, but by the situation in which the observer is placed. This is what Bourdieu calls the 'economy of logic', the fact that a person will use no more of the overriding system of oppositions than is absolutely necessary for their specific purposes. What is important therefore in thinking about space, time, human relationships etc, is the perception of oppositions. Exactly which oppositions are chosen, however, is a function of the issue that needs to be stressed.

At first sight this may not seem to have very much to do with the understanding of belief in the Anglican church. What interests me, however, is the concept of the 'economy of logic' and the implications that this has for the understanding of belief. Is it not possible for individuals to use only as much 'belief' as is necessary for their particular purpose? A complex and coherent 'system' of beliefs may well exist in academic theology but there is no reason why this whole system should be invoked every time any one person makes a particular statement of belief. The statement of belief itself will, as I have already argued, be made for a purpose. Could not the person making the statement use only that aspect of the total system that suits their present needs? If this is the case, and I think that it can be easily shown to be so, then what implications does this have for the way in which 'belief' itself is understood? Let me try and draw together a few of the ideas that I have already presented in this chapter and attempt to give my view of the way that beliefs are being held and used by the ordinary member of the congregation within the Anglican church and, by implication, within the other churches.

Earlier in the chapter I restated Sperber's notion that belief statements are a different kind of statement from the ordinary, everyday, views of members of the congregation. To say 'I believe...' implies that what is 'believed' cannot be proved empirically and that its empirical truth is largely irrelevant. To say 'I believe...' is to make a 'symbolic' assertion (Sperber 1975). However, I suggested that Sperber's own assumption that what is asserted, or, as he would put it, what is 'evoked', by such a statement is a 'system' of beliefs (Sperber 1982) to be somewhat distracting. If we take Bourdieu seriously we will see that the statement itself will only express as much of any system as is needed at any one point. This may well imply a wider system or it may not. What is important, however, is not the system but the statement. If this is the case then the distinction that has been made between superstition and official belief becomes irrelevant. A person, we are assuming, will state any belief, official or popular, that is of value at any particular moment and in any particular situation. From this I would want to argue, and my own experience of talking to the members of the various congregations would back this up, that most ordinary worshippers do not think in terms of systematic beliefs, and systems of theology, at all. Rather, they think almost entirely in terms of specific belief statements as and when these are needed. This is probably impossible to prove, not least because one of the belief statements that members of the Anglican church find most helpful to express is that 'we believe that there is a logical system to our beliefs'. They believe this statement and it is this that gives each individual statement its own authority. This, however, is a belief that is stated. This is not how the members of the congregation actually work.

I would argue that this distinction between the regular use of disconnected belief statements and the need to assert the existence of a system of beliefs is just as relevant for the Catholics and the Independent Christian Fellowship as it is for the Anglicans. In all these churches the need for authority reinforces the assertion that there is a coherent system of beliefs, whether this is based upon tradition or upon the Bible. In the everyday thinking of individuals, and especially in the way that belief statements are used, we see the isolation of specific statements, each being used within a particular situation at a particular time. This creates what might be called 'situational belief' (Stringer 1997b). What we need to ask now, of course, is why these people need such statements at all and, perhaps more importantly, why they need the statement that all the statements form a coherent whole. Here I think that we must come back to Sperber. Sperber argues that we use a statement of belief when our minds cannot cope with the irrationality of the situation, when an empirical statement no longer makes sense (Sperber 1982). Belief statements are used to deal with illness, misfortune or grief. Belief statements are used to express the sense of something beyond our own selves over which we have no control. Belief statements are used to provide security and to justify actions that are largely unjustifiable. In all these cases the assertion of a 'belief' transfers the argument away from the everyday to the 'sacred', to the special, to the other. It gives the argument a special power and relevance. This is, of course, just as true for superstition as it is for official beliefs. There is, I would argue, no real distinction.

I will come back to these questions later in the chapter; for now I wish to change tack and look at another area of discontinuity within the worship of the Anglican church: that of festivals.

FESTIVALS AND CELEBRATIONS

Whenever I talked to members of the Anglican church about worship it was not long before they came round to reminiscing about past festivals. They told me all about services that had been held at their church or those that they had attended at other churches. They could very rarely remember the content of the sermon, which hymns they sang or any other details about these services. Occasionally some particular item might stand out as being extra special, such as the well-known hymns that are sung only at a Marian feast, a particularly amusing sermon by a visiting preacher or an Easter garden or Christmas crib. What was remembered, however, was the 'festival', that is the association of worship, the liturgy that they knew through its repetition every Sunday, with the special experience of the festival itself, as something out of the ordinary. But what is it that characterises the 'festival' as a memorable experience?

My thinking on the question of festivals arose originally from my reading of a book called simply *Worship* by John Burkhart

(1979). This is one of a number of books produced in the 1970s and early 1980s that could go by the collective title of 'popular liturgy' (Perry 1977, Gelineau 1978, Kendrick 1984, Dunstan 1984, and others). These books seem to be attempts, in one way or another, to revitalise people's interest in worship. The writing in such books is 'charged' and the whole message is one of joy and excitement. Worship is something to be enjoyed, something to excite us and stimulate us. We should all go out, therefore, and get on with it. On the whole all books of this type have similar ways of saying similar things. They all seem to focus on our need to worship God and not God's need for our worship. They all try to relate worship to some of the main trends in modern society by the use of material from the social sciences. They all try to emphasise the 'thanksgiving' nature of worship, the 'communal' nature of worship, the 'festive' nature of worship, and so on. Lastly, they all try to inspire us to a more expansive use of symbols and the idea of worship on a grand scale. Burkhart's book, *Worship*, is one of the better examples of the style.

On all the issues raised by such books the priest and core members of the Anglican church I studied would be in full agreement. They would say that we do need to put more life into our worship. The Eucharist, they would agree, is a feast. We are supposed to be celebrating God. The whole service ought to lift off and we should not stop at the church door. Our worship should overflow into the community and into all their various social concerns. We should all bring our own particular gifts into worship and we should emphasise ideas such as participation, drama, singing, dancing and the more expansive use of real symbols, light and colour. And yet all this bears very little resemblance to what was actually going on Sunday by Sunday, or what was actually wanted by most of the congregation. As I talked to ordinary members of the congregation the words that were used to describe worship were not 'life', 'joy' and 'festivity', but 'order' and 'formality' and this, I am told, was what the congregation really wanted. As far as I can gather the main issue behind all these ideas is the type of 'experience' that is expected from our worship.

The subtitle of Burkhart's book is 'A Searching Examination of the Liturgical Experience'. Worship for Burkhart is essentially an experience and not simply a series of specific words or actions. The first chapter is framed as a critique of the theory that we worship God because of any benefit such worship may offer either to us or to God. Worship, for Burkhart, is not 'effective' in that it does not 'do' anything as such; it is a celebration of God in response to God's gifts to us. In the chapters that follow Burkhart shows us that worship is primarily corporate, that it is the act of the assembled people of God. He indicates the great importance of weekly worship and the place of Sunday in our understanding of God and of God's people. He emphasises the importance of eating and drinking in all celebration and especially from the Christian perspective. He stresses that the Eucharist is above all else a 'feast' and not just a pious nibble. He looks at the idea of the 'service of the Lord' and the basic equality of the Christian assembly with each member bringing their own gifts to share within the worship of that assembly. And lastly he comes to baptism and the symbolism of water and the Jordan. Baptism we are told is the Lord's welcome, not just an initiation into the church but also an ordination into the royal priesthood and a welcome into the assembly as one who can respond with that assembly in worship. In all these topics the emphasis is firmly on the 'overemphasis' of symbol and communal worship. We are given the feeling of a very lively, almost charismatic, group that is taken up in the Spirit with huge amounts of singing and rejoicing and large expansive gestures. The book concludes with a quote from Aiden Kavanagh's *The Shape of Baptism*. 'Baptism into Christ demands enough water to die in, oil so fragrant and in such quantity that it becomes the easter aroma, kisses and abrazos, bread and wine enough to feed and rejoice heart. And rooms of glory filled with life rather than crumpled vestments and stacks of folding chairs' (Kavanagh 1978: 179–80).

This is a wonderful vision and one that most contemporary worship leaders would probably find appealing. This is not just the vision of a few charismatic liturgists, however. Similar visions can be seen within many of the major works of liturgical study. Kavanagh, for instance, is not what might be called a 'popular liturgist', and the trend can easily be traced back to Gregory Dix himself whose infectious enthusiasm for the liturgy is well known (Dix 1945). If we pick up any liturgical book that is not too much of an academic text on some obscure ancient liturgy, we will find the same enthusiasm and the same emphasis on a more expansive liturgical style to bring out the heart of the worship. However to say that this is what 'ought' to happen, or that this is what we would like to happen, is one thing, to say that this is what worship actually 'is' is another. Burkhart sets out to discover what worship 'is' and he draws this exciting picture of lively assemblies and expansive symbolism. That, however, is not what the churches I studied would claim for their own worship on the average Sunday. Their worship is staid and formal and really rather dull.

THE EXPERIENCE OF FESTIVITY

The question of experience sits at the heart of Burkhart's study, but what kind of experience is this and is it really an appropriate experience for worship? During the course of my research I came across a very interesting article in *Theology Today* by J. Randal Nichols (1985), which takes up some of Victor Turner's ideas from *The Ritual Process* (1969) and applies them to the field of liturgical study. Randal Nichols' conclusions are very similar to those of Burkhart and the 'popular liturgists' that we have just been looking at. The article claims that Turner's thesis is that all societies need some kind of 'liminal' period during which the members of that society can get away from the structure of their own society, as they know it, and enter into a state that Turner refers to as 'communitas' or 'anti-structure', that is total freedom from social rules and hierarchy (1969: 82–3). This liminal period is entered into by the manipulation of symbols that evoke the experience of communitas and so help the participants to recreate it, and we are told that Turner states that religion and ritual are the traditional areas in which this communitas, or anti-structure, is experienced. Randal Nichols takes up these ideas and applies them to Christian ritual by claiming that this should also create a sense of communitas, the experience of anti-structure.

Personally, I think that Randal Nichols may have distorted some of Turner's ideas to his own ends.[1] That, however, is not particularly relevant. The point I am trying to make is that through an emphasis on Turner's concept of the 'communitas',

Randal Nichols is suggesting that there is a specific type of 'experience' that can be called 'religious'. This experience is ecstatic, egalitarian, free from social rules and so on. Having made this assumption he then has to claim that worship is simply one attempt to recreate this experience. Put like this we can see that such an argument is obviously unhelpful. Most leaders of worship will say quite firmly that the last thing that they are trying to do is to create any kind of specific 'religious' experience. In many ways the emphasis that is placed on 'formalism' and 'order' in our churches is precisely an attempt to get as far away as possible from the whole idea of 'religious experiences'. However if we are to believe Randal Nichols' interpretation of Turner then such an experience is vital to us and to our society.

According to the traditional views of this 'liminality theory' the experience of the liminal is one which is the opposite of our experience of society, it is one of freedom, of equality, of oneness with the crowd. It is an experience that Turner sums up by the word 'anti-structure' (1969: 82–3). Essentially, therefore, we are talking about a 'communal' experience. However, communal experiences of the kind that we are discussing are not purely religious. In fact, I would argue that in our society they are typically not religious at all. We feel this way at a football match, or perhaps at a party, during a carnival or at any other time when a large crowd has come together for the sole purpose of enjoying itself. We are, I would claim, well used to this type of experience. However such experience has become very 'secular' for modern society, even to the extent that we complain when it is 'misused' at large evangelistic rallies. The experience of the liminal is not, therefore, an essentially religious experience; it is for contemporary society a decidedly secular one associated with all that we would traditionally place over and against religion.

In our own society, therefore, this liminal experience is the experience of 'play' and of games. Seen in this way I would agree with Turner that such experiences are essential to our society. In the Anglican church that I studied, for example, the 'church social' and the party that followed all major festivals were vital to the community life of the church, as were cricket matches, exchanges with other churches and other, similar, 'liminal' experiences. However, it is in these 'play' activities that we primarily find communitas in Western society and not in the worship

184

itself. Of course the anthropologists will tell us that for 'primitive' tribes, and in many other parts of the world today, 'play' and 'ritual' are one. This may be so but that does not mean to say that this is so in our own society and it does not necessarily mean that it 'should' be so. It has generally been assumed by the anthropologists that this liminal experience is one that is essentially 'religious', whilst also being found on occasions outside of religion. I would argue, on the other hand, that the experience of the liminal is essentially the experience of 'play' and that this can sometimes be found within religion, whilst not being essential to it.

Obviously some people, Burkhart and the popular liturgists amongst them, are telling us that we should get back to the idea of ritual as 'game' and I would tend to sympathise with them, but this is not really the point at issue. Many people in the churches I studied would cringe if I suggested that belief is all about telling fairy stories and ritual is really only about the acting out of pantomimes. Up to a point such statements will always be true, but they are superficial, and they equate two concepts that seem to be essentially different. Harvey Cox takes this line in his book *The Feast of Fools* (1969). He claims that our society needs a re-emphasis on festivity and fantasy and that without it we cannot function clearly as a society. He claims that for men and women to be human they must be able to laugh at themselves and at their world, they must be able to celebrate that world and they must be able to dream up new worlds. Societies must also be able to celebrate their own history and fantasise about the future if they are to have any credibility at all. So far I would agree with this. However, Cox then goes on to say that if a religion is going to mean anything to anybody then that religion must be a religion of 'festivity and fantasy'. A sober religion, he claims, is of no use to anyone and, in the end, is, in fact, no religion at all. The language used is very similar to that of Burkhart: 'we must celebrate', 'we must say 'Yes' to God and to the world', 'we must dream and rehearse our future vision', 'we must feast and we must fantasize'.

This is all very well but festivity, celebration, liminality or whatever, is only one aspect of religion and is not essentially religious in itself. I think that this is something that a church such as the Anglicans that I have been looking at can tell us. It is also for this reason that we all tend to cringe when this kind of exuberant, expansive liturgical style is suggested. We like it, we want it, and occasionally I would argue that as a social group we need it, but worship must go on every Sunday and in no church can we have a festival or feast every week otherwise it would become shallow and lose all sense of occasion. Feasting is fine for special occasions and in that sense it is no coincidence that all churches observe some kind of liturgical year.[2] We need to feast but we also need the everyday common meal in between. We must therefore acknowledge the presence of the festival whilst realising that this does not take us any nearer to an understanding of the weekly worship. Can we, however, continue to argue, in the light of all that I have been saying, that it is the weekly worship that is the central focus for most people's understanding of worship? Or could we say that it might be the big one-off festivals that are, in fact, the most important factor?

TOWARDS A THEORY OF FESTIVITY

What are the implications of defining the experience of the festival as that of 'play', or of 'liminality', for the understanding of worship? What is the relationship between festivals and ordinary Sunday worship? The answers to both these questions should provide us with the basis for a 'theory of festivity'. What I would wish to argue is that the 'liminal' experience of the festival, the sense of the festival as something out of the ordinary, as something more akin to 'play' than to the normal experience of 'worship', sets the festivals apart in the minds of the worshipper. Because of this difference, it helps the worshipper to remember the festival when the average service of an ordinary Sunday morning is long forgotten. Such a statement may well seem to be stating the obvious but I would argue that this is an 'obvious' that is all too easily forgotten and one which has a number of further implications. Let us therefore go on to look at this situation a little more closely and pursue some of its implications.

Most festivals in the Anglican church were related to specific days or seasons in the church's year: Christmas, Easter, Pentecost, Creation Sunday, Harvest Thanksgiving etc.. Each season of the church's year focuses on a different aspect of belief, be it incarnation, resurrection, creation or whatever. Each of these festivals, therefore, being associated with a specific season, is also linked with a specific statement of belief. These statements of belief will usually be emphasised during the festival's worship, through music, visual images, readings, dance and so on. The special nature of the festival, therefore, allows the worship to highlight, to set apart and to 'spotlight', a particular point within the Christian faith, be it incarnation at Christmas, resurrection at Easter or other elements at other times. These statements of belief will generally be remembered along with the festival, usually in the form of a story about the festival, and will therefore be recalled whenever the festival itself is recalled. The festival, however, is also only an exaggerated form of ordinary worship, having the same basic structure and content as the average Sunday morning service. The festival, therefore, can be recalled through that ordinary worship at any time. The 'extraordinary' and 'exaggerated' is remembered each time the 'ordinary' is performed. It is, therefore, the memory of the 'special', the 'festival', the 'celebratory', the 'liminal', that underlies the average worshipper's understanding of the ordinary Sunday worship. All this implies that we cannot, in fact, understand ordinary worship without at least acknowledging the presence of the festival, but also that ordinary worship cannot, in itself, be 'festive'.

It is, I would suggest, the association of 'experience', as we have defined it in terms of play and liminality, with 'event' that is remembered. The specific impact of this is seen when the members of the congregation come back to the everyday and the mundane, those services that do not share in the festive experience. At this point the memory of the past experience underpins the current mundaneness and raises it above the ordinary. Having said this, however, I do not wish to imply that the only factor to sit at the heart of ordinary worship is a 'good' experience at some particular festival. What I am suggesting is that the 'experience' is the means by which 'that which is special' is remembered. It is the medium, not the message. The 'experience' simply creates a relationship of recall between the ordinary and the festival, opening the way for a whole range of more significant connections.

The festival, therefore, is essential to an understanding of worship in the Anglican church because it is the festival that gives all other worship its sense of something out of the ordinary. This simple statement leads us on to two conclusions that I have already indicated in passing. Firstly, it must follow that there cannot be a festival every Sunday. If there were, then the festival would no longer be unusual. Secondly we must realise that this theory in no way predetermines what the particular memory of any one festival may be. I have said that festivals are often connected with calendrical feasts which celebrate, in themselves, the major truths of the Christian faith and that these truths are often restated and brought home in some way during the festival. This is undoubtedly true, and yet, even though these messages may well be taken in and remembered by some members of the congregation, this can not be assumed for the congregation as a whole. The specific memory of the festival is often the memory of an 'experience', simply of something out of the ordinary, of something that was 'good fun'. It was very rare for an individual to refer to a specific memory of the message. Here again, as with a number of other aspects of worship that I have been dealing with, the most important element exists beyond the possibility of verbalisation. The memory, and the communication, may well be one of experience, one that cannot be put into words, but that experience is related to the message, can trigger the message and, therefore, allows access to the message when this is needed. It is this that gives all worship its ambiguous quality and yet it is this that gives that same worship whatever power or significance it may have. It is at this point, therefore, that I must come back from this discussion of festival to the discussion of belief with which I began this chapter.

BELIEF AND RITUAL

In the last few pages of this chapter I wish to offer one possible way in which my ideas about festivity can suggest how ritual and belief may be related. I began this chapter by commenting on the disjointedness of Anglican worship and I related this to a similar disjointedness of Anglican belief. This was simply an observed correlation, I did not mean to suggest, at that stage, that these two were in any way related. I then went on to look at beliefs and to show why these are necessarily disjointed. Each belief statement, whilst relating to the possibility of a grand system of beliefs which somehow gives the statement its power, must, in itself, be separate and related to the specific situation in which it is presented. If worship is also disjointed, can we go on from this position to say something similar about worship. Can we claim that the disjointedness of worship is 'necessary', or perhaps only claim that it is related to the necessary disjointedness of belief?

The argument that I want to present here is that many of the actions that become important during the worship can be seen as visual belief statements and therefore work in a very similar way to that which I have already described for beliefs. The high point of any Eucharistic service in the Anglican church was the moment of consecration during the Eucharistic prayer. The priest may well argue, with certain theological justification, that the reception of communion was the high point or that there is no single high point within the rite, but this is not the way in which the rite appears from the point of view of the congregation. At the moment of consecration the priest, after saying the words of institution, elevated the host, and later the cup. This elevation was very pronounced. The host and the cup were shown to all members of the congregation, sitting on two sides of the altar, by a slow circular movement of the priest. Then, once the host or cup had been replaced on the altar, the priest and his two assistants at the altar genuflected deeply before the prayer was continued. This action was 'large' and 'bold' and was not easily missed. It was also a clear and precise event that was largely self contained. The 'elevation' could, therefore, be described as a specific ritual act within the liturgy.

The elevation was, in fact, only one of many such specific self-contained actions within the Anglican worship. As I have mentioned before there was a deliberate attempt within this church to place an emphasis on the visual aspects of the liturgy, and all such actions were performed with considerable exaggeration of movement, as I have described for the elevation. Similar actions could include the censing of the Gospel, the offertory procession, blessing of people or things with holy water, anointing children at a 'thanksgiving for childbirth', or even baptism itself which was done with great panache and a threefold total immersion for infants. These actions were obvious, unmissable and immediately recognisable. They could be said to form a series of specific ritual statements that punctuated the worship. In this sense such ritual actions have a great deal in common with belief statements. I described belief statements as statements that are set apart from ordinary discourse, that relate the ordinary to the 'other'. Ritual actions were also, by their formality and boldness of presentation, set apart from ordinary action and could also be said to relate to that which is 'other'.

So far I have simply defined, in very traditional terms, a 'symbol', or we could say 'symbolic action'. This is not coincidental, as I have arrived at this point via Sperber's own discussion of 'symbols'. Sperber, however, leaves us in the realm of belief statements and symbolic utterances; he fails to show how his argument can have any impact on visual and performative symbols (Sperber 1975). I would like, therefore, to move on from this position to show how the visual symbol, the symbolic action, acts in a very similar way to the symbolic statement, with the single exception that there are, usually, no words. Sperber claims that the important thing about symbolic statements is that they do not actually mean anything, they have no implicit empirical truth (1975: 98–101). If a symbolic statement does not 'mean', however, then why does it have to consist of words at all? Could not an action perform the same function just as well? Perhaps it could perform the function even better, as an action does not have the overtones of 'meaning' that we usually associate with words (Humphrey & Laidlaw 1994: 2–5).

I would want to suggest that the specific symbolic or ritual actions that punctuated the Anglican worship were simply evoking a response without recourse to words. The example that Sperber offers of 'evocation' in his book, when he is trying to draw the distinction between this and 'meaning', is that of smell (1975: 115–19). Smells evoke responses. The smell of bacon and eggs cooking conjures up an image in our mind, a particular time and place, or perhaps just an ideal image of the 'English breakfast'. This is done almost entirely without recourse to words and, as Sperber points out, it is impossible to define a smell in terms of words. We do not have the classificatory terms. We cannot talk about blue smells or loud smells, simply the smell of bacon and eggs, the smell of incense or whatever. If this immediate non-verbal association can occur with smell, then something similar could easily occur with visual images, actions or even words, where these are defined in a symbolic statement as having no implicit, semantic meaning of their own. Once again, therefore, we return to the sense of evocation and response that I am arguing is the centre of our experience and understanding of worship.

This also brings me back to the question of festivals. Festivals, as I have already said, were high points in the year, services to look forward to, something special and out of the ordinary, a time to let the congregation's liturgical hair down and produce liturgy of the kind that Burkhart and his colleagues would have been proud of. Festivals also contained more than their fair share of symbolic or ritual statements of the kind that I have just been discussing.

Apart from Christmas and Easter, neither of which I celebrated with this particular church, the most important festival for the church was the Patronal Festival. This was the 'birthday' of the church and was a time to 'celebrate' the church, as a community and as a building, and also a time for the congregation to celebrate itself. On the occasion that I attended the church had invited a bishop to preside at the Eucharist and to preach. This in itself set the festival aside as something unusual, as something 'out of the ordinary'. Apart from the bishop, the priest and an assistant priest from the church, a number of other local clergy, about ten in all, had also been invited to sit in the sanctuary and to concelebrate. The church had been able to borrow a set of matching vestments for the occasion so that all the priests were dressed alike and the visual effect remained consistent. In more general terms, in terms of content and of structure, the service was much like those that were celebrated on any ordinary Sunday but there were noticeable differences. Everything was done with that little extra enthusiasm, with a certain panache and verve. The hymns were lively and the organ blared out, almost drowning the congregation. The thurifer swung the thurible through full circles on his way up the aisle. After the communion a member of the congregation performed a liturgical dance. The bishop's sermon was more lighthearted than the usual, and so on. It was small points such as these that made the service come alive and remain embedded in the memory. The festival, however, did not finish with the service. After the service the members of the congregation were all invited into the hall for a party which went on into the evening. This party was as much a part of the Patronal Festival, the birthday of the church, as any act of worship.

This was just one amongst a number of festivals, or special services, that occurred constantly throughout my time with the church. On Creation Sunday we had the chance for any member of the congregation to contribute in whatever way they wished to the service. Here again we had a dance, various people brought examples of their 'creativity' to the altar during the offertory, and a number of the West Indian members sang a freedom song from South Africa during the distribution of communion. All the major church festivals were celebrated with something special: there were baptisms, processions around the church, special blessings, lively songs, contributions from the children, and so on. Each of these acted as a ritual statement in their own right and as such stuck in the memory of some members of the congregation to function much like the belief statements that I have been discussing above. The year was constantly punctuated by services which had a special significance and which were highlighted in one form or another. The festival, therefore, was an important part of church life, and the experience, belief and significance that became associated with it was fundamental to understanding how worship was perceived within this church.

CONCLUSION

If we compare the kind of theory that I have just been developing with what I have said about the other churches I studied, then it should be obvious that there are many elements of this theory that are clearly recognisable from previous chapters, although I have presented them here from a slightly different point of view. By this point, therefore, it should also be reasonably clear that the basic arguments in all the chapters in this section of the book are essentially the same. The patterns by which the liturgy works in each of the churches are, I seem to be suggesting, of a similar kind. It would seem to be only the specifics, the details, that change. As a brief conclusion to this chapter, therefore, I would like to draw a few of these ideas together and to lay out, at the risk of simplification, what I felt at the time of the original fieldwork to be the basic underlying pattern.

When I began my study, I set out to find the common ground between the four churches and their worship. About half way through the research, having studied three of the churches, I despaired at the lack of common ground that existed. In my final thinking, however, and as I looked more closely at the material from each church and began to work on this material, deriving theories that I felt were relevant for each specific congregation, then some kind of common ground began to emerge. This became even more apparent as I wrote the work up. It is this common ground which I wish to lay out here.

Such a 'common ground', based on what I would be the first to describe as very disparate material, is liable to open itself to the criticism of being the lowest common denominator or, alternatively, of coming to generalised conclusions that are probably too obvious to be of any real value for an understanding of worship within any one of the four churches. There probably are such fundamental ideas and obvious statements that I could uncover and lay out. I do not feel, however, that this would be of any value in itself and it certainly would not go very far to help any serious understanding of worship. I hope, therefore, that it can be seen that these ideas have been derived from a detailed study of some particular aspect of each of the four churches. I hope that this will be seen as a study that has been developed, in depth, beyond the obvious, to that which, in most cases, could not be expressed verbally anyway. It is by this method of looking at each church independently, and in depth, that I have arrived at the common theory. The fact that each church has, when studied in detail, produced an understanding of worship which is essentially identical, is largely coincidental from a methodological point of view. It was certainly not pre-determined. From a theoretical point of view, however, this identicalness should not really surprise us and should add at least some weight to the theory itself.

The theory is simple and can be expressed very clearly. What I hope to have shown throughout the presentation of my research is that worship 'works' primarily through the memory of past experience. What is essential in worship is its repetition over a number of weeks, months, or years. The constant replaying of the same sequence within the worship, whether highly organised as within the Roman Catholic church, or totally unorganised but with common themes as within the Independent Christian Fellowship, allows the individual to build up a store of memory around a particular series of ideas, images and statements. This memory will consist of many things and will be constantly added to over time. At its root, however, is an 'experience' of one kind or another that sets this particular store of memory apart from the ordinary or the everyday. The source of this experience is going to be different in each church and this, more than anything else, gives each church its specific character. The exact way in which the memory is recalled and utilised will also be different. This does not matter. What is important for the understanding of worship is the recall of experience, and the drawing together of disparate memories within the scope of that experience, so giving a special significance to all other memories. It is this, I would argue, that is at the core of the worship in each of the churches studied.

I have tried to argue in this particular chapter that the core experience of the Anglican church is that of ritual statements within the regular round of festivals. These are the special events in the church's life, those times that are remembered by members of the congregation and those services that underlie their understanding of the ordinary worship. Within the Baptist church I argued that memory is contained within the 'story' and the cumulation of stories over time. With the Catholics memory is associated with the cumulative effect of 'tradition'. Lastly, with the Independent Christian Fellowship the root memory is the experience of conversion and the understanding of response that this creates. All these memories are then recalled, if not every Sunday, then often enough, and are brought, over and over again, in to the forefront of the mind.

From this list it is obvious that no one element is exclusive to any one church. Stories and tradition, in one form or another are found in all churches, and festivals and experiences of conversion and response are found in most. It should also be noted that stories and tradition are the means by which the 'experience' and the memory are transmitted, the way in which they are contained, passed on and added to. Festivals and conversion, on the other hand, are sources of experience, the root of the memory. From all these disparate ideas, therefore, it should be possible to derive a complete theory of worship and the way worship works which will, in its essentials at least, be relevant for all the churches I have studied, and, by implication, for most other churches as well. In one sense I have already completed this task within these four chapters. In another sense, I have constantly avoided the temptation to do just that.

I did not begin at Chapter Four by claiming to set out a complete theory of worship. This is partly because I did not think that I had come anywhere near completing such a theory (I have only made a few suggestions of where we might begin). It was also because by creating a complete theory of worship I think that I would have failed in the very concept of the project. To have laid out all my ideas in terms of sociological or psychological language, to have wrapped the theories up within the intricacies of detailed analysis, would I feel, have killed them dead, fossilised them in such a way as to make them meaningless in terms of actual worship. It is the very ambiguity of the work, the qualifications and contradictions that exist within my analysis, that give it any authenticity that it may have. Throughout these chapters I have claimed that whatever we may say about the way in which worship may or may not 'work', we can never say with any kind of conviction what it is that worship is 'about' for any one person. The memories that I have constantly referred to are personal to each and every person who comes to any one of these churches to worship. Their specific content is none of my business and I have made no attempt to uncover them. The specific experience that lies at the heart of worship will never be the same for any two people and, by its very nature, can never be communicated fully to any other person, let alone laid out in a neat and precise formulation. Lastly the specific relationship of memory to experience will, obviously, be unique for each worshipper, and may often be beyond their own ability, or mine, to articulate. This should not surprise us. It should not worry us. It should only warn us against too great a precision. All I will claim for any of the ideas that may be expressed within these chapters is that they are simply suggestions for how memory and experience may be related within worship, and how such a relationship may help us to understand and develop our faith, and the relation of that faith to the world, through worship. This, then, is my conclusion, such as there is a conclusion. The full implications of this will be explored in the chapter entitled 'Conclusion' that follows.

NOTES

1   Despite the title of his book, *The Ritual Process*, Turner was not really interested in ritual at this stage of his writing and was far more concerned to see signs of the liminal, communitas and anti-structure in society as a whole. By applying this specifically and uniquely to ritual Randal Nichols appears to have misunderstood the basic drift of Turner's book (Randal Nichols 1985, Turner 1969).

2   One exception to this was the Independent Christian Fellowship that resolutely refused to acknowledge any festivals (including Easter, which fell during the time that I was studying them).

PART III

CONCLUSION

In this concluding chapter I wish to draw together a number of the themes within the book as a whole and to refocus on the question with which I began my introduction. That is the question deriving from my conversations with Mark Searle in Notre Dame concerning the place of 'meaning' in relation to worship. Throughout my analysis of the field situation in Part II I have continually stressed that if individuals do create for themselves a meaning for worship then this meaning is beyond our reach as ethnographers and is unique to the individual concerned. I have tried, therefore, to explore the way in which individual meanings could be generated within the context of worship rather than exploring the nature or form that those meanings may take.

In order to provide a framework for this conclusion, and to develop my ideas on meaning a little further, I want to focus specifically on Caroline Humphrey and James Laidlaw's book *The Archetypal Actions of Ritual, A Theory of Ritual Illustrated by the Jain Rite of Worship* (1994). This text, as the subtitle suggests, is an attempt to develop a theory of ritualisation drawing on the ethnographic fieldwork that these two scholars undertook among the Jain community in Jaipur in southern India. The main issue that Humphrey and Laidlaw address is the question of meaning as this relates to ritual. They develop a theory in which they argue that the process of ritualisation creates events that are, in themselves, meaningless. It is for those who take part in these events, therefore, to provide meaning from other sources. At a superficial level there is much in this theory that relates very directly to the kind of analysis that I have been pursuing within this book. I want to suggest, however, that the authors of this theory only go some way along the direction that I would want to follow and are still working within an essentially intellectual understanding of meaning. By developing their ideas further, in relation to my own fieldwork, I want to focus on the question of 'mind' that I raised briefly at the end of Chapter Two. I want to show how an ethnographic study of worship such as this can develop the understanding of mind, and of meaning further than may at first sight be obvious.

RITUAL AND RITUALISATION

Humphrey and Laidlaw's book is set out as a critique of the principle theories of ritual within anthropology, the kind of theories which I discussed in Chapter One. This critique is based on their own fieldwork within a Jain community in southern India and takes the form of two, closely related, arguments. Among the Jain community there is clearly some ambiguity about the nature and role of ritual, which takes the form of 'Puja', or short actions performed in front of idols either in the temple or at home (1994: 16–63). Some Jain sects clearly disapprove of all ritual, claiming that enlightenment comes through a rejection of the things of this world and involves intellectual activity and an inward-looking focus on the mind. Others do still allow the performance of Puja but claim that it has no intrinsic value in itself in terms of ultimate salvation. The people who go to the temple accept this latter position up to a point. It becomes very clear, however, that there is a sense in which the Puja is felt to be beneficial for those who perform it, and that it can even lead to healing and other functional ends in certain very specific circumstances. Puja is never performed, however, by the ascetics, the spiritual elite, and those who have rejected the ways of the world; it is clearly not a necessary ritual.

This ambiguity towards ritual leads Humphrey and Laidlaw to question the very nature and purpose of ritual in itself (1994: 64–87). Much of the book consists of a critique and reworking of the basic understandings of ritual within anthropology. The problem with many of the anthropological theories, according to Humphrey and Laidlaw, is that they set out to try to define ritual and then derive the functions and purposes of ritual from their definition. The difficulty with this position comes from the fact that there is very little that is common to all those activities which anthropologists might want to define as 'ritual'. Some anthropologists, such as Lewis, have tried to get around this problem by proposing a definition to the effect that ritual must contain one or more of a list of characteristics but may not contain them all (Lewis 1980). This, however, is something of a fudge from the point of view of Humphrey and Laidlaw who conclude that to define ritual in terms of its content is a hopeless task, that there are no commonalities which can enable us to do this successfully. What Humphrey and Laidlaw suggest, therefore, is that rather than defining 'ritual' as a particular type of 'activity' we should rather define 'ritualisation' as an approach to any kind of activity such that it defines a particular way of doing things, not a set of things which are done. In this view any action can be ritualised, from eating and drinking, through washing (which is the core action of the Puja), to combing hair and numerous other actions in other societies. Seeing ritualisation as a way of doing things, however, rather than in terms of the thing that is done, also has implications for the way in which these actions are approached and understood.

Humphrey and Laidlaw's main criticism is reserved for those theorists who, on rejecting a functionalist approach to ritual, have argued that ritual is essentially about communication, about the transmission of messages, or meanings. In presenting this critique the authors cover much of the same ground that I have already covered in Chapter One while placing a particular emphasis on the critique that asks if ritual is a means of communication then who is communicating what to whom? They reject out of hand the suggestion that in ritual a society is sending messages to itself as being patently nonsensical. In the context of the Puja among the Jains, then, there is no other being (God, spirit, guru or whoever) who might be thought to be the recipient of the message.

This emphasis on the lack of meaning within ritual derives in part from the ethnographically observed distinction between 'meaning' and 'action' among the Jains themselves, but also from their definition of ritualisation as an approach to any action. Ritualisation for Humphrey and Laidlaw is an attitude to action that strips that action of any meaning that it might have had. The ritualised action is such that it no longer performs its original function adequately, and therefore lacks any kind of functional meaning. It also acts in what Humphrey and Laidlaw define as an 'archetypal' way (1994: 89). That is, it is performed because it has to be performed and for no other reason. The action itself just is. It has no obvious logic, intention or purpose. The meaning, or function, that it might be given by a particular community is simply that. It is given. It is read into the action by the community and is not intrinsic to that action. It is necessary, we are told, for the Jains to give meaning to the actions of the Puja and most will do so on request. What is clear, however, is that these meanings are given by the individual concerned, based on their own reading, on listening to others, or on their own imagination, they do not relate in any obvious way to the action itself.

For Humphrey and Laidlaw, therefore, ritual, or the ritualised act, does not contain any kind of meaning for itself. It is not a sign or symbol within a process of communication. It is fundamentally a 'space', an archetypal action, into which, or onto which, any number of meanings – traditional, social or individual – can be placed. The meaning for Humphrey and Laidlaw is contained in the reflection on ritual by those who take part in it. Clearly, for the Jains, the need to provide meanings for their ritual actions is an imperative. Even those sects which allow for the performance of the Puja claim that it is pointless unless some kind of reflection on its meaning is undertaken alongside, or usually after, the performance of the ritual itself. Humphrey and Laidlaw offer the possibility, therefore, that their theory of ritual is only applicable to this specific Jain situation and may make no sense of other forms of ritual where meanings may be more closely interrelated to the ritualisation of action itself. It is interesting to note, however, that many of the comparisons which Humphrey and Laidlaw give from other, non-Jain contexts, relate primarily to Protestant Christianity. They clearly see a similarity in process between the thinking and ritualisation of the Jains and the approach to ritual taken up by Protestant thinkers following the Reformation. Is there anything in Humphrey and Laidlaw's critique, therefore, that can offer an understanding of worship in contemporary British Christianity?

RITUALISATION AND MEANING IN CHRISTIAN WORSHIP

Where I would agree with Humphrey and Laidlaw, and support their argument, is in the critique which they offer of the idea of ritual as a type of action, and in the development of their theory of ritualisation. Where I would want to question their theory, however, is in relation to the understanding of the place of meaning within the process. This, as Humphrey and Laidlaw explain it, is, I would suggest, specific to the Jain context in which their research was conducted.

If we take the idea of ritualisation, for example, we can see that this offers an ideal framework within which to understand the kind of ritual actions within the worship of the Anglican church as discussed in Chapter Seven. These actions are 'ritualised' in the way that Humphrey and Laidlaw suggest. They are distillations of other, everyday, kinds of actions. They are stylised and undertaken with a certain deliberateness of purpose. They are also archetypal in that they are given, they are the actions of the rite. They do not, therefore, contain any kind of meaning or communicate any kind of message in and of themselves. In this sense Humphrey and Laidlaw's theories ought to be able to help us in understanding what is going on within the worship of this particular church. Unfortunately this is not the case. The Anglicans within this congregation, unlike the Jains of southern India, have no reason to attribute meaning to these actions and, from my experience, they would never think of doing so. It is not necessary. What is more these actions are performed, during communal worship, by the priest and are not, therefore, the ritual actions of individuals in the way that Puja is for the Jains. Individual ritual actions do exist within this Anglican church, in the form of making the sign of the cross with baptismal water as they enter the building or lighting candles in front of images of particular saints or icons. These actions are very similar to those of the Jain community studied by Humphrey and Laidlaw but, unlike for the Puja, I never witnessed any obvious attempt to provide meanings for these actions on the part of the Anglicans involved.

Another view on this can be seen if I take a slightly different, and not so obvious, example from the Independent Christian Fellowship. Here there was very little ritualisation to speak of, but Humphrey and Laidlaw's theory can, I would suggest, be applied not just to actions, but also to language. In the case of the Independent Christian Fellowship I noted the way in which the members of the congregation used clichés and stock phrases to communicate with each other about certain experiences which they could not articulate in any other way. There are some senses in which these evangelical clichés act in the same way as the ritualised actions of the Jains. First, these phrases are, to use Humphrey and Laidlaw's term, 'archetypal', they are given, they exist prior to and independently of the individuals who choose to use them. I would also argue that, in and of themselves, such phrases are meaningless, or at the least the semantic meaning of the words (like the functional meaning of ritualised actions) is irrelevant to the use of those words in this 'ritualised' context. Thirdly, therefore, these phrases, like the ritualised actions of the Jain worshippers, provide a space into which the individuals who use them can place any kind of experience or 'meaning' that they should choose to place there. Clearly, there are limits to this, as there are limits to the kind of meaning that the Jains can choose to use to explain their actions. However, it must be the case that the experience of conversion expressed by the phrase 'coming to the foot of the Cross' cannot be the same for any two people. The phrase itself, therefore, is used to contain that experience without the individual actually having to articulate for themselves, or for others, the details of the experience.

There is some association, therefore, between Humphrey and Laidlaw's theory of ritual and the use of phrases such as those used by the Independent Christian Fellowship. The same kind of argument could, therefore, be used to develop a link between ritualisation and the kind of approach to belief statements, symbolic statements and fundamental truths that I discussed in relation to the Anglican and Roman Catholic churches and the theories of Sperber and Southwold. There is clearly a range of ideas and approaches here which all come together around a particular approach to either words or actions that are in some way treated as 'significant', that are distilled in some way that makes them 'meaningless' in themselves, and which are 'archetypal' in that they are given, they exist to provide significance, or need to be filled with meaning by those that use them. Such phrases or actions are central to my own analysis in Part II of this book and therefore what Humphrey and Laidlaw have to say about such ritualised events has to be significant to my own thinking on this subject. Where I would part company with Humphrey and Laidlaw, however, is in the way they assume that it is 'meaning', in an intellectualising sense, that has to be given to these kinds of event. From the context of my own fieldwork I would place far more emphasis on 'experience', that which cannot be expressed in words, than on 'meanings' and it is here that perhaps southern Indian Jains and contemporary British Christians have a different approach to, and understanding of, their worship.

'CAPTURING' EXPERIENCE

At this point I wish to go back to the kind of discussion and arguments that I was working with at the end of Chapter Two, specifically to the idea that there are two kinds of reality involved in worship which are beyond empirical study. The first of these I defined as the reality within the mind of other people, the second as the reality that is supposed to lie behind worship. I will come back to the second of these in the following section. For now I wish to concentrate on that which exists in the mind of individuals involved in worship, that which cannot be expressed in words. This will include, but may not be entirely made up of, 'experience'. I have discussed experience in relation to each of the churches that I studied but at no point have I actually tried to draw the different discussions together and to say anything very specific about the possible relation between experience and worship.

Experience will always raise difficulties for the ethnographer (and for other kinds of researcher for the same reasons). Experience exists beyond words and cannot ever be fully expressed within words. Experience, therefore, stands opposed to 'meanings' and other means by which we try to understand worship, or any other kind of activity, in terms of words. Ever since the 'linguistic revolution' of the early years of this century, led by figures such as de Saussure and Wittgenstein, academics have been trying to understand social and personal life in terms of words, or by using language as a model for all other kinds of activities. This has developed throughout the century even when words no longer seem to be the most appropriate medium or analogy. I would want to propose, however, that there are large areas of our lives as human beings which do not, and cannot, either be captured in words, or likened to words.[1] There are, to phrase this in a very different way, many aspects of our lives that go beyond meaning. Experience, I would suggest, is by far the most important of these.

I am not suggesting at this point that experience cannot be captured in words. My whole analysis of the story in relation to Baptist worship in Chapter Four made it very clear that the 'story' is an ideal way in which to try to communicate, through words, the essential nature of experience. I did go on to suggest, however, that the story was probably the only way to communicate experience. I suggested that what is communicated with the story is not a true account of the experience itself but an analogy that allows the listener to empathise with that experience and to have some kind of sense, for themselves, of what the experience in question might be like. I also suggested that experiences can be associated with stories in ways that do not relate directly to the content of the story at all, or to the experience which is expressed within that content. An individual, for example, might associate a particular story, or the sense of a story, not with the content of the story, but rather with the context within which that story was heard. In other words the experience evoked by the story could be the experience of hearing the story, or recalling the story and not the experience that is actually contained within the story.

I would suggest that if we take this last possibility a little further it would not take us long to come back to Humphrey and Laidlaw's concept of ritualisation. As soon as the story becomes objectified, in that the experience associated with the story no longer relates to the content of that story but rather to the context of its telling, then that story can be evoked at will and takes on a status within the life of the individual such that the meaning of the story is entirely divorced from the experience that the story evokes. If we substitute 'beliefs', 'symbolic statements', 'ritual statements' or 'ritualised actions' for 'story' within this context than clearly we are back to the meaninglessness of ritual, but now we are talking about the evocation of experience as opposed to the improvisation of meaning.

At this point, therefore, I need to become much more clear about what it is that I am actually talking about when I refer to 'experience'. It is clear that in the different kinds of analysis that I presented in Part II experience plays a subtly different role in each of the acts of worship that I studied. In some cases, as with the Independent Christian Fellowship and the Anglicans, I was trying to relate to specific 'experiences', either that of conversion or that of the festival. I was not trying to define these experiences as such but I was suggesting that these experiences had some kind of significance for individuals and that they would be recalled in subsequent acts of worship. In the case of the Baptists, however, I was not being as specific about the kind of experiences that I was dealing with, I was simply suggesting that stories communicate experiences and that we can sustain experiences of stories. In the case of the Catholic church I took a slightly different line. Once again I focused on a particular kind of experience, that of repetition, and related this to a wide range of possible experiences within the worship that could build up over time to create a complex understanding, at the level of experience, in the minds of the worshippers.

There is clearly a great deal of complexity in all these approaches and it would be difficult for me to draw them all together into one single theory, nor would I want to. To do so would, in fact, do what I have tried to avoid doing up to now, that is turning experiences into words, or capturing experiences within a web of language. One thing I can do, however, is to be fairly clear, with reference to other writers, what kind of experience I am *not* talking about.

First of all I am not, in any way, trying to define the nature or content of any of the experiences that I have been discussing. I am not, in this sense discussing 'religious' experience as this has been understood by writers such as David Hay (1990). Hay tries to clarify and to classify experiences on the basis of accounts of those experiences provided by the individuals who had them. Hay catalogues these experiences in terms of the form, nature or content of the experience as they relate to that which the holder of the experience claims to be 'religious'. Hay, therefore, provides a classification of 'religious' experiences. Having done this, however, he is uncertain as to what to do next. Classification in itself gets us nowhere and produces a process that

Edmund Leach likens to butterfly collecting, curious but pointless (Leach 1961). Richard Schechner (1986, 1993) takes this
kind of approach somewhat further when he tries to associate
classical definitions of 'religious experience' with particular stances and motions within ritual and therefore tries to construct ritual in such a way that a series of predetermined experiences can
be generated and manipulated. In this case the experience is
not that which is captured in a story by the one who experiences, but rather it is defined psychologically according to the chem-
ical workings of the brain and then manipulated in a practical
context.

Related to both of these approaches is the classic 'religious'
experience as outline by Rudolf Otto (1928) and developed in
different ways by William James (1912) and Ralph Hood (1985)
among others. Here *the* religious experience is the experience
of awe, of the numinous or the transcendent, the *mysterium tre-
mendum* (Otto 1928: 13). This experience, either treated as 'the
sacred' and so related to a Durkheimian sociology of religion,
or treated as 'mystery' and so developed through Eliadian approaches to comparative religion, has been incredibly influential in discussions of religion, ritual and even liturgy in many
different disciplines (but not, interestingly enough, within anthropology). Keiren Flanagan develops this kind of experience
(in both its numinous and its mystery guises) as the root of liturgy in his book *Sociology and Liturgy* (1991). The problem with
the experience itself, however, is that it is practically impossible
to say what it is, or even what kind of thing it is. At the root of
this problem, I would suggest, lies a confusion between a definition, like Hay's, which is based on the recounting of experience
in the form of a story, and a definition, like Schechner's, which
roots the definition in an innate psychological or biological phenomenon. The experience of the 'numinous' may be either or
both of these, but neither actually helps us to get any closer to
what ordinary people are actually experiencing. As Flanagan's
book shows so clearly, we actually have to assume the nature
and form of the experience of the numinous in an entirely abstract fashion before we can ever begin to use it as an explanatory element in our analysis (Flanagan 1991).

I am not, therefore, talking about any specific kind of experience. Nor am I trying to define experience in terms of its con-

tent. I do, however, want to talk about specific experiences and not 'experience' in general as a kind of ongoing sensory perception.[2] What I am attempting to get at is that experience which is associated with what Humphrey and Laidlaw define as 'action' (Humphrey and Laidlaw 1994: 4–5). Humphrey and Laidlaw propose what they, following Charles Taylor's discussion of Hegel, call a 'qualitative' view of action. This proposes a subjective view of action such that the actor is the being 'for whom and through whom action is directed as it is' (1994: 4). This then produces an 'inarticulate', 'dim' or 'partly subliminal' knowledge of the action in the actor. Humphrey and Laidlaw do not develop this any further, except to use this kind of approach to suggest that ritualisation consists of taking a particular attitude towards action based on the kind of knowledge that they have just been discussing. It is this dim, partly subliminal, and above all 'inarticulate' knowledge, however, that I am trying to grasp when I use the word 'experience'. We cannot say what it is. We can never define it or even describe it in any articulate sense, but it must be there and it must be important.

One of the problems that we still face at this point is that we still instinctively want to talk of knowledge and thinking in terms of language. Real thinking, all our common sense and instinctual processes tell us, is done with words. But is this necessarily so? Dan Sperber suggests one context in which it might not be when he talks about the way in which smells evoke memories of other similar smells, or the idea of that which produces the smell (Sperber 1975: 113). There is never any need for the smell itself to be articulated. We could not do it if we tried. Could not the same be said, therefore, of experiences, this inarticulate knowledge of action described by Humphrey and Laidlaw? Can we not think with experiences, remember experiences, juxtapose and recreate experiences without ever needing to articulate those experiences or to relate those experiences to any particular kind of verbalisation? I can see no reason why we should not. And if this is possible then I would suggest, it may also be possible that the ritualised act, or even the ritualised statement, can offer the 'space', in Humphrey and Laidlaw's terms, not to be filled with 'meaning', but in which to contemplate experience without ever feeling the need to articulate that contemplation in words.[3]

THE 'OTHER REALITY' OR THE REALITY OF THE 'OTHER'

In Chapter Two I talked about two kinds of reality that were beyond the scope of the ethnographer. The inner life of those being studied was one of these, the other was the possibility of the reality of the Other. Clearly these 'other realities' are of a very different order from each other. It should be obvious that there *is* something going on in the minds of those we are claiming to study, as there is clearly something going on in our own minds (see Cohen 1994). We may never know exactly what it is. We may ultimately be reduced to the kind of speculation that I have just been exploring in the previous section. From an empirical position, however, there *must* be something there and we do need to take that something seriously. The 'other reality' that lies behind worship, however, is of a very different order. This is an *assumed* reality. It is the reality of the Other which is brought in to make sense of worship by those who take part in that worship. It is, of course, impossible to study this Other empirically, but it is also, following my exploration of Sperber, impossible to dismiss it on empirical grounds as well (see Chapter Five).

One of the points about this second 'other reality', is that it is perfectly possible to undertake a study of worship with the assumption that this kind of 'other reality' does not exist in any empirical sense. There is some sense in which much of my own analysis has been undertaken in this way. I have never drawn on this 'other reality' as part of my explanation, either for what is going on within worship, or for deciding how worship works. In many ways, therefore, I have avoided the issue. It is also clear that at times, in my discussion of all four churches, I have drawn on the language of this 'other reality', of God, and related my own discourse to that of the people whom I am studying. I have said, very clearly, that I am a practising Christian and that the language of God comes naturally to me both as an explanation of, and an explanation for, worship. Within this study, however, I have tried to go beyond this language to an understanding of what is actually going on at the level of discourse and of experience without any direct reference to this Other.

One of the problems of ignoring the possibility of the 'other reality' beyond the worship is that our account of worship can very easily begin to sound like an account of many other activities in contemporary society where this kind of 'other reality' is certainly not postulated as an explanatory tool. I have already shown in Chapter Seven how the understanding of the liminal and the experience of communitas makes much more sense of the football match, and other events where large crowds come together with a single focus, than it does of what happens in Christian worship. It is possible, therefore, that many of my other theories and insights might also be more applicable to the context of watching football, following a pop group, watching a soap opera, attending an all-night rave, or any number of other contexts in which memory and experience interact in a significant way, than they are to the context of worship which I am supposed to be studying.

Does the possibility of an 'other reality' behind or within worship make any difference, therefore, to that worship, or does it simply work at the level of discourse, a common way in which language about worship is constructed and articulated? To understand this I think that we need to explore very briefly the concept of 'significance' that I have used throughout this book but have seldom set out in any systematic form. In doing this I am aware that I am leaving the realm of description and entering into the field of speculation. I cannot authenticate any of what I am about to argue through the use of evidence. What I am proposing is, I would suggest, merely a logical continuation of the kind of argument that I have developed up to this point.

One of the problems of bringing the question of 'meaning' to the fore in this book has been that I have tended to define it, and use it, almost entirely in its semantic sense. Meaning, I have assumed, implies a specific, definable, something which an action or a statement 'means'. This is not, however, the only way in which 'meaning' has been used within the literature on ritual and liturgy (although it has become the most common use of the term since the linguistic turn in explanation that I discussed earlier in this chapter). Something can be 'meaningful' for a person without containing any specific 'meaning'. An event or a story can give 'meaning' to a person's life without that event or story actually containing any coherent 'meaning' of a semantic kind. It is this slippery nature of the word 'meaning' that has, to some extent, I would suggest, caused all the problems over the possible 'meanings' inherent in ritual in the first place. My problem, however, was a problem of terminology. How could I convey the second, less specific sense of the word 'meaning' without using the word itself and so leaving the concept of 'meaning' within my analysis for the linguistic, semantic sense of the word? In order to do this I have fixed on the word 'significance'. A rite or phrase can have significance without ever carrying meaning. Such an event can also give significance to a person's life without that person ever needing to ask what it might actually 'mean'.

Having said all this, I am still conscious of the fact that I have appeared to use 'significance' itself in a decidedly slippery way by relating it to different aspects of the worship in each of the chapters in which I have used it. I would suggest, however, that this apparent inconsistency is not as real, or as important, as it might seem. If I take three contexts in which I use the word as examples then I can begin to show something of what I am trying to suggest.

In the case of the Anglican church I gave primary significance to the experience of the festival which I portrayed as a 'significant' experience in and of itself. I then went on to suggest that it was the 'significance' of this experience which gave 'significance' to the belief and ritual statements which were used within that context. These statements, with their borrowed 'significance' could then transfer some of that 'significance' to any context in which they might subsequently be used either within worship or elsewhere. In the case of the Catholic church, however, I suggested a different kind of association such that the unquestioned truths of the Catholic faith were given 'significance' through the 'authority' of the tradition and that these truths, subsequently, gave 'significance', through the process of repetition, to the otherwise rather dull experience of attending mass. I also suggested, towards the end of that chapter, that there was some kind of circularity at work within this context such that the experience of repetition itself lent 'significance' to the understanding of tradition, which then gave authority to the truths, which then gave 'significance' to the mass. Something similar can be seen when I was talking about the Independent Christian Fellowship. In this context I used the word 'significance' to refer to the experience of conversion. This was seen to be 'significant' both because it was a powerful experience in itself, and also because the structure of story that was used within the congrega-

tion to discuss this experience was given a certain level of 'significance' through its repetition and reflection within the worship.
This worship, however, gained its own 'significance' because of
the way in which it constantly referred back to, and made present
for the congregation, the experience of conversion itself.

What can be seen from each of these cases, and that of the
Baptist chapel if I was to lay it out in the same kind of way, is that
experience, basic truths (belief statements, structures or stories)
and significance are all intimately related in a complex, and
sometimes apparently confusing, way. What I am describing,
however, appears to be a classic 'chicken and egg' kind of situation. One thing leads to another, and then to another, and then
back to itself in a circular fashion without any obvious beginning or any clear-cut ending. All that changed, within each of
the specific contexts that I have tried to describe, was that I began the analysis in a different place and so I went round the
circle from a different starting point. In each case, however, the
structure of the process was clearly circular and the individual
had to place themselves fully within that circle, had to be caught
up within the worshipping context, for that situation to make
any sense whatsoever.

Put in a different way, with slightly different language, what I
think I have been describing within each of the worship situations that I have been studying, is a process of positive feedback
such that significance, belief statements and experience each feed
off one another and provide back up for one another. Once
into the loop then the process generates its own momentum
and appears to be unstoppable, self-sustaining, and totally complete. It is only once we pull ourselves away and stand outside
the system that the process itself can be understood. Linked to
this system, however, are two further features which are necessary to its functioning, and which I have explored in passing in
each of the chapters in Part II. The first is 'repetition' which is
clearly necessary for any loop system, as the whole process must
go round and round, each time coming back to the same, or to
a similar, place. The second is 'memory'. Memory is needed to
provide the continuity between each revolution of the circle. We
have to 'remember' the experience, the significance or the truth
each time we go around or else the three could never interact.
Memory, however, is only ever partial, and it is, I would suggest,

this partial nature of memory, the slippage that occurs between one revolution and the next, which sustains the system and keeps it in motion. If we remember the experience perfectly each time we come around then we would never give it any significance. If the memory of the belief statement included all the details of its construction then its merging with the experience would be impossible. Some slippage is necessary for the full feedback mechanism to work.

It is at this point, therefore, that the concept of the Other, the 'other reality' which worshippers claim to be present behind their worship, becomes relevant and vital to a full understanding of what might be happening. What I have described so far sounds extremely mechanistic, even painfully so, despite the necessity for some flaws in memory to make the process work. This flaw, however, or perhaps I should use the word 'slippage' as being somewhat less negative, actually provides a space, a gap, a pause in the process within which the individual becomes suspended and disorientated. This 'space' is important. In some cases, as with the Roman Catholic emphasis on order and habit, the space is minimised and passed over as quickly as possible. In the case of the Independent Christian Fellowship, however, this 'space' is the space produced by montage. It is expanded, and allowed to disturb the participant, before it is filled once again with new layers of significance and experience. This 'space' demands to be filled and, I would suggest, it is the Other (however that is defined within the context of the worship) which fills it. Where a ready model of the Other exists (either in terms of truths, stories or experience) then the space can be easily dealt with, where it is not, then the individual is left struggling. However, I would suggest that some kind of Other (not always in any articulated form) is always needed to make sense of that gap, the 'space' produced by the slippage in memory between repetitions of significant experiences.

The use of the word 'space' clearly links this line of speculation with Humphrey and Laidlaw's discussion of ritualisation, which also proposes a 'space' which needs to be filled. All that I have attempted to do here, therefore, is to add a certain dynamic to that process; to show that what fills that space, whilst being understood in terms of an Other, does not in itself need to be articulated at any point and can be allowed to remain at the level of significant experience. Alternatively, in certain kinds of tradition, that space can lead to articulation, either through pre-determined, 'archetypal', stock phrases and basic truths, or through personal improvisation on given themes within the tradition (the process which is proposed by Humphrey and Laidlaw themselves).

WORSHIP AND THE MIND

I suggested in Chapter Two that the process of detailed ethnography could lead, through listening to discourse and an understanding of the different kinds of reality which can and cannot be grasped within or through that discourse, to a theory of the mind. I do not wish at this stage to be dogmatic and to construct a complete and uncontestable theory. As I said at the time such a theory needs to be built up over time through dialogue between ethnographers and others working within this field. Much of this chapter, however, has already taken the form of speculation, most of which is probably beyond empirical proof of any kind. The conclusions that I can draw from it, therefore, must themselves exist at the level of speculation and I must leave it for others to play with these ideas and test their usefulness in other situations and other contexts. Drawing on what I have been trying to say within this conclusion, there are three things that I think I can say about the nature of the human mind in relation to worship. I want to develop each of these briefly before drawing to a final conclusion and showing how this kind of analysis might lead us to ask other questions which require further research in order to develop these speculations.

The first point that I would like to stress is related to my discussion of the concept of 'experience'. The point is actually very simple and, by this stage, very obvious. It is, however, often forgotten in many discussions of the mind that I have read. My point is simply that not everything that happens within the human mind can be articulated in words. I am not referring here to any concept such as the sub-conscious or even the subliminal. Both of these assume that the human mind, when conscious and thinking, would normally function with language. Anything that happens within the mind without language, therefore, is thought to be subsidiary and beyond comprehension. Put another way, 'consciousness' is nearly always understood in linguistic terms. This is not always stated in so many words. However, until we begin to explore ways in which the basic elements of experience are felt, reflected upon, juxtaposed or whatever, without the mediation of language, then, I would argue, we are not going to understand the nature of consciousness. It is very clear to me that within worship, and within ritualisation more generally, much of what is going on in the mind is going on at the level of experience, unmediated by words, and beyond the articulation of language. A thorough study of this process, therefore, may be able to help us to rethink what consciousness is and how it functions at an everyday level.[4]

The second point relates to the process of positive feedback, of significance and experience, that I discussed in the previous section, and particularly to the possibility of a 'space', or a gap, or of slippage, within the feedback process. While I have expressed this in a highly mechanistic fashion, the point that I would want to make about the human mind in relation to this process is actually far more 'human', if I can be allowed to use that phrase. It is the gap itself that interests me. This gap is necessary, I suggested, to the working of the feedback process. It is necessary to the development of significance within worship. It is necessary, therefore, to worship. What this gap suggests to me, however, and I cannot put it any stronger than that, is that there is a 'sense of incompleteness' within the human mind. This is not to say that the mind itself is 'incomplete' in any biological sense, but that an important element in the understanding of the human mind is the need to understand the 'sense of incompleteness' that leads human beings to enter into the process of worship. The gap, the space, is created externally, within worship or ritualisation, but what that gap reflects, I would suggest, is a sense of uncertainty, an inquisitiveness, a desire for otherness (the language to express this is inevitably imperfect) within the human mind itself.

This leads to my third point, and the point that goes beyond the analysis I have developed in this chapter so far. If the human mind contains within itself a 'sense of incompleteness', then clearly the human person possesses within themselves the desire for completion. At this point, however, we move beyond the mind to something much larger, and on to a position that many other people have held before. There are many things which can provide a 'sense of completion'; other people and personal relationships, elaborate structures and systems of cosmology, God. The choice is wide open and I would not want to speculate as to what any one individual might care to turn to in order to find that completion for themselves. This clearly takes me beyond the scope of this study as I have defined it, and begins to deal with the details of individual meaning systems that I have studiously avoided discussing throughout the book. All I would want to say at this point, however, is that something must fill the space that this study of worship has uncovered and that this 'something' will inevitably lead us back from the individual towards the communal, the congregation and possibly even God.

CONCLUDING REMARKS

One of the things that I was forced to do within this study, as I have already suggested at the end of Chapter Seven, was to find the common ground, the generalisable theory, beyond the specifics of each of the four different congregations which I have studied. This has led me, probably inevitably, into a discussion of process and of mind that is, theoretically, generalisable even beyond the context of Christian worship, or even the British context, to the level of humanity as a whole. Human beings, however, do not exist at this abstract level. To some extent, therefore, my attempt to generalise at such a level has meant that many aspects of the worship that I studied, and of the process that I have outlined, have had to be ignored or placed on one side. In order to understand what is happening, therefore, not in each and every situation, but in one particular situation, then other levels of analysis need to be built up on top of that which I have outlined within this chapter.

I have tended, for example, to focus on the individual, although no individual can ever exist in isolation and the context of worship is primarily a collective context. The experience of any one individual is clearly influenced by the experience of others, and an understanding of the relationships between worshippers is vital for a full understanding of the nature of the experience and significance of worship. When we come to look at ritualisation, fundamental truths and significant stories then,

217

clearly, we must not only take into account the collective nature of the event but also the power relations within the worshipping arena. We must investigate questions of authority, oppression and liberation that are inevitable within any collective context. I have not developed these themes to any great extent within this study because to do so would inevitably lead me from the general to the specific. Such factors do exist, however, and inevitably so. They are going to make an impact on the worship, on the ethnographic context, and on the mind of any individual we may care to focus on, ourselves included. These elements all need to be developed far more and explored in depth in relation to many different specific contexts, and in relation to the basic argument that I have put forward within this book. This, however, I would suggest, provides a 'space', an agenda for further study, rather than a 'gap', or sense of incompleteness, within the present one.

Finally I must come back to my discussion with Mark Searle and the question of where we should be situating meaning within the context of worship. Clearly both of us were wrong if what I have been suggesting in the last few chapters of this book are correct. Both of us were still working primarily within a linguistic understanding of meaning and both of us were assuming that some kind of articulated meaning was going to be necessary. I hope that I have shown both that the act of worship itself, with its actions and its words, is best understood as being a space without meaning in its linguistic sense, and that the individuals who come to worship have no need or imperative to fill that space with meaning in any but an experiential, 'significance', kind of way. Within the Christian tradition liturgy and worship is given meaning, that is undeniable, but that is done by liturgists, theologians, and even by sociologists, and, it would appear, the ordinary worshipper is more than happy for that to continue.

NOTES

1   In doing this I am explicitly rejecting the approach to discourse as developed by Foucault and his followers. Such an approach I would suggest denies the individual any place of their own within the discourses that surround them and captures everything within the concept of language (see Nightingale 1996: 126–44

for an exposition of this view). Personally I see the individual as an active agent in the world and 'discourse', as I explained in Chapter Three, as an empirical part of the world which can be recorded, listened to and responded to, not as some all-encompassing net, or structure, which holds all those within it at its mercy.

2   This distinction is based on Victor Turner's reading of Wilhelm Dilthey for whom 'mere experience' is a kind of background perception and 'an experience' is, to use Turner's example, 'like a rock in a Zen sand garden' – it stands out from the background as something special (Turner 1986: 35). Dilthey, and Turner, go on to speculate as to how specific 'experiences' relate to the background experience in a way that is not unlike my discussion of the experience of festivals and ordinary worship in Chapter Seven. For my present purposes, however, the distinction itself is useful.

3   This does not mean that people will never fill this space with meanings. Many will and, as in Humphrey and Laidlaw's case of the Jain community, some may feel compelled to do so, or be strongly encouraged to do so. All I am suggesting is that the construction of meaning is a secondary process, as Humphrey and Laidlaw imply, which may or may not take place. What is primary, and in my view must always be present, is the experience and the thinking with experience that is part of the action itself.

4   The emphasis on experience may also begin to draw us away from an understanding of 'mind' that separates it from 'body'. Experience does not occur simply within our heads, it is a whole-body activity and, I would suggest, is often 'remembered' within the body rather than within the brain. A theory of consciousness that takes experience seriously must also be a theory of consciousness that takes the body seriously. In order to get at this then we should perhaps pay far more attention to the body in worship than I have been able to do within this book (see Chauvet & Lumbala 1995).

BIBLIOGRAPHY

Abrams, M., Gerard, D. & Timms, N. (eds) (1985) *Values and Social Change in Britain.* Macmillan, London.

Allen, R.C. (ed.) (1987) *Channels of Discourse.* Methuen, London.

Alternative Service Book 1980 (1980) Collins, London.

Archbishop of Canterbury's Commission on Urban Priority Areas (1985) *Faith in the City, A Call for Action by Church and Nation.* Church House Publishing, London.

Archbishop's Commission on Rural Areas (1990) *Faith in the Countryside, A Report Presented to the Archbishops of Canterbury and York.* Churchman, Worthing.

Balthasar, H.U. von (1988) *Theodrama: Theological Dramatic Theory: I Prolegomena.* Ignatius Press, San Francisco.

Barth, F. (1975) *Ritual and Knowledge among the Baktaman of New Guinea.* Yale University Press, New Haven.

Baumann, G. (1996) *Contesting Culture, Discourses of Identity in Multi-Ethnic London.* Cambridge University Press, Cambridge.

Baumstark, A. (1958) *Comparative Liturgy.* Mowbray, London.

Bell, C. (1989) 'Ritual, Change, and Changing Rituals' *Worship,* Vol. 63, No. 1, pp. 31–41

Belmont, N. (1982) 'Superstition and Popular Religion in Western Society' in M. Izard & P. Smith (eds) *Between Belief and Transgression: Structuralist Essays in Religion, History and Myth.* Chicago University Press, Chicago, pp. 9–23.

Berger, P.L. & Luckman, T. (1966) *The Social Construction of Re-*

ality, A Treatise in the Sociology of Knowledge. Penguin, Harmondsworth.

Bernier, P. (1981) *Bread Broken and Shared, Broadening our Vision of Eucharist.* Ave Maria Press, Notre Dame.

Bishop, E. (1918) *Liturgica Historica, Papers on the Liturgy and Religious Life of the Western Church.* Clarendon, Oxford.

Bishop's Conference of England and Wales (1991) *Celebrating the Paschal Mystery, A Syllabus of Liturgical Formation for those Setting up Courses in Liturgy.* Liturgy Office of the Bishop's Conference, London.

Botte, B. (1988) *From Silence to Participation, An Insider's View of Liturgical Renewal.* The Pastoral Press, Washington.

Bourdieu, P. (1977) *Outline of a Theory of Practice.* Cambridge University Press, Cambridge.

Bradshaw, P. (1992) *The Search for the Origins of Christian Worship.* SPCK, London.

Bradshaw, P. (1993) 'Liturgy and "Living Literature"' in P. Bradshaw & B. Spinks (eds) *Liturgy in Dialogue.* SPCK, London, pp. 138–53.

Bradshaw, P. & Spinks, B. (eds) (1993) *Liturgy in Dialogue.* SPCK, London.

Brierely, P. & Hiscock, V. (eds) (1993) *UK Christian Handbook 94/95 Edition.* Christian Research Association, London.

Brightman, F.E. (ed.) (1896) *Liturgies Eastern and Western, being the Texts Original or Translated of the Principal Liturgies of the Church.* Clarendon, Oxford.

Brightman, F.E. (1915) *The English Rite.* Clarendon, Oxford.

British Council of Churches (1986) *Views from the Pews, Lent '86 and Local Ecumenism.* BCC/CTS, London.

Bruce, S. (1995) *Religion in Modern Britain.* Oxford University Press, Oxford.

Bryant, A.W. (1983) 'Lay Communicants' Attitudes to the Eucharist in Relation to Liturgical Change in the Church of England' in D. Newton (ed.) *Liturgy and Change.* Institute for the Study of Worship and Religious Architecture, Birmingham.

Buckingham, D. (1987) *Public Secrets: Eastenders and its Audience.* BFI Publishing, London.

Bugnini, A. (1990) *The Reform of the Liturgy 1948–1975.* The Liturgical Press, Collegeville.

Buono, A.M. (1982) *Liturgy, Our School of Faith.* Alba House, New York.

Burkhart, J.E. (1979) *Worship: A Searching Examination of the Liturgical Experience.* Fortress Press, Philadelphia.

Cairncross, H., Lamburn, E.C.R. & Whatton, G.A.C. (1935) *Ritual Notes, A Comprehensive Guide to the Rites and Ceremonies of the Book of Common Prayer of the English Church Interpreted in Accordance with the Recently Revised 'Western Use'.* W. Knott & Son, London (8th edn).

Caldecott, S. (ed.) (1998) *Beyond the Prosaic, Renewing the Liturgical Movement.* T&T Clark, Edinburgh.

Carr, W. (1985) *Brief Encounters, Pastoral Ministry Through the Occasional Offices.* SPCK, London.

Chauvet, L.-M. & Lumbala, F.K. (eds) (1995) *Liturgy and the Body.* (Concilium 1995/3) SCM, London.

Clark, D. (1982) *Between Pulpit and Pew, Folk Religion in a North Yorkshire Fishing Village.* Cambridge University Press, Cambridge.

Clifford, J. & Marcus, G.E. (1986) *Writing Culture, The Poetics and Politics of Ethnography.* University of California Press, Berkeley.

Cohen, A.P. (1994) *Self Consciousness, An Alternative Anthropology of Identity.* Routledge, London.

Cotton, R. & Stevenson, K. (1996) *On the Receiving End, How People Experience What We Do in Church.* Mowbray, London.

Coulthard, M. (1985) *An Introduction to Discourse Analysis.* Longman, London.

Cox, H. (1969) *The Feast of Fools, A Theological Essay on Festivity and Fantasy.* Harvard University Press, Cambridge, Mass.

Crow, G. & Allan, G. (1994) *Community Life, An Introduction to Local Social Relations.* Harvester Wheatsheaf, New York.

D'Aeth, L.J.H. (1999) 'Can Soap Opera Care for its Audience?'. Unpublished PhD Thesis, University of Birmingham.

Davie, G. (1994) *Religion in Britain since 1945, Believing without Belonging.* Blackwell, Oxford.

Davies, D. (1994) 'Introduction: Raising the Issues' in J. Holm & J. Bowker (eds) *Worship.* Pinter, London, pp. 1–8.

Davies, J.G. (1973) *Every Day God, Encountering the Holy in World and Worship.* SCM, London.

Davies, J.G. (1983) 'Opposition to Liturgical Change' in D. Newton (ed.) *Liturgy and Change.* Institute for the Study of Worship and Religious Architecture, Birmingham.

Davies, J.G. (ed.) (1966–83) *Annual Research Bulletins.* Institute for the Study of Worship and Religious Architecture, Birmingham.

Dix, G. (1945) *The Shape of the Liturgy.* Adam & Charles Black, London.

Douglas, M. (1973) *Natural Symbols, Explorations in Cosmology.* Penguin, Harmondsworth.

Duffy, R.A. (ed.) (1987) *Alternative Futures for Worship, Vol. 1, General Introduction.* The Liturgical Press, Collegeville.

Dunstan, A. (1984) *Interpreting Worship.* Mowbray, London.

Durkheim, E. (1995) *The Elementary Forms of Religious Life.* The Free Press, New York.

Evans-Pritchard, E.E. (1956) *Nuer Religion.* Oxford University Press, Oxford.

Evans-Pritchard, E.E. (1965) *Theories of Primitive Religion.* Clarendon, Oxford.

Fenwick, J. & Spinks, B. (1995) *Worship in Transition, The Twentieth Century Liturgical Movement.* T&T Clark, Edinburgh.

Finnegan, R. (1977) *Oral Poetry: Its Nature, Significance and Social Context.* Cambridge University Press, Cambridge.

Flanagan, K. (1991) *Sociology and Liturgy, Re-presentations of the Holy.* Macmillan, London.

Flannery, A. (ed.) (1975) *Vatican Council II, The Conciliar and Post Conciliar Documents.* Dominican Publications, Dublin.

Fortescue, A. (1919) *The Ceremonies of the Roman Rite Described.* Burns Oates and Washbourne, London.

Foucault, M. (1972) *The Archaeology of Knowledge.* Routledge, London.

Franklin, R.W. (1976) 'Gueranger and Pastoral Liturgy: A Nineteenth Century Context' *Worship.* Vol. 50, No. 2, pp. 146–62.

Frazer, J.G. (1911) *The Golden Bough, A Study in Magic and Religion.* Macmillan, London (3rd edn).

Frere, W.H. (1906) *The Principles of Religious Ceremonial.* Longmans, Green & Co., London.

Gadamer, H.-G. (1979) *Truth and Method.* Sheed and Ward, London (2nd edn).

Geertz, C. (1971) 'Deep Play: Notes on the Balinese Cockfight' in C. Geertz (ed.) *Myth, Symbol, and Culture.* W.W. Norton & Co., New York, pp. 1–38.

Geertz, C. (1973) *The Interpretation of Cultures.* Fontana, London.

Gelineau, J. (1978) *The Liturgy Today and Tomorrow.* DLT, London.

Gell, A. (1975) *Metamorphosis of the Cassowaries, Umeda Society, Language and Ritual.* The Athlone Press, London.

Gellner, E. (1974) *Legitimation of Belief.* Cambridge University Press, Cambridge.

Green, R. (1987) *Only Connect, Worship and Liturgy from the Perspective of Pastoral Care.* DLT, London.

Griaule, M. (1965) *Conversations with Ogotemmeli: An Introduction to Dogon Religious Ideas.* Oxford University Press, Oxford.

Gusmer, C. (1989) *Wholesome Worship.* The Pastoral Press, Washington.

Hammersley, M. (1992) *What's Wrong with Ethnography? Methodological Explorations.* Routledge, London.

Hammersley, M. & Atkinson, P. (1983) *Ethnography, Principles in Practice.* Tavistock, London.

Hammond, C.E. (ed.) (1878) *Liturgies Eastern and Western, being a Reprint of the Texts, either Original or Translated, of the Most Representative Liturgies of the Church, from Various Sources.* Clarendon, Oxford.

Hay, D. (1990) *Religious Experience Today, Studying the Facts.* Mowbray, London.

Hobson, P. (1993) *A Voice in the City: Worship for Urban People.* CPAS, Warwick.

Hood, R.W. (1985) 'Mysticism' in P.E. Hammond (ed.) *The Sacred in a Secular Age, Toward Revision in the Scientific Study of Religion.* University of California Press, Berkeley.

Hopewell, J.F. (1987) *Congregation, Stories and Structures.* SCM, London.

Howard, J. (1984) 'Bishops Might but Anthropologists Do Not' in J. Howard (ed.) *Margaret Mead, A Life.* Harvill, New York, pp. 340–54.

Hugh-Jones, S. (1979) *The Palm and the Pleiades, Initiation and Cosmology in Northwest Amazonia.* Cambridge University Press, Cambridge.

Humphrey, C. & Laidlaw, J. (1994) *The Archetypal Actions of Ritual, A Theory of Ritual Illustrated by the Jain Rite of Worship.* Clarendon, Oxford.

Irvine, C. (1993) *Worship, Church and Society, An Exposition of the Work of Arthur Gabriel Hebert to mark the Centenary of the Society of the Sacred Mission (Kelham) of which He was a Member.* Canterbury, Norwich.

James, W. (1912) *The Varieties of Religious Experience, A Study in Human Nature.* Longmans, Green & Co., London.

Jasper, R.C.D. (1989) *The Development of the Anglican Liturgy 1662–1980.* SPCK, London.

Jhally, S. & Lewis, J. (1992) *Enlightened Racism: The Cosby Show, Audiences and the Myth of the American Dream.* Westview Press, Colarado.

Jordon, L.H. (1905) *Comparative Religion, Its Genesis and Growth.* T&T Clark, Edinburgh.

Kaberry, P. (1957) 'Malinowski's Contribution to Field-Work Methods and the Writing of Ethnography' in R. Firth (ed.) *Man and Culture: An Evaluation of the Work of Malinowski.* Routledge & Kegan Paul, London, pp. 71–92.

Kavanagh, A. (1978) *The Shape of Baptism: The Rite of Christian Initiation.* Pueblo, New York.

Kavanagh, A. (1984) *On Liturgical Theology.* Pueblo, New York.

Kendrick, G. (1984) *Worship.* Kingsway, Eastbourne.

Langer, S. (1942) *Philosophy in a New Key.* Harvard University Press, Cambridge.

Leach, E.R. (1961) 'Rethinking Anthropology' in E.R. Leach *Rethinking Anthropology.* The Athlone Press, London.

Leach, E.R. (1968) 'Ritual' in *International Encyclopaedia of the Social Sciences.* Macmillan, New York.

Leach, E.R. (1976) *Culture and Communication, The Logic by which Symbols are Connected.* Cambridge University Press, Cambridge.

Leach, E.R. & Aycock, D.A. (1983) *Structuralist Interpretations of Biblical Myth.* Cambridge University Press, Cambridge.

Leege, D.C. & Gremillion, J. (eds) (1984–87) *Notre Dame Study of Catholic Parish Life. Reports 1–10*, University of Notre Dame, South Bend.

Leslie, J.H. (1983) 'Lay Conceptions of Liturgical Practice in the Roman Catholic Church' in D. Newton (ed.) *Liturgy and Change.* Institute for the Study of Worship and Religious Architecture, Birmingham, pp. 54–66.

Lewis, G. (1980) *Day of Shining Red, An Essay on Understanding Ritual.* Cambridge University Press, Cambridge.

Lewis, I.M. (1989) *Ecstatic Religion, A Study of Shamanism and Spirit Possession.* Routledge, London (2nd edn).

Livezey, L.W. (ed.) (1996) *Religious Organizations and Structural Change in Metropolitan Chicago: The Research Report of the Religion in Urban America Report.* University of Illinois at Chicago, Chicago.

Lowie, R.H. (1936) *Primitive Religion.* George Routledge & Sons, London.

Malinowski, B. (1922) *Argonauts of the Western Pacific, An Account of Native Enterprise and Adventure in the Archipelagoes of Melanesian New Guinea.* Routledge & Kegan Paul, London.

Manly, G. & Reinhard, A. (1984) *The Art of Praying Liturgy.* Spectrum Publications, Melbourne.

Marett, R.R. (1914) *The Threshold of Religion.* Methuen, London.

Martin, D. (1980) *The Breaking of the Image, A Sociology of Christian Theory and Practice.* Blackwell, Oxford.

Moloney, R. (1995) *Problems in Theology: The Eucharist.* Geoffrey Chapman, London.

Moore, R. (1974) *Pit-Men Preachers and Politics, The Effects of Methodism in a Durham Mining Community.* Cambridge University Press, Cambridge.

Morley, D. (1992) *Television Audiences and Cultural Studies.* Routledge, London.

Morris, B. (1987) *Anthropological Studies of Religion, An Introductory Text.* Cambridge University Press, Cambridge.

Myerhoff, B.G. (1974) *Peyote Hunt, The Sacred Journey of the Huichol Indians.* Cornell University Press, Ithaca.

Neale, J.M. (1843) 'Introduction' in J.M. Neale & B. Webb (eds) *The Symbolism of Churches and Church Ornaments, A Translation of the First Book of the Rationale Divinorum Officiorum, written by William Durandus.* T.W. Green, Leeds.

Neale, J.M. (1863) *Essays on Liturgiology and Church History.* Saunders, Otley & Co. London.

Neale, J.M. & Littledale, R.F. (1869) *The Liturgies of SS. Mark, James, Clement, Chrysostom, and Basil, and the Church of Malabar, Translated, with Introduction and Appendices.* Griffith

Farran & Co., London.

Needham, R. (1972) *Belief, Language and Experience.* Blackwell, Oxford.

Neibuhr, H.R. (1952) *Christ and Culture.* Faber & Faber, London.

Newton, D. (ed.) (1983) *Liturgy and Change.* Institute for the Study of Worship and Religious Architecture, Birmingham.

Nichols, B. (1996) *Liturgical Hermeneutics: Interpreting Liturgical Rites in Performance.* Peter Lang, Frankfurt.

Nightingale, V. (1996) *Studying Audiences: The Shock of the Real.* Routledge, London.

Okely, J. & Callaway, H. (1992) *Anthropology and Autobiography.* Routledge, London.

Otto, R. (1928) *The Idea of the Holy, An Inquiry into the Non-Rational Factor in the Idea of the Divine and its Relation to the Rational.* Humphrey Milford, Oxford.

Owen, D. (1980) *Sharers in Worship.* National Christian Education Council, Redhill.

Palmer, W. (1832) *Origines Liturgicae, or Antiquities of the English Ritual, and A Dissertation on Primitive Liturgies.* Oxford University Press, Oxford.

Perham, M. (ed.) (1993) *The Renewal of Common Prayer, Unity and Diversity in Church of England Worship, Essays by Members of the Liturgical Commission of the Church of England.* SPCK, London.

Perry, M. (1977) *The Paradox of Worship.* SPCK, London.

Pickstock, C. (1997) *After Writing, On the Liturgical Consummation of Philosophy.* Blackwell, Oxford.

Platten, S. (1981) 'The Bible, Symbolism and Liturgy' in K. Stevenson (ed.) *Symbolism and the Liturgy: II, The Anglican and Methodist Contributors.* Grove, Bramcote, pp. 4–16

Pouillon, J. (1982) 'Remarks on the Verb "To Believe"' in M. Izard & P. Smith (eds) *Between Belief and Transgression: Structuralist Essays in Religion, History and Myth.* Chicago University Press, Chicago, pp. 1–8.

Power, D.N. (1984) *Unsearchable Riches: The Symbolic Nature of Liturgy.* Pueblo, New York.

Ramshaw, E. (1987) *Ritual and Pastoral Care.* Fortress Press, Philadelphia.

Randal Nichols, J. (1985) 'Worship as Anti-Structure: The Contribution of Victor Turner' *Theology Today.* Vol. 41, No. 4, pp. 401–9.

Richards, A.I. (1956) *Chisungu: A Girl's Initiation Ceremony among the Bemba of Zambia.* Tavistock, London.

Ricoeur, P. (1976) *Interpretation Theory: Discourse and the Surplus of Meaning.* The Texas Christian University Press, Fort Worth.

Ricoeur, P. (1981) 'What is a Text? Explanation and Understanding' in J.B. Thompson (ed..) *Paul Ricoeur, Hermeneutics and the Human Sciences: Essays on Language, Action and Interpretation.* Cambridge University Press, Cambridge, pp. 145–64.

Rite of Christian Initiation of Adults (1985) ICEL, London.

Robertson Smith, W. (1907) *Lectures on the Religion of the Semites, First Series, The Fundamental Institutions.* Adam & Charles Black, London (2nd edn).

Saussure, F. de (1959) *Course in General Linguistics.* Philosophical Library, New York.

Schechner, R. (1986) 'Magnitudes of Performance' in V.W. Turner & E.M. Bruner (eds) *The Anthropology of Experience.* University of Illinois Press, Chicago, pp. 344–72.

Schechner, R. (1993) *The Future of Ritual, Writings on Culture and Performance.* Routledge, London.

Searle, M. (1986) 'The Notre Dame Study of Catholic Parish Life' *Worship*, Vol. 60, No. 4, pp. 312–33.

Searle, M. & Leege, D. (1985a) 'The Celebration of Liturgy in the Parish' in D.C. Leege and J. Gremillon (eds) *Notre Dame Study of Catholic Parish Life*, Report No. 5. University of Notre Dame, South Bend.

Searle, M. & Leege, D. (1985b) 'Of Piety and Planning: Liturgy, the Parishoners and the Professionals' in D.C. Leege and J. Gremillon (eds) *Notre Dame Study of Catholic Parish Life*, Report No. 6. University of Notre Dame, South Bend.

Southwold, M. (1983) *Buddhism in Life: The Anthropological Study of Religion and the Sinhalese Practice of Buddhism.* Manchester University Press, Manchester.

Sperber, D. (1975) *Rethinking Symbolism.* Cambridge University Press, Cambridge.

Sperber, D. (1982) 'Is Symbolic Thought Prerational?' in M. Izard & P. Smith (eds) *Between Belief and Transgression: Structuralist Essays in Religion, History and Myth.* Chicago University Press, Chicago, pp. 245–64.

Stringer, M.D. (1989) 'Liturgy and Anthropology: The History of a Relationship' *Worship.* Vol. 63, No. 6, pp. 503–20.

Stringer, M.D. (1991) 'Situating Meaning in the Liturgical Text' *Bulletin of the John Rylands University Library of Manchester.* Vol. 73, No. 3, pp. 181–95.

Stringer, M.D. (1994) 'Antiquities of an English Liturgist: William Palmer's Use of Origins in the Study of the English Liturgy' *Ephemerides Liturgicae,* Vol. 108, pp. 146–56.

Stringer, M.D. (1997a) 'Style against Structure: The Legacy of John Mason Neale for Liturgical Scholarship' *Studia Liturgica,* Vol. 27, No. 2, pp. 235–45.

Stringer, M.D. (1997b) 'Towards a Situational Theory of Belief' *Journal of the Anthropological Society of Oxford.* Vol. 27, No. 3, pp. 217–34.

Tambiah, S.J. (1981) *A Performative Approach to Ritual.* The British Academy, London.

Taussig, M. (1987) *Shamanism, Colonialism, and the Wild Man, A Study in Terror and Healing.* University of Chicago Press, Chicago.

Thompson, K. (1988) 'How Religious are the British?' in T. Thomas (ed.) *The British, Their Religious Beliefs and Practices 1800–1986.* Routledge, London, pp. 211–39.

Turner, D. (1995) *The Darkness of God: Negativity in Christian Mysticism.* Cambridge University Press, Cambridge.

Turner, V.W. (1967a) *The Forest of Symbols, Aspects of Ndembu Ritual.* Cornell University Press, Ithaca.

Turner, V.W. (1967b) 'Muchona the Hornet, Interpreter of Religion;' in V.W. Turner *The Forest of Symbols, Aspects of Ndembu Ritual.* Cornell University Press, Ithaca, pp. 131–50.

Turner, V.W. (1968) *The Drums of Affliction, A Study of Religious Processes among the Ndembu of Zambia.* International African Institute, London.

Turner, V.W. (1969) *The Ritual Process, Structure and Anti-Structure.* Penguin, Harmondsworth.

Turner, V.W. (1974) *Dramas, Fields and Metaphors: Symbolic Action in Human Society.* Cornell University Press, Ithaca.

Turner, V.W. (1986) 'Dewey, Dilthey, and Drama: An Essay in the Anthropology of Experience' in V.W. Turner and E.M. Bruner (eds) *The Anthropology of Experience.* University of

Illinois Press, Chicago, pp. 33–44.

Turner, V.W. & Bruner, E.M. (eds) (1986) *The Anthropology of Experience.* University of Illinois Press, Chicago.

Turner, V.W. & Turner, E. (eds) (1978) *Image and Pilgrimage in Christian Culture, Anthropological Perspectives.* Columbia University Press, New York.

Tylor, E.B. (1871) *Primitive Culture: Researches in the Development of Mythology, Philosophy, Religion, Art, and Custom.* John Murray, London.

Underhill, E. (1911) *Mysticism, A Study in the Nature and Development of Man's Spiritual Consciousness.* Methuen, London.

Underhill, E. (1937) *Worship.* Nisbet & Co., London.

Van Gennep, A. (1960) *The Rites of Passage.* Routledge & Kegan Paul, London.

Visweswaran, K. (1994) *Fictions of Feminist Ethnography.* University of Minnesota Press, Minneapolis.

Walsh, C. (ed.) (1979) *Instructions on the Revised Roman Rites.* Collins, London.

Ward, C.K. (1965) *Priests and People, A Study in the Sociology of Religion.* Liverpool University Press, Liverpool.

White, J.F. (1962) *The Cambridge Movement, The Ecclesiologists and the Gothic Revival.* Cambridge University Press, Cambridge.

Willett, J. (1959) *The Theatre of Bertolt Brecht, A Study from Eight Aspects.* Methuen, London.

Winstone, H. (ed.) (1975) *The Sunday Missal, Sunday Masses for the Entire Three-Year Cycle, Complete in One Volume.* Collins, London.

Worgul, G.S. (1983) 'Sociology's Contribution to an Understanding of Liturgical-Sacramental Efficacy' in D. Newton (ed.) *Liturgy and Change.* Institute for the Study of Worship and Religious Architecture, Birmingham, pp. 38–53.

Young, D.E. & Goulet, J.-G. (eds) (1994) *Being Changed by Cross Cultural Encounters.* Broadview Press, London

Young, M.W. (ed.) (1979) *The Ethnography of Malinowski, The Trobriand Islands 1915–1918.* Routledge & Kegan Paul, London.

INDEX

action, 26, 36, 58, 189–90, 201–4, 209
altar servers, 62, 64, 65, 110, 114, 116, 119
Alternative Services Book 1980, 35, 117
ambiguity, 100, 117–18, 174, 188, 195, 200
anamnesis, 120
Anglican congregation, 16, 140, 167, 168–92, 194, 203, 204, 207, 212
Anglican priest, 169, 172, 177, 181, 189, 191
anthropology, 6–10, 24–9, 32–6, 39, 42–3, 48, 54, 64–5, 66, 77–8, 85–7, 117–18, 123, 127, 135, 142–4, 173, 185, 200, 208
anti-structure, 183–4
archetypal, 202–4, 215
audience analysis, 45–7, 49
authority, 69–70, 76, 110, 130–6, 179, 212, 218

Balthasar, H.U. von, 37

baptism, 103–5, 170, 182, 189, 192
Baptist congregation, 15, 68, 71, 83–107, 113, 115, 140, 141, 166, 170, 171, 194, 207, 213
Baptist minister, 84–5, 98–100, 103, 170
Barth, F., 65, 87, 120
Baumann, G. 61, 68
Baumstark, A., 30, 35
beatitudes, 97–9
belief, 11, 15, 171–80, 187–92, 204, 206, 212–14
Belmont, N. 177
Bible study groups, 83–4, 139
Bible, 69, 72, 76, 99, 101, 103–4, 117, 119, 126, 147, 148, 156, 171, 179
Bishop, E., 23
Bourdieu, P., 177–9
brain-washing, 154–5
bread, in the eucharist, 117–18, 128–30, 134, 182
Brecht, B., 152–4
Brightman, F.E., 23, 34
Brookside, 47–9, 54

Burkhart, J., 180–3, 185, 191

Catholic congregation, 15, 33, 71, 109–36, 139, 140, 143, 152, 166–7, 170–2, 175, 179, 194, 204, 207, 212, 214
Catholic parish priest, 109–10, 113–14, 132
celebrant, 62, 64, 114, 116, 119, 121
celebration, 182, 185, 187, 191
ceremonial, 23, 110, 169
chaos, 96, 107, 143, 159, 162, 164
children, 110, 138, 142, 168, 170, 192
choruses, 141–2, 146–7, 149–50, 154
Christ (see *Jesus*)
Church of England, 7–8, 32,
circular arguments, 133–6, 212–13
Clark, D., 14–5, 175–7
class, 45, 109, 154
clichés, 156, 167, 204, 215
coherency, 74–5
collective (communal) discourses, 66–9, 72, 74–6
communal worship, 30–2, 182
communication, 27–8, 33, 201–2, 206
communion ministers, 119, 132
communion, 119, 132, 142, 149, 189, 191–2
communitas, 183–4, 211
comparative liturgy, 29–30
comparative method, 30, 35
comparative sociology, 13–14
confession, 116
confessional groups, 139
consciousness, 216

consecration, 189
conversations 113, 116, 119, 121–2, 131, 155, 157, 172 (see also *interviews*)
conversion, 152–65, 194, 204, 207, 212
Coronation Street, 46
Cosby Show, 45
Cotton, R., 63
Cox, H., 5, 7, 185
Cross, 153–4, 158–9, 204
cultural studies, 37, 42–3
culture, 135
cumulative meaning, 120–2, 194

daily office, 30, 168–9
dance, 25, 169, 181, 186, 191–2
Davies, J.G., 5–7
description, 54–5, 57, 211
dialogic, 75–6
Diana, Princess of Wales, 25
discontinuity, 170–1, 175, 180, 188–9
discourse analysis, 61
discourse, 17, 53, 57–8, 61–76, 135–6, 157, 211, 215
discussion groups, 67, 70–1, 86, 93
disjointedness (see *discontinuity*)
dislocation, 154, 158
disorder, 143–4, 152–3, 170
Dix, G., 35, 182
dominant discourse, 67
doubt, 174–5
Douglas, M., 4–8, 120
Durkheim, E., 26, 34, 208

Early Session Discussion Group, 83–4, 89–90
EastEnders, 44
economy of logic, 177–8
ecstatic rituals, 142–4, 184

elders, 139, 143, 145, 148, 158
elevation, 189
Eliade, M., 208
emotion, 24–6, 28, 105–6, 134
empathetic merging, 105–6
empathy, 99, 101–2, 106, 206
empirical reality (truth), 23, 47, 128–9, 175, 179, 190, 210
ethnic minorities, 44, 67, 109, 169
ethnography, 2, 9, 14–17, 42–4, 47–58, 61–2, 66, 72–5, 77–8, 119, 123, 199–201, 205, 210, 215, 218
Eucharist, 35, 168–70, 181–2, 189, 191 (see also *mass*)
Eucharistic prayer, 114–16, 126, 189
Evans-Pritchard, E.E., 26, 173, 175
experience, 38–9, 73, 78, 97, 99–102, 106–7, 136, 140, 155, 157, 159, 161–7, 180–8, 191–5, 204–17
explanation, 49, 54–8, 210–11

Faith in the City, 12
Faith in the Countryside, 12
faith, 103, 155–7, 174, 195
families, 83–4, 109–10, 132, 168
fantasy, 185
festivals, 169, 171, 180–1, 183–8, 191–2, 194, 200, 207, 212
festivity (see *festivals*)
fieldwork, 15–16, 76, 78, 193, 205
Flanagan, K., 8–9, 62–5, 72, 208
folk theologies, 71, 75, 176
football, 124, 184, 211
formulations, 91, 93, 95, 102, 195

Fortescue, A., 23
Foucault, M., 61
framing, 48–9, 53, 72, 163–4
Frazer, J., 24
freedom, 71, 143–4, 146, 151, 183–4
Frere, W., 23
functionalism, 24, 56, 210–12

Gadamar, H.G., 36
Geertz, C., 4, 36
generalisation, 54–7, 193, 217
God, 11, 95–6, 104, 107, 115, 129–30, 135–6, 140, 147–8, 154, 158, 160, 164, 174–5, 181–2, 185, 201, 210, 217
Gospel, 121, 189
Gueranger, P., 30, 32, 34

habit, 110–14, 116–19, 122, 125–6, 133–4, 136, 214
Hay, D., 207
healing, 152–4, 172, 200
Hebert, G., 32
hermeneutics, 36–8
Hopewell, J., 67
Humphrey, C. & Laidlaw, J., 40, 56, 65, 73, 76, 199–206, 209, 214
hymns, 88, 95, 103–5, 110, 112, 114, 119, 141–2, 146–7, 149, 154, 163, 180, 191

identity, 67, 69, 94
implicit (intuitive) knowledge 92, 94–5, 101
incense, 169, 189, 190–1
incompleteness, 216–17
inconsistency, 117–18
Independent Christian Fellowship, 15, 71–2, 77, 136, 138–67, 170–1, 173–4, 179, 194,

203–4, 207, 212

individual discourses (meanings), 66–8, 70, 72, 74, 75, 125, 127

informal texts, 123–4, 145

Institute for the Study of Worship and Religious Architecture, 5–6

institution narrative, 117

interaction of stories, 103, 105

intercessions (see *prayers*)

interpretation, 36, 45, 51–2, 54–8, 61–2, 65–6, 69–70, 74, 100, 148

interviews, 12–13, 72, 74, 86, 88–95, 101, 103, 107 (see also *conversations*)

Jains, 40, 65, 73, 199–205

James, W., 39, 208

Jesus, 98–9, 101, 120, 126, 130, 147, 153–4, 156–9, 162

John XXIII, 131

Joint Liturgical Group lectionary, 84, 98

Justice and Peace group, 110, 113

juxtaposition, 117–19, 121–2, 209, 216

Kavanagh, A., 6, 62–5, 96, 107, 162–3, 165–6, 182

Langer, S., 26

language, 26–7, 61, 69, 71–2, 90, 92–3, 95, 101, 156–8, 204–5, 207, 209, 211, 215–6

Leach, E., 27, 117–18, 121–2, 208

leadership, 145–6, 169

lesbian viewers, 47–9, 54

levels of engagement, 115–17, 121, 133

Lewis, G., 65, 201

liminality, 36, 183–7, 211

linguistic revolution, 205, 211

linguistics, 95

listening, 12, 57, 61, 63, 65–6, 74, 78, 87, 99–100, 116, 172, 215

liturgical committees, 131

Liturgical Movement, 30–2

liturgical revisions, 6–8, 31–5, 120, 124

liturgical year, 186, 188, 191–2

liturgy, the study of, 4, 6–9, 21–3, 29–41, 72, 123, 182, 218

Lowie, R., 25

Luther King, M., 160–1, 165

Malinowski, B., 43, 54

Manchester, 1–3, 15–16, 77, 168

Manley, G. (see *Reinhard, A.*)

Marett, R.R., 24–5, 28

Martin, D., 7–8, 120

mass sheet, 114–16, 119

mass, 54, 109–26, 128, 130–2, 134, 143, 212 (see also *Eucharist*)

Mead, M., 7

meaning, 2–3, 10, 16–17, 26–8, 33, 36–40, 44, 49, 51–2, 55–6, 61, 65–6, 72–5, 89, 91, 97, 105–6, 117–22, 125, 127–8, 134–5, 157, 171, 189, 191, 199–206, 209, 211–12, 217–18

meaninglessness, 23–6, 28–9, 32–3, 38, 199, 204, 206

media studies, 42–3, 47

memory, 51, 100, 105, 119, 140–2, 157, 186–8, 191–5, 207, 209, 211, 213–14

methodology, 2–3, 9–10, 15–17, 42–4, 64–5, 192

mind, 47, 53–4, 57–8, 134, 194, 200, 205, 207, 210, 215–18
Ministry of the Sacrament, 132, 170
Ministry of the Word, 110, 132, 170
missal, 126
mistakes, 121–4
model, 161–3, 165
montage, 77, 152–4, 214
Moore, R., 15
Muchona the Hornet, 64, 72
multi-vocality, 117–18
Myerhoff, B., 64
mystery, 208
mystical theology, 96
mysticism, 39

narrative, 75, 102–4
native exegesis, 10, 65, 127
native's point of view, 43, 54
Neale, J.M., 23, 29–30, 32
New Testament (see *Bible*)
Nichols, B., 2, 37, 51, 56
Notre Dame Study of Catholic Parish Life, 13–14
Notre Dame University, 1, 13, 77
numinous, 25, 208

offertory, 114, 116, 170, 189, 192
official belief (discourse, meaning), 66–72, 74–6, 112, 123, 125, 127–8, 130–1, 172, 176–7, 179
Old Testament (see *Bible*)
order, 142–5, 150–1, 153, 159, 184, 214
other realities, 52–3, 56–8, 205, 210, 214
Otto, R., 24, 208

Palmer, W., 29
Parish Communion Movement, 32
parish council, 169
parish studies, 14–15
participant observation, 13–14, 50, 79, 140
participation, 28–9, 31–2, 50, 52, 73, 95, 123, 131, 140–2, 144, 146, 183
pastor, at the Independent Christian Fellowship, 138–42, 145, 148, 158
pastoral theologians, 12
pentecostal worship, 143–6
perception, 10, 14, 17, 51–2, 65, 112, 144
performance, 33, 35–9, 44, 50–2, 69, 112, 119, 122–4, 153, 187, 190, 202
phenomenology, 39
pilgrimage, 8, 36, 64, 168
Platten, S., 117–18, 120
play, 184–7
popular liturgists, 12, 96, 111, 125, 181–3, 185
positive feedback, 213, 216
post-modernism, 8, 37, 152
Pouillon, J., 173–5, 177
Prayer Book language, 7, 32
prayer meeting, 139
prayers, 69, 84, 103–5, 119, 141–2, 144, 146–9, 153, 156, 160–2
processions, 189, 192

questionnaires, 13, 43, 45, 50, 86–7
quotations, 91, 157

Randal Nichols, J. 183–4
rationality, 23, 134, 180
readings, 103, 116, 121, 142,

187 (see also *Gospel*)
reality, 44, 46–7, 50, 53, 55, 57–8, 164, 205, 210, 215
reflexive anthropology, 78
Reinhard, A., 160–6
religious experience, 21, 184–5, 207–8
religious language, 93
religious studies, 39–40, 208
repetition, 112, 120, 158, 180, 193, 207, 212–13
representations, 44–9
response, 113, 122, 144, 154, 158, 160–4, 166–7, 182, 190–1, 194
Ricoeur, P., 36, 57, 61
Rite of Christian Initiation of Adults, 35
rites of passage, 35
rites, the study of, 21–2, 34–40
ritual actions (statements), 172, 190–2, 194, 202, 206, 212
ritual specialists, 64, 87
ritual, the study of, 21–9, 33–41, 64–6, 72, 87, 117, 122–3, 152–3, 173, 183–5, 199–203, 208
ritualisation, 40, 65, 199, 201–6, 209, 214, 216, 218
Roberston-Smith, W., 25–6, 28, 173
Roman Catholic Church, 7–8, 13, 23, 31–33, 70, 110–1, 124–5, 131–2, 134, 163, 175
rosary, 115

sacredness, 106, 180, 208
sacrifice, 26, 126
Saussure, F. de, 27, 205
Schechner, R., 208
Searle, M., 1–3, 13, 16–17, 77,

199, 218
Second Vatican Council, 7, 31, 125–7, 130–1
secularisation, 5, 8, 184
seeing more, 163–4
self-consciousness, 53
semiotics, 1, 27
sense of a story, 104–6, 206
sequence, 143, 144, 149–51, 194
sermon, 69–72, 84, 86–7, 97, 100, 103–4, 111, 114, 116, 132, 141–2, 145, 148, 150, 153–4, 156, 158, 171, 180, 191
significance, 103, 105–6, 119–23, 126, 130, 133, 164, 167, 188, 192, 194, 204, 207, 211–18
sin, 157–8
singing in the Spirit, 143
situational belief, 180
smell, 190, 209
soap operas, 43–6, 50–2, 211
social club, 110, 124
social psychology, 42–3
sociology, 4, 6–8, 21, 23–4, 32, 34, 36, 42–3, 62, 66, 73, 95–7, 175, 195, 208, 218
Southwold, M., 129, 135–6, 174–5, 204
space, for meaning (experience), 202, 204, 209, 214, 216, 218
speaking in tongues, 143, 148–9
Sperber, D., 127–30, 134, 175, 179–80, 189, 204, 209–10
Spirit, 71, 142, 144, 149, 182
St. Vincent de Paul Society, 110, 113
stance, 62–3
statistics, 11, 14, 47, 88
Stevenson, K., 1–3, 12, 63
story, 67, 69, 75, 97–107, 121,

155–60, 162–3, 165, 167, 187, 194, 206–8, 213–14, 218

Strathern, M., 2, 77

structuralism, 27–8, 37, 117, 121, 135

structure, 32, 35, 100–1, 141, 143–4, 150–1, 153, 156–9, 161–2, 165, 187, 213

superstition, 172, 175–7, 179–80

surveys, 43, 45, 47, 50

symbol, 26–8, 33, 64, 72, 117–18, 120–2, 127–8, 134, 160, 167, 181–3, 190, 202

symbolic meaning, 27–8, 32–3, 36, 100

symbolic statement, 129, 157, 175, 179, 190–1, 204, 206

symbolist analysis, 9, 28, 34, 37

tape recording, 86, 97, 140–1

Taussig, M., 77, 152–4

testimony, 141, 146–51, 153, 156

text, 2, 29, 31, 33, 36–9, 44–50, 52, 57, 61, 69–71, 75, 77, 84, 86, 89, 91, 122–4, 140–1, 170

textual analysis, 44, 46–7, 49–50, 57

theological meaning, 29, 33, 37

theology, 4–6, 21, 29, 34, 38, 63, 69–70, 72–4, 85, 93, 96–7, 99, 129, 132, 174, 178–9, 189, 218

theoretical frame, 3, 55

theory, 11, 37, 45, 49, 54–8, 64–6, 192–3, 195, 207, 215, 217

time, 48–9, 116, 124, 130, 152, 177–8, 194, 207

togetherness, 71, 127

tradition, 110–12, 124–7, 130–6, 179, 194, 212

translation, 31–2, 54–5, 57, 127

transubstantiation, 71, 127

Tridentine Mass, 62, 125

truth, 33, 111–12, 124, 128–30, 133–6, 167, 174–5, 188, 204, 212–14

Turner, V., 4–5, 7–8, 26–8, 33, 36, 64, 72, 87, 116–18, 121–3, 125, 183–4

Turton, D., 2

Tylor, E., 24, 30

Underhill, E., 39–40

understandability, 32–3

unknowable, 97, 100, 106–7

unofficial discourses, 69

Van Gennep, A., 35

verbalisation, 188, 209

verification, 164–6

vestments, 169, 191

video, use of, 86

Ward, C., 14

Wesley, C., 147

words, 141, 146–8, 154, 156

worship space, 95, 138, 145

worship, the study of, 37–41

writing, 49, 75, 77–8

youth groups, 83